Ask Steve

Everyday business advice from a successful CEO

By

Steve Sanghi

Table of Contents

Dedication

To My Readers:

I dedicate this book to the readers of the Arizona Republic newspaper, who supported my column "Ask Steve" in the Sunday business section for seven years.

Acknowledgments

I wish to acknowledge the business editors of the Arizona Republic, who saw the value in creating a business advice column that became a very popular "Ask Steve" column.

I extend my heartfelt thanks to the readers of the Arizona Republic. Their active participation, continuous questions, rebuttals and comments have been the driving force behind the success of the "Ask Steve" column for seven years.

I want to thank the employees of Microchip Technology, who keenly read the column and asked many of their own questions, some of which appeared in the column.

I want to thank Marcy Hatch-Padilla for editing and marketing support, Michael Wikan for cover design and David Cunningham for final edits.

I wish to acknowledge Kim van Herk, Microchip's in-house General Counsel, who researched and provided some answers to legal questions.

I want to thank Lauren Carr, Microchip's Senior Vice President of Global Human Resources; Mitch Little, retired Senior Vice President of Sales: Eric Bjornholt, Chief Financial Officer: and Ganesh Moorthy, current President and CEO of Microchip for their help in proofreading some of the columns where their individual expertise was needed.

I thank my wife, Maria; my two children, Christie and Jason; my four grandchildren, Sophia, James, Nina and Kimi; and my daughter-in-law, Miwa. All of them have contributed meaningfully to my life.

Author's Note

This book is the work of Steve Sanghi and represents his personal thoughts and views, not those of Microchip or any of its other officers, directors or employees. Neither Microchip nor any of its officers, directors, or employees has confirmed the accuracy or completeness of any of the answers in this book. The advice contained herein may not be suitable for your situation. The author wishes to advise you to seek the help of your own human resources professional, attorney, financial advisor, certified financial planner, or estate planning attorney for your specific needs.

Chapter 1: Introduction

I am Steve Sanghi, Retired President and CEO of Microchip Technology Inc., a public semiconductor company with over $6 billion in annualized sales. For many years, Microchip has been one of the best-performing companies in its industry. However, this is very different from its tumultuous beginnings in 1989. When I took over as CEO of Microchip in 1990, the company was in a crisis. It was hemorrhaging money, its technology was outmoded, its factories were inefficient and its employees lacked morale.

A parade of consultants marched through my office, offering every kind of cure. But there was no single cure for what ailed Microchip. I recognized that our situation required a novel approach to improve all aspects of the enterprise and involve every employee in the quest for improvement. As a result, we designed and implemented The Aggregate System, to simultaneously improve all of a company's business processes by aligning and uniting the processes and elements that lead to success. It is a big-picture approach that creates an exceptional business culture and a management model that institutionalizes and perpetuates improvement across the entire business.

Microchip became a leader in the semiconductor industry. My two books, "Driving Excellence, how the Aggregate System Turned Microchip Technology from a Failing Company to a Market Leader," published in 2006, and "Up and to the Right, My Personal and Business Journey Building the Microchip Technology Juggernaut," published in 2023, explain the story of Microchip, how The Aggregate System works, the foundations of a true values-based corporate culture, and how you can put it to work in your own organization.

After publishing my first book, "Driving Excellence," I made many presentations, speeches, book signings, roundtable luncheons and conferences. I was asked many questions at each venue about the book, leadership, management styles, employee relations, career choices, strategic formulas, guiding values, raising capital, motivating employees, employee empowerment, business legislation, and business and professional ethics. I answered many of these questions using my 30+ years of business experience, where I had encountered all these challenges.

However, the book did not address every business issue somebody could encounter. So, an idea occurred to me: Why not try to create a forum where many of these questions and their answers could be posted so that there would be a wider dissemination of the knowledge? I proposed the concept of an "Ask Steve" business advice column to the Arizona Republic, my hometown newspaper. The head business editor of the Arizona Republic loved the idea, and the column became a reality.

With the weekly column called "Ask Steve," I offered my services to share the practical business know-how I had gained over many years I had led Microchip to the top of a highly competitive industry. I offered practical advice on the genuine business issues the readers were wrestling with. From individual career advancement to global trade dilemmas—I invited the readers to "Ask Steve" by posting their questions to my blog on the Arizona Republic's Business Web site or sending me the questions in my email. Most of the questions for this column came directly into my email box. I also received questions through telephone conversations and even one from a passenger sitting next to me on an airplane. I received questions from other CEOs, managers, non-managerial employees, students, teachers, the unemployed, investors, head-hunters, retired people, and marketers. I drafted the answers to the questions during long plane trips, weekends, and lunch breaks. I considered my time donated as a community service to use my experience in helping others.

This column was a significant achievement for Microchip, boosting its corporate branding and status worldwide. A column of this magnitude in the Sunday business section of Arizona's only statewide newspaper (a sister publication to USA Today) is not easy to achieve and many companies would love to have the opportunity.

The variety of questions very much exceeded my original expectations. I answered questions on funding sources, layoffs, promotions, 401(k) plans, pensions, discrimination and harassment (age, gender, race and religion), politics, overtime & vacation pay, higher education, change in the workplace, outsourcing, networking, marketing, confrontation, pay raises, dividends, executive perks, investing your money, gender-biased environments, leadership and hiring from ex-employers. These are only a subset of the questions I received, and I answered many more questions privately by email.

I received a tremendously positive response from readers, friends, business associates and other business leaders in the community. At the same time, I received several rebuttals and people disagreed with my answers. I published some of these rebuttals because they added to the discussion of the subject matter.

It was common to run into someone who asked me while hiking at Piestewa Peak or the airport, "Are you the Steve who writes the column in the Arizona Republic?" My wife or associates would always chuckle, and another conversation about the column would begin. And sometimes, they pop a question that ended up in the column.

This column lasted for about seven years, during which I wrote over two hundred columns. In this book, I have organized these columns by chapter for related topics. I hope the readers use this book as a reference for many of the daily business challenges they face.

Chapter 2: Job promotion at work

I received many questions from employees regarding job promotions, layoffs, benefits, discrimination, harassment and the effects from the merger of the company. I will devote several chapters to answering these questions. This chapter deals with questions regarding job promotion.

The weakness principle

Question: I am a middle-level manager in a technology company. I am doing really well in my job but cannot seem to get another promotion. I have a lot of strengths, but my boss keeps pointing out my weaknesses. I have always been told to develop and use my strengths. What should I do?

-Henry, Phoenix

Answer: Your question touches on one of my favorite topics. I call it "The Weakness Principle." It is quite common to see employees leveraging their strengths to achieve their career aspirations. Their strengths are the "upward force" that drives or advances their career. However, enhancing your strengths to advance your career addresses only half of the success equation. The lesser-known portion of the equation for success centers on eliminating your weaknesses. Your weaknesses represent the "downward force" that constantly acts to slow your career progression. Consequently, the downward force generated by your weaknesses eventually limits your opportunity to advance.

The profound impact employees' weaknesses have on their eventual success led us to develop "The Weakness Principle," which I discuss at length in Chapter 10 of my book "Driving Excellence". To summarize, "The Weakness Principle," states that as employees progress upward through the company hierarchy, it is their weaknesses that ultimately limit success and stall their careers. This occurs when the upward and downward forces created by an employee's strengths and weaknesses reach equilibrium and the employee reaches the career stall-point.

Ask your Human Resources executive to conduct a 360-degree review, utilizing feedback from your peers, subordinates, and supervisor to evaluate your strengths and weaknesses. Then, construct a plan to improve your weaknesses to at least an acceptable level. Usually, the executives with strong strengths and strong weaknesses recognize their strengths but rarely see and agree with the assessment of their weaknesses. Committing to seeing your weaknesses and reducing them will pave the path for further advancement.

Rebuttal from the above column

In the column above, I answered a question from Henry by explaining "The Weakness Principle." I said that his strengths will not be enough, and he should improve his weaknesses to get the next promotion at work. I received a rebuttal from another reader.

Question: Henry came to you for support and sympathy. His strengths should be enough to get him the next promotion. Instead, you supported his mean boss. It was hard enough for him to write to you and confess in public, and you just put him down.

-John

Answer: First, I want to thank you for your rebuttal because it gives me a chance to have a dialogue. The original questioner, Henry, did not come to me for support and sympathy. He came to me for advice on how to get his next promotion. By agreeing with his boss, I did not put him down. Instead, I explained the best course for him to follow.

I do not know why, but employees often get very defensive about their weaknesses. I see more employees blocked from promotions because of their weaknesses than from a "lack of strengths." We need to break this counterproductive cycle, where employees are focused on strengths while ignoring their weaknesses. Companies need to put a formal process in place to routinely conduct 360-degree feedback that identifies employee weaknesses and then put a plan in place to rectify such weaknesses. If this practice becomes routine, then an employee will not feel singled out and the single-minded focus on strengths will start to fade.

I received significant positive feedback on "The Weakness Principle" column. However, your rebuttal was unique and, therefore, deserved further explanation.

I did not see Henry's question as a public confession. If you want a confession, visit a priest. If you want practical business advice, then "Ask Steve."

Hired employee not showing leadership potential

Question: I am the CEO of a small business employing twenty-five people. I hired a young, bright man Dave with the understanding that he may grow to be the group leader. Since he could not handle the work effectively for our growing company, I had to hire a senior person as group leader. Dave still thinks that he is going to be the group leader after the current one retires in a few years. Though Dave is OK at what he does, I do not see him maturing in his attitude nor in his abilities to see the big picture needed for the group leader's position. I do not want to mislead him about his growth opportunities. On the other hand, if I tell him my true assessment of his capabilities, he is bound to argue and not accept it and may turn into a disgruntled employee. What is the right thing to do?

-Bill, Phoenix

Answer: The situation you described is quite common, and there are a few ground rules you should follow. First, you should not promote someone you do not find to be qualified. At the same time, you should not automatically assume that he cannot grow up and mature in a few years to assume the leadership role. And third, you should not mislead him about his growth opportunities. How do you accomplish this without these ground rules being in conflict with one another?

The answer lies in asking the question, "Where does the ownership and responsibility lie for Dave to get promoted to the group leader position?" The responsibility lies with Dave. It is your job to provide growth opportunities in the company. However, it is the employees' responsibility to take advantage of those opportunities.

Please get a copy of my book, "Driving Excellence," published by Wiley. (Trust me; it is not about selling you a book.) Then read Chapter 10, "The Weakness Principle," twice.

Employees' strengths are the "upward force" that drives their careers. Their weaknesses represent the "downward force" that constantly acts to slow their career progression.

"The Weakness Principle" states: as employees progress upward through the company hierarchy, it is their weaknesses that ultimately limit success and stall their careers. This occurs when the upward and downward forces created by an employee's strengths and weaknesses reach equilibrium, and the employee reaches a career stall-point.

Conduct a 360-degree review to evaluate Dave's strengths and weaknesses. Then, construct a plan to improve his weaknesses. Usually, the employees with strong strengths and strong weaknesses recognize their strengths but rarely see and agree with the assessment of their weaknesses. If Dave sees his weaknesses and commits to reducing them, then it will pave the path for further advancement. You will have shifted the responsibility back to Dave without misleading him.

Who to promote with fear of discrimination

Question: I manage a department store and need a supervisor to run the operations so I can spend time on strategic and promotional planning. I have two employees that are equally qualified for this job. One is a Caucasian male, and the other is an African American male. I am concerned that no matter whom I promote, I will be accused of discrimination or reverse discrimination. Should I just hire someone from the outside?

-Lori, Phoenix

Answer: You should not hire someone from the outside. First, it is not fair to either of your employees. Secondly, you would deprive your store of the talents of an inside employee who already knows your business. Thirdly, what kind of message will you be sending? Employees will read into an outside hire that there are no promotional opportunities in your store.

You should develop a selection process for the employee to be promoted. Start with a comprehensive resume, including all prior experience. Then, conduct a 360-degree feedback analysis on both employees. For this, you should interview other store employees, other supervisors, repeat customers, vendors, and security staff. If these steps still do not create a clear-cut differentiation between the two employees, then you can create a trial period where each employee will act in the supervisor's capacity for a period. After the trial, you should be able to compare performances and select your next operations supervisor.

If you run an honest and fair process like this, then you are not likely to be accused of discrimination or reverse discrimination. Employees will see and respect your leadership in trying to be thorough and fair.

You are fortunate to have two qualified employees to choose from. Bypassing them both to hire someone from the outside-that is a cop-out.

Friends as subordinates

Question: I work for a large construction company, and I recently got promoted. Now, one of my best friends works for me. Both of us are increasingly uncomfortable with each other. He uses our friendship and does not easily take direction from me. Our friendship outside of work is compromised, too. What should I do?

-Harold, Phoenix

Answer: You are facing a common dilemma created by friends working together when one of them is promoted. The solutions are not easy and will require some work and adjustments from both of you.

One option is that you should not make friends at work because it may interfere with your career. I believe that it is too harsh. You spend so much time at work and know people the best at work. That is where you are most likely to meet people you can make friends.

The second option is that you should only socialize with people from work who are at a similar or higher level. I do not like that, either. First, by that logic, your seniors should not socialize with you. Second, every time someone gets promoted, the friendships have to be rearranged. That way, you would never have a deep friendship with anyone with whom you could confide and have a life-long relationship.

So, the only other option is to make the situation work as it stands. You should have a heart-to-heart conversation with your friend. Make it clear that you have always enjoyed his friendship and continue to do so now. The changes at work should not come between the friendship. At work, you will give him an equal say and listen to his input, just like everyone else—no more and no less. At times, you may not support his requests. But you would like to continue to be friends with him outside of work. It is quite possible that your friend feels the same way but cannot bring himself to start that conversation with you. By taking the lead, you may have an amicable discussion and find a good compromise.

Whether in this case or later in life, you will encounter a circumstance where you cannot make it work. In that case, you need to find your bias. Either you are career-minded and will sacrifice your friendship, or you are extremely sociable and will compromise your career. I cannot tell you which path to take. But, if you cannot make a compromise work, then you will have a tough choice to make.

After all, there is a reason why someone said that it is lonely at the top.

Sharing in company's values may trump job skills

Question: I just received my performance review. My manager gave me a good score on my performance. But he was overly critical of my values, the way I conduct myself, the way I treat others, my lack of people skills. I do not understand what he is talking about. I should have been promoted to manager and I was not, because of what he claims are my values. If my company does not promote high performers, they will leave. Do you not agree?

-Daniel P., Phoenix

Answer: Actually, I agree with your manager. I consider a company's culture to be at the center of what it stands for, including how its employees conduct themselves and the image it projects to both employees and external audiences. It is a manager's job to be the role model of that culture. Additionally, managers should evaluate their direct-report employees on their values, skills, and results at every performance review. There needs to be a check on all three.

If an employee has the values and skills but does not achieve satisfactory results in one year, I will give that employee another chance. If the employee lacks skills, I would offer training before taking other actions. But if the employee does not share our company's values, he or she will not be successful.

Managers in senior positions who lack shared values can bring a department down. In fact, depending on how this lack of values is expressed (e.g., no respect for legal requirements, financial impropriety, poor quality discipline), they could bring down the whole company. So, I would not compromise on values.

I know that many companies and many managers will give a pass to an employee who has terrible values but achieves good numbers. That is the most dangerous kind of employee, as they can undermine the whole culture. Everyone around these people can see that management is paying lip service to the culture by giving them a pass or, even worse, a promotion.

I applaud your manager for upholding the company's values and standards of behavior. He is telling you that practicing the company's values is not optional. I suggest you put yourself on a corrective action program to learn, adopt and practice those values. Then, in combination with your high performance, you will soon be on your way to that promotion you desire.

My honest advice may not be what you wanted to hear. But when you "Ask Steve," that is what you will receive.

Be understanding of commitments broken due to a bad economy

Question: I am an engineering supervisor for an electronics company. Our company was growing rapidly. Just six months ago, the division manager told me they would divide the group into two groups along the product lines. And I would be promoted to the new division's engineering manager.

Then came the recession, and the company is now laying people off. The plan to break up the division has been shelved, and I got screwed. I asked my boss for a promotion, or at least the salary and benefits of an engineering manager. My company does not agree. Can you help?

-David, Scottsdale

Answer: David! David! David! You could not have been more wrong. I wish you had written to me prior to asking your company for a promotion.

Your company told you about the promotion during strong business conditions. Then came the financial meltdown, and your company was seriously affected. Your fellow employees are being laid off through no fault of their own. And you are asking for a promotion and benefits to which you feel entitled. How dare you be so unsympathetic to the problems faced by your company and the plight of your fellow employees who are being laid off?

Becoming the engineering manager of a division is usually two levels away from the CEO in most medium-sized companies (i.e., the CEO, the division manager and then the engineering manager). As an engineering manager, you would be part of the company's management team. When business conditions change, it would be part of your job, along with the senior management, to steer the company, save costs, cut production, and make whatever hard decisions need to be made.

Asking the company for a promotion and salary increase at this point raises the question of your qualifications as a leader. I am sure you are qualified technically and that is why your company has chosen you for a promotion. You are qualified to manage your people. The question is whether you are qualified to lead your people.

I am sure you wear your company's badge on your shirt pocket. As a candidate aspiring for a management position, you should also wear the company's badge in your heart. That involves understanding its problems, supporting the hard decisions, having empathy for your fellow employees you wish to lead and being willing to make personal sacrifices.

In times like these, ask not what your company can do for you. Ask what you can do for your company.

You should have gone to your division manager and said, "I know that the company is going through tough times. I assure you that you have my support to do whatever is needed to navigate through these rough times. It is not the correct time to give me a big salary increase." That would have dramatically raised your profile in the eyes of your management. And, you would have received the promotion sooner than you are likely to now.

Chapter 3: Layoffs

I received many questions on layoffs, ranging from how to select employees to let go to the effect on the employees who survive a layoff.

Question: I am the CEO of a small manufacturing company facing layoffs because of the weakening economy. Please help me with the process.

-Rick, Phoenix

Answer: Dear Rick, in a cyclical economy, layoffs sometimes become necessary. First, squeeze out all non-critical discretionary spending. Then, decide how much downsizing is required and how many employees will be impacted.

Use sound and defensible criteria for selecting which employees to lay off. First, ensure that you keep critical skills. Then, consider high job performance and, finally, length of service as a tiebreaker. Also, be careful not to affect the distribution of minority employees. After selecting targeted employees, decide on severance packages--paying higher severance for longer service. Additionally, offer job-placement assistance.

Next, prepare exit packages for the affected employees, including severance checks, explanations of benefits, etc. During the exit interview, be courteous and respectful to departing employees. It is not their fault that they are losing their jobs. It is preferable that the layoff be completed within one or two days once it begins to avoid mass fear and unrest.

Remember that layoff survivors need help, too. After completing the layoff, it is extremely important that you have a company-wide communication meeting. Share your analysis on why the layoff was necessary, what was done to avoid a layoff, the criteria for selecting employees and the severance offered--and always show empathy for effected employees. Then, explain the business plan going forward, how and why the company will do well, and why employees should not look for a job. You will be seen by some as having let your employees down. It is your job to pick up their spirits and get them to recommit to the task going forward.

Once it is all done, you will be physically and emotionally exhausted. Do not look for sympathy. You are a CEO and are expected to rise above the situation.

Solving layoff dilemmas

Question: I am the owner of a small private business with 16 employees. My business is facing hardships because of the weakening economy. Unfortunately, I need to lay off one of my employees. My dilemma is how to select the employee to lay off because of the gender and racial mix. Eleven of my employees are Caucasian males, two are Caucasian females, one is a male from India, one is an African American male, and one is a Hispanic male.

My two worst performers are one of the Caucasian females and the only African American male. First, I cannot find a way to decide between those two. And secondly, whatever I do, I will be accused of discrimination and may potentially face a wrongful termination lawsuit.

-Duncan, Peoria

Answer: Title VII of the Civil Rights Act of 1964 prohibits discrimination based on gender or race in any non-governmental organization with fifteen or more employees. If you had less than 15 employees, then your legal dilemma would not be there. But you would still have an ethical dilemma.

So, my first piece of advice is that when you have fourteen employees, you need to be careful. You should try to serve your needs through one or two temporary employees so that you do not face a legal dilemma when you must downsize.

Secondly, you should have implemented a formal system of employee assessment, which is normally called "Performance Appraisals." Smaller employers like you are more likely to overlook this need. Periodical performance appraisals would help you to document your employees' performance, strengths, and weaknesses.

Such documented appraisals would help defend yourself with the Equal Employment Opportunity Commission or in any lawsuit from the laid-off employee. Regardless of your final decision, you should institute a process to deal with poor performers. Often, managers/owners overlook the impact that poor performers can have on the morale of the rest of the team.

In the absence of any documented track record, you have the risk of a potential discrimination lawsuit if you lay off the only African American male or one of the two females. Even if you defend the lawsuit and win, your legal fees may be more than the salary savings from one employee.

My best advice is to refrain from letting any employees go involuntarily. I suggest two options. The first option is to meet with all the employees and ask if anyone would like to voluntarily resign for a severance package.

If no one accepts the offer, your second option is to cut every employee's salary by about 6%. Over sixteen employees, you will save the salary of one employee. You will keep everyone employed and solve your legal and ethical dilemmas. Then, you can reinstate the salaries when your business returns to good health. With this plan, it would be advisable to devise a bonus system, should all employees pitch in and produce great results for the business. This way, everyone will have skin in the game.

Layoff selection criteria

Question: I worked for five years for an engineering company suffering financially from the weak economy. I was recently laid off from my job. What angers me is that certain recently hired employees from other companies are still there. I cannot get any answers from my company. Can you help?

-Scott, Phoenix

Answer: First, I am sorry that you have become the victim of a layoff because of the weakening economy. It is understandable for a laid-off employee to be confused and angry at his company. The most frequently asked question is, "Why me?"

Sometimes, it is the first layoff for a new company. In that case, the criteria for selection were recently developed and probably not yet communicated to the employees. But, in most cases, the laid off employee either did not agree with the criteria or did not agree with how he or she was evaluated against that criterion.

Most employees would like length of service to be the number one criterion. However, in a brutally competitive global environment, that method does not work.

The first criterion is often "critical skills." If the company is going to have fewer employees, it is important to keep the ones with the most critical skills. If your company was not doing well and still hired employees from other companies, I am sure that this was done to acquire skills that were critical for its success.

The second criterion is often job performance. Imagine that there are two employees with similar critical skills. The first one applies his skills and gets good results. He gets along with everyone, helps others succeed, is well-engaged and is seen as an excellent employee. The second one has a chip on his shoulder, does not get along with others, is not engaged and is seen as a disruptive influence. If you were the manager, it is clear whom you would choose.

The third criterion is length of service, which should be used only as a tiebreaker.

The next issue is how to apply the above criteria fairly. Prior performance appraisals may give some guidance. However, critical skills and job performance are not absolute measures. My experience has been that when a laid-off employee disagrees with the application of the first two criteria on him, then in most cases, he also disagrees with prior performance appraisals. In those cases, there were warning signs all along for the employee to improve his skills and job performance. However, the areas of improvement were not acknowledged or internalized and, therefore, never improved upon.

There is one other scenario. Anti-discrimination laws require that a company may not impact the distribution of minorities, females, and employees over forty after a layoff. During the application of these laws, a more qualified employee can sometimes get laid-off.

Is that fair? I think not! But that is the subject for another column.

How to avoid a layoff?

Question: I am the department manager in our company, which is suffering because of the weak economy. Our management is considering layoffs. Can you suggest some best practices to help avoid a layoff for as long as possible?

-Jennifer, Phoenix

Answer: I am sorry to hear that your company is suffering and considering layoffs. In this column, I will discuss how to avoid or postpone layoffs.

Of course, the best way to avoid a layoff is to have a strong business model in which your company is gaining market share. However, such a market position is achieved over many years. In this column, I will address how to cope with decreased business and avoid layoffs.

1. <u>Reduce discretionary expenses:</u> First, companies should reduce discretionary expenses—travel, entertainment, conferences, tradeshows, advertising, and temporary labor. It looked foolish when the auto-manufacturing executives showed up in Washington D.C. on private jets and asked for $25 billion in bailout funds. Microchip executives fly in coach class during these difficult times.

2. <u>Reduce capital expenditures:</u> Review your capital-expenditure budget. Do not spend just to flush the budget.

3. <u>Forced shutdowns:</u> You can have an unpaid shutdown. This technique is very effective for a manufacturing company. In addition to the payroll savings, the company saves on all other

costs—raw materials, utilities, gases, chemicals, repairs, and transportation. The company also keeps its inventory lower while sales are falling.

Arizona employees can apply for unemployment insurance for that week. They do not get paid for the first shutdown week, which is the qualifying week. Then, during any subsequent shutdown, the employees can claim unemployment insurance from the state.

4. Pay cuts: A company can decide to institute a pay cut for all employees to save on costs or roll back a previously announced round of pay raises.

5. Voluntary unpaid time off: There are always employees who would like to take some unpaid time off for personal reasons. But they are afraid to ask because they fear losing their jobs. Such personal reasons may be to take care of ailing parents or siblings, bond with a new child, complete education, travel abroad or religious commitments.

   Companies should consider allowing employees to apply for extended time off without pay without fear of reprisal. This would help the company save money and it would have its trained employees back by the time the business recovered.

Can these actions prevent a layoff? That depends on how deep the downturn is and how strong your company's market position is. Such actions allow all employees to share in the sacrifices, which builds a stronger team; versus using layoffs as the first tactic. This stronger and more committed team will go the extra mile to help your business succeed.

Layoff survivors need attention too

Question: Our company recently had a layoff. But the management had no communication with the rest of us still working. While we are glad to have our jobs, we are all very nervous. We do not know exactly who is gone and whether the layoff is complete. We do not know whether there is another layoff coming. And we do not know whether any projects have been reprioritized because of the reduction in force. The stress level is very high. Management just tells us to shut up and do our jobs, and that we are lucky to not be on the layoff list. Is this the correct way to handle things?

-Tanya, Mesa

Answer: Very succinctly, this is not the correct way to handle things. In fact, it is a terrible way to conduct a layoff. While we do not expect managers to be experts in conducting layoffs, some simple steps must be taken to relieve the anxiety of those still employed. Layoff survivors need help, too.

First, any layoff should be completed in just one or two days. After completing the layoff, the management (preferably the CEO) must hold a company-wide communication meeting. They should share the analysis of why the layoff was necessary, what was done to avoid it, the criteria for selecting employees and the severance offered. The management should always show empathy for affected employees. Then, explain the business plan going forward, how and why the company will do well, and why the remaining employees should not look for a job.

One of the questions on employees' minds will be whether another layoff is coming. The CEO needs to be very honest with the employees. If he or she believes that the downsizing has been completed, then he or she should say so. If another layoff is possible, the CEO should set the appropriate expectations and define some metrics that could trigger another layoff. Finally, the CEO should challenge the employees to give their very best and perform better than the competition so that the need for a second layoff does not arise.

The remaining employees are indeed lucky to have their jobs. However, they still need direction, project prioritization, stress relief and the knowledge that the layoff is complete. This will allow them to return to their jobs and concentrate.

Some will see the CEO as having let the employees down. It is his or her job to lift their spirits and get them to recommit to the task, going forward.

Once it is done, the CEO will be physically and emotionally exhausted. While a CEO is expected to rise above the situation, it is lonely at the top. And it would not be a bad idea for you to drop him or her a short note of support.

Manager refuses to lay off employee

Question: I am the purchasing manager for an engineering company. Our company is downsizing, and the management is planning a layoff. I was told to lay off one of my employees out of seven that I manage today. While the volume is down, I still manage the same number of line items. I cannot manage the department with one less person. Besides, all my employees are good, hard-working employees and I do not feel morally right about laying off one of them. My boss disagrees and thinks every department needs to participate in the cuts. What should I do?

-Jonathan, Phoenix

Answer: First, I am very sorry to hear that your company is planning a layoff. In a layoff, it is critical for a company to preserve its most crucial assets to ensure its survivability and eventual prosperity. The best criteria are to preserve critical skills first, then look for job performance and only use length of service as a tiebreaker.

You said that you work for an engineering company. What do you believe that your customers pay for? Do they pay for engineering output, or do they pay for managing the purchasing of line items? I am sure that it is the former.

Do the most valuable assets of your company lie in engineering talent or purchasing? Should the company lay off one more engineer, so you do not have to do the hard work of letting go of one of your purchasing agents? Surely you do not think that. The fact that all of your employees are good, hard-working people does not figure into the equation. A layoff does not only affect non-performers. In a reduction, many good performers have to be let go. If every soldier asserts his moral rights on the battlefield, then every war will be lost.

So, if your company is having a layoff and you have been asked to reduce your headcount by one, you must choose one of your employees using the criteria I defined above. If you continue to insist that your department be spared from the layoff, I see one option for you and another for your boss.

The option for you is to propose another way to achieve the same payroll savings that laying off one employee would produce. Including you, there are eight in the department. If you, and all of your employees take a 12.5% pay cut, that would be the equivalent of laying off one person.

If you do not produce any suitable alternatives, then there is only one option for your boss. He or she should add your name to the layoff list and groom another individual to be the leader of your department. Next time, he or she should choose one more capable of seeing the bigger picture than you seem to be.

Like they say, if you cannot take the heat, then stay out of the kitchen.

Can I hire my nephew instead of recalling a laid-off employee?

Question: I own a small business and provide painting and other minor repair services to residential, commercial, and industrial customers. Several months ago, I had to let 25% of my employees go because of lower business activity. I recently got a large job and now need to rehire one employee. Do I have to rehire one of the employees that I laid off, or can I hire my nephew, who has recently been laid off from another job and has some prior experience in painting?

-Scott

Answer: First, I must say that I have been getting a lot of questions about layoffs and who to fire. It has been a long time since I received a question regarding who to hire. That is a welcome change and hopefully a small sign of a bottoming economy and job growth ahead.

The answer to your question depends on several facts about the situation, that I do not know from your question. Since this type of question will likely come up often as job openings reappear, I will give a broad-based answer under several scenarios.

There are several key factors that could apply to your situation. 1. Does your company have fifteen or more employees? 2. Were any minority or over-forty employees let go? 3. Is your nephew a Caucasian male under forty? 4. Does your company have a formal or informal policy for recalling employees from a layoff?

Let us address these one at a time…

If your company has fifteen or more employees, they are covered by Title VII of the Civil Rights Act of 1964, which prohibits discrimination. So, if you laid off an employee who is a minority or over forty and then hired a Caucasian male under forty, you may have some legal exposure. If you let several employees go, including a mixture of Caucasian and minority employees, then it is less of an issue.

The second factor is whether your company has a formal or informal policy of first recalling the employees who were let go. If there was such a policy, deviating from your own policy may cause legal exposure.

I am bringing up these issues to include several circumstances where different factors may be in play. In many cases, if an employee is bitter or feels that he or she was inappropriately selected for the layoff, then this employee may be particularly watchful when the rehiring takes place. If you are on the borderline of any Title VII issues or your own internal policy, you have a higher risk of drawing a legal challenge.

In small non-governmental businesses with less than 15 employees, which likely describes your operation, you may hire your nephew at will without any concerns of a legal challenge. I will leave any moral dilemmas for you to sort out.

Loyalty alone is not enough

Question: In your column, "Understanding Layoff Criteria," you answered my question by saying that in a layoff, managers should look for critical skills first, job performance second and length of service as a tiebreaker. Where does loyalty fit into this equation?

Scott, Phoenix

Answer: Ah, loyalty! It is such a warm word but is often ill-defined and misunderstood.

The dictionary definition of loyalty is "unswerving in allegiance." Some describe it as loyalty to the boss. For others, loyalty is synonymous with length of employment. Still, others say attendance is loyalty—always showing up for work. During a layoff, people often ask the following question based on their contrived definition of loyalty, "Did my loyalty not mean anything?"

Many managers are delighted by employees who show personal loyalty to them. These managers protect such employees, even though their performance may be marginal. Such managers lack confidence and draw strength from employees who are personally loyal to them. Many managers will use "fear and reward" tactics to force such loyalty. Often, these managers get caught up in a layoff, leaving their "loyal" employees feeling very vulnerable. Managers should coach employees to be loyal to the company, not themselves.

Good companies engender loyalty by creating a culture and system where ordinary employees can produce extraordinary results. During good times, employees share in the profits of those extraordinary results. This culture also creates a groundswell of support for the shared sacrifices required during difficult times. Over time, a virtuous spiral of loyalty develops between employees and the company.

I have written a lot about how to avoid layoffs. During this recession, Microchip has chosen to reduce employees' work hours, pay and benefits. But we have not laid anyone off. During such periods of uncertainty, employees are closely watching how well a company follows its values. One of Microchip's guiding values is, "Employees are our greatest strength." And, even in this extremely difficult business environment, we are demonstrating how much we truly value our employees by remaining the only company in the semiconductor industry that has not done a layoff in several downcycles in business.

This may not always be possible for every company. Once a company has decided that a layoff is necessary based on its business prospects, the selection criteria come into play and loyalty comes up.

Many people would use the slogan "Loyalty is dead." This slogan originated when employers first faced low-cost foreign competition and began outsourcing certain jobs to low-cost countries. I do not believe that loyalty is dead, but loyalty alone is not good enough.

In times of distress, a company needs results to avoid getting into a death spiral. And results come from employees with critical skills and good job performance. If the employees possessing critical skills deliver good results and are loyal, then you have a dream team. If that is not the case, then loyalty alone is not enough.

Have you seen a football coach sideline a long-term quarterback when he is no longer producing results? Similarly, managers should select their most qualified resources to get the best results. Marginal employees, whether they are loyal or not, should move on.

Small employer facing second layoff

Question: I own a small engineering services company with twenty-five employees. When the recession hit last year, I had to lay off fifteen of my forty employees. Then, I committed to no further layoffs. I just lost another major contract from a customer who decided to cut back on outsourcing. I need to lay off another three employees. What should I do?

Edward, Phoenix

Answer: First, I am sorry that you are facing the possibility of a second layoff. As an owner/CEO, you have learned that it was a mistake to commit to no further layoffs. In business, there are things like the economy that you cannot control. You should always leave a door open to address the issues of an uncertain economy. The best way to do so is to add "conditionality" to your commitment to no further layoffs. This allows you to change your commitment if the circumstances change. So, what should you do now?

As an owner/CEO, it takes many years to build trust with your employees. Employees compare every word you say to the actions that you take. If you conduct a layoff now, you will suffer a significant blow to your credibility. If your business were to be at stake unless you lay off half or a third of your employees, you would not have a choice. You must save your business, even if it destroys your credibility. However, regarding your question, you have a 10% payroll problem that you need to solve by laying off three employees. I will suggest two alternatives, which I have previously used at Microchip Technology.

The first option is implementing a mandatory one to two weeks off without pay. This can be the entire company off at one time or the employees scheduling it individually, or whatever is more suitable for your business.

The second option is to introduce a 10% pay cut for all employees. You can also mix and match these two options. For certain employees when there are several with similar skills, you can have time off without pay. For others where you have only one of two employees with a certain skill, you can institute a pay cut.

You made a no-layoff commitment. You did not make a commitment concerning pay cuts or unpaid time off. So, these options would let you keep your commitment while achieving the payroll savings that your business needs.

You will suffer some loss in credibility. But, if you make a good case in a company-wide communication meeting and sell it as a shared sacrifice rather than laying off three poor souls, your employees may even rally around your decision and get a morale boost.

Trust me, I have been there. When I announced a similar program at Microchip, the employees applauded the concept of shared sacrifices versus a layoff.

Chapter 4: Benefits at work

Supervisor asks overtime to not be reported

Question: I am an hourly employee eligible for overtime. Our company has clamped down on overtime. However, my supervisor regularly asks me to work overtime and then requires that I not put overtime on my timecard. Is that illegal and unfair to me?

-Deborah, Peoria, Arizona

Answer: Dear Deborah, it is absolutely illegal and also unfair to you. I respect a company's right to clamp down on overtime to control costs. Your supervisor then needs to prioritize the work so that the work can be accomplished without overtime. If that is not possible, then he or she needs to appeal to the management for a waiver from the overtime clamp down. I have two suggestions.

First, you should try to reason with your supervisor. You are employed at an hourly rate of pay. Why should you have to work extra hours without pay?

The second is you should talk to the employee relations person in your human resources department. Illegal practices like this by renegade supervisors can expose the companies to class action suits, government inquiries, union drives, etc. Your employee relations person is likely to be very sensitive to your complaint and will intervene on your behalf. It is always a good idea to put your complaint to human resources in writing and keep a copy. Whistleblower laws will safeguard your interest if your company or your supervisor retaliates in any way.

Your ultimate avenue will be to complain to the Department of Labor. But I think that any professional human resources department will understand the seriousness of this violation of law and will nip this problem in the bud.

Ask your supervisor about your performance review, not for a raise

Question: I started a new job a year ago. I have worked very hard and believe my performance has been very good. Yet, I have not received a pay raise from my boss. Should I ask him about it or just wait for it to come my way?

-Sue, Tucson

Answer: Half the honor of getting a raise is gone if you have to ask for it. Similarly, half the pleasure of delivering a pay raise or promotion is gone for your boss if you must ask for it. Therefore, do not ask for it yet.

Your company, depending on its size and culture, must have a practice of giving pay raises. Some companies give raises on employees' anniversaries, while others do so on the same day for all employees. You should ask your colleagues discreetly about your company's practices.

If the practice is that you get a raise on your anniversary, then you should wait for a few weeks past the anniversary. Your boss may be occupied or traveling, and your pay raise might be on its way. Meanwhile, you could ask the human resources department if your pay raise is due.

If the practice is that you get a raise on a date along with everyone else (usually called Focal), then that date should be announced soon. Again, you can ask human resources for that date.

As far as your boss is concerned, I would not ask him for a pay raise. Instead, I would ask him about your performance review. If your company does not have a formal performance review process, then ask your boss the following question: "I have been here a year. I would like to know how I am doing. Are there areas where you would like me to improve? And are there areas where I have done well?"

The question will prompt your boss to talk. If your pay raise is in the works, he will tell you so. If it is not, he will give you feedback on your performance and will likely tell you he'll get back to you with a pay raise. Good luck.

Vacation policy varies from state to state

Question: I am an hourly employee eligible for earned vacation. Once earned, can an employee forfeit his vacation?

-Tony, Superior

Question: My sister works for a company as an hourly employee. The company closes on the Friday following Thanksgiving and forces its employees to use a vacation day for that closure. They have no choice. They cannot even take the day as an unpaid day. This just does not seem right to me. Is this practice legal?

-Delores, Phoenix

Answer: Vacation is a voluntary benefit that an employer provides. US labor law does not mandate a vacation or sick benefit. However, if an employer establishes a policy, then the law states that they must enforce that policy fairly. Additionally, if an employer establishes a policy of accruing vacation by time spent working, the law says the employee is entitled to that vacation. Therefore, if an employee quits, they are entitled to be paid for unused vacation.

An Arizona employer can establish a "use it or lose it" policy. It is legal in Arizona, but not in every state (it is illegal in California). For example, at Microchip, we allow our Arizona employees to roll their unused vacation at the end of the year to March 31 of the following year before they lose it. Again, it is so because we have written the policy at Microchip to be this way. Arizona law gives wide discretion to the employer in establishing the policy.

The employer can also mandate using that vacation during a shutdown, as Delores' sister's company has done. At Microchip, we always offer an option to the employee to take an unpaid day or use a vacation day, but we do not have to. So, if the company forces the employee to take a vacation day, is it legal? Yes. Is it an employee-friendly policy? Definitely not.

COVID-19 company policy

Question: I am an executive with an engineering firm in Scottsdale. We have been struggling with figuring out our COVID-19 policy for absences from work. Obviously, we do not want infected employees to be at work to avoid the spread of disease. But how should we address these absences in our attendance policy, and who should pay for the sick time?

-Arthur, Scottsdale

Answer: First, I am not a doctor. So, any comments on the medical side are based purely on information from government Web sites and advice from my doctor. I will focus mainly on workplace policy.

The COVID-19 virus spreads mainly through the droplets from a sick person who is sneezing and coughing. Therefore, it is important that anyone infected stays at home and does not expose others to the virus at work. Currently, many flu cases are COVID. At Microchip, we require any employee with flu symptoms to stay home. We are giving them a break from the attendance policy by not counting it as unscheduled absenteeism. However, the employee is paid from his or her fixed personal-absence allotment.

The obvious question is, what if an employee tries to take advantage of the lax attendance policy? The answer lies first in the culture that you have developed at your company. With all that we have done for our employees through business cycles, I am confident that they will not misuse our generosity. If you are concerned, you could require a note from the doctor for each affected employee.

If you do not relax your policy, the employees are likely to show up at work sick. This will infect more employees, and it will cost you more in the long term.

You should consider some other precautionary measures that you should consider. Several years ago, we installed hand-sanitizer dispensers in all common areas, such as outside the restrooms, and near copy machines, water fountains, cafeterias, building entrances, etc. (We have also encouraged employees to make liberal use of these hand sanitizers.) As a direct result, we have seen a noticeable decrease in employee sickness during the last three years.

A few years ago, we dedicated a janitor at each site to continuously wipe down and sanitize the doorknobs, handrails, cafeteria tables and other common surfaces. We believe this is a very cheap insurance policy to prevent the spread of flu.

Lastly, communicate your real concern for their health and the continued prosperity of the company yourself and through your management team. And remind them and encourage them to take prudent precautions.

Should my company pay my home office expenses?

Question: I work for an engineering company and often take work home. I also occasionally work out of home when I do not have a meeting in the office. I use my internet, printing and copy paper, ink cartridges and other office supplies while working at home. I tried to take some office supplies home, but the company did not like that practice. Should I not be compensated for my home office expenses?

-Anonymous, Phoenix

Question: I live in Tucson and work for a company in Phoenix. I visit the company once or twice a week, and work from home the rest of the time. When the company hired me, it was understood that I would work from home for three to four days a week. I am an engineer, and I have a lab set up at home. Should the company not pay for my home-office expenses?

-Randall, Tucson

Answer: Should you be compensated for your home office expenses? Yes. Should you ask to be compensated? No.

If you were a remote employee in a town where the company had no facilities and you ultimately worked out of your home, then the situation would be different. If you just work out of home occasionally and in the evenings, then the expenses you are talking about are minimal and are intertwined with your personal use of those items.

You probably still need internet for yourself, your spouse and your kids even if you do not work out of home. Most broadband expenses are not per user, so you have no incremental expenses. The expenses for copy paper and other supplies are minimal.

If you use your telephone to make long-distance calls for work, then your company should give you a phone card, or you can use the company cell phone or bill them for actual long-distance calls. However, all the other expenses are small, and you should offset them against the benefits you receive by occasionally working out of home. Such benefits include saving on driving time, saving on automobile expenses, proximity to spouse and kids, being able to temporarily watch a child when spouse runs out for an errand and best of all, being able to work in your PJs. You will not want the company to dock your pay for the time spent on those breaks. Nor should you dock the company for very small office expenses.

In the case of Randall, you are a remote employee in a town where the company has no facilities, and you primarily work out of your home. In addition, you have a lab at home, which will regularly need engineering supplies and small components. In this case, you should be compensated. However, you should have discussed such compensation as part of your job offer when you made the agreement to work from home three to four days a week. It is likely that the company buys its services in bulk, so compensating you at retail prices may cost the company extra money. However, with your supervisor's permission, you may be able to take some office and lab supplies from work and use them at home.

Your work-related unreimbursed expenses were deductible above 2% of your adjusted gross income till 2017. However, the Tax and Jobs Act took the deduction away from 2018 to 2025.

My bottom line is this: If you can occasionally work from home, enjoy that privilege and do not sweat the small stuff.

How do we contain health care costs?

Question: I am a plant manager for an international company with $2B in annual sales. This is the time of year again when our employees are offered open enrollment for medical and other benefits. Once again, costs to the employees are going up. I am concerned that my yearly explanation that medical costs are going up everywhere will not sit well with the employees. The increased costs will essentially wipe out all raises given last year. And for employees on the lower end of the wage scale, it will cost them a good portion of their take-home pay.

How can I sell this to the employees? And is there a way to contain health care premium costs?

-Shawn, Casa Grande

Answer: Health cost inflation is one of the biggest issues facing our corporations and our nation. Healthcare costs have been rising double-digit rates, well above the inflation rate.

There are really no tricks to selling it to employees. The best way is to show them that you are doing everything possible to lower the cost increases.

All you can do in the short term is for your company to take a larger share of the increase to keep employees' costs manageable. Another thing that you can do is play with deductibles, control expensive prescriptions and promote the use of generics. All these are tricks that your benefits manager may already know.

The next step is to investigate self-insurance with a rider for catastrophic stop loss. With $2B in sales, your company is large enough to insure itself. Any insurance company will charge you equal to what it will cost you, plus a healthy profit for the insurance company. By self-insuring, you are saving by acting as your own insurance company. You should buy a rider for catastrophic stop loss so that your company is financially protected in case of a serious one-time illness or accident.

The next thing to do is to aggressively shop for a medical group and negotiate deep discounts from that group. Then, you should limit your choice of doctors to those available in this group. Many groups with deep discounts have excellent doctors. I have found that most of the doctors that employees see are already in those groups.

The final area is to look into having an onsite health clinic. Our company, Microchip Technology, opened an onsite health clinic with a nurse practitioner in May 2007 and the response has been overwhelming. I was surprised to see how cost-effective the clinic is, and it saves employees significant time traveling to doctors' offices and delays in the waiting rooms. The visit to the clinic is free to employees and their covered spouses. This gets them to see a doctor early before major complications and significantly higher costs, thus saving us money in the longer term.

One point to note is that the onsite clinic idea only works if you are self-insured.

Christmas gift from your employer

Question: I work for a large employer. It is a good place to work. But, every Christmas season, we do not receive anything from our employer to show their appreciation for our hard work.

What do you do to show your appreciation to Microchip's employees during the holiday season? Does management send them a signed card? Do they get a certificate for a ham or turkey? Or do they get a cash bonus?

-Frank

Answer: What seems to be a very simple question is quite complex. What a company can do for its employees can change based on the size of the company, its international makeup, the status of the economy and the current performance of the company.

Let me walk you through the stages of Microchip's growth and how this decision has changed over the years. When we were a small company, we held an annual Christmas party for our employees, which was well appreciated. As we grew and began 24/7 manufacturing operations, it became more difficult.

When we held the Christmas party on Saturday night (a traditional night for parties), we got complaints from the weekend shift. Then, we held a second party on Monday night for the weekend shift. We got complaints again that the party was smaller, had fewer menu choices, and all the executives did not attend. So, no matter what we did, a section of the employee workforce was unhappy.

Then, a couple of years ago, we had a record year at a time when gas prices shot through the roof. So, we gave every employee a $100 gas bonus to help with their holiday shopping. That went well, but it is not affordable every year. Yes, I have written Christmas and holiday messages for them during certain years, but not consistently.

Although I have not experienced this problem at Microchip, other companies have received complaints about using the word "Christmas" at Christmas parties, Christmas trees, Christmas bonuses, Christmas cards and Christmas gifts. It seems that some would like to cancel Christmas and just call it "Holiday." Other companies have also received complaints about major holidays important to other faiths. There are kosher and vegetarian dietary restrictions that can make giving food certificates complicated.

The situation gets more complex for an international company, with employees in forty countries. Each country has a different culture, customs, and holidays. It is nearly impossible to keep it all fair and square.

So, you should not necessarily look for something special from your company for Christmas. The employees need to be appreciated every day, not just at Christmas. I personally appreciate and thank my employees at every communication meeting and at every other opportunity I get throughout the year.

Work is no place for public display of affection

Question: Have you ever encountered a situation where two men or two women were involved with each other and displaying affection? It is probably only a matter of time, and they'd probably holler, "discrimination based on sexual orientation." This could happen in hiring and promotions. The biggest issue is in the benefits that a spouse is entitled to. Just wondering if you have a policy in place if that should happen.

- *Nate*

Answer: This question can stir controversy faster than any other question I have answered. However, I am not going to take a position on homosexuality, same-sex marriage, or gay and lesbian rights. So, whatever your position is on these subjects, you are entitled to your position and there are other avenues through which you can voice your opinion. Instead, I am going to focus on the workplace as it relates to gay or lesbian employees.

First, I do not think that any specific policy is needed for homosexual conduct in the workplace. It is a place of work where everyone is supposed to be busy doing their jobs, whether it is research, manufacturing, marketing, or serving clients. Open displays of affection should be discouraged in the workplace, whether heterosexual or homosexual.

Secondly, it is illegal to ask anyone during any interview whether they are married. A person's marital status should not affect their candidacy for a job. It should be the same for their sexual orientation—this should have no bearing on a person's candidacy. After an employee starts working, their colleagues usually know through social contact whether the person is married. Similarly, colleagues usually know the person's sexual orientation. However, these things should not affect the employee's role at work. Similarly, marital status and sexual orientation should have no bearing on promotions, layoffs and merit raises.

Suppose a person is disruptive at work and engages in debates about homosexuality, dresses inappropriately, or displays inappropriate posters. In that case, he or she should be governed by the existing workplace rules. Just make sure that you interpret the rules in the same manner for heterosexual as well as homosexual behavior.

Now comes the hard part. What about benefits? Should the same-sex partner be covered under the employee's medical benefits, just like married spouses are? I answer that question by asking whether the employer covers heterosexual couples living together but not married. The same treatment should be applied to cohabitating homosexual couples.

This is the point where the debate usually rages on. I am not offering an opinion as to whether employers should cover unmarried couples living together. Arizona state law does not require them to do so; the rest is up to the employer's policy. If you do not like this law, call your congressperson. All I am saying is that a company's benefits policy should be applied in the same manner to both heterosexual and homosexual unmarried couples.

Employers should accommodate new mothers

Question: I am a new mother who just went back to work. I need to pump my milk during work hours and save it in a refrigerator for later use by my new baby. Should my employer provide an adequate room for new mothers?

-Marisol, Phoenix

Answer: It is fully understandable that mothers who are breastfeeding will sometimes want to extract their own milk and save it for their baby's later use. I think the most reasonable size employers would provide a private room with a sink and a refrigerator to facilitate this.

Microchip provides a mothers' room in all of the large facilities. However, it is difficult to provide a dedicated room in many of our small sales offices of eight to ten employees around the world. Although, there is always a small kitchenette with a refrigerator. So, in smaller facilities, the new mother can extract her milk in the women's restroom and then keep it in the refrigerator.

I would simply say this to employers: employees are under tremendous stress in the current environment. Layoffs are rampant because of the deteriorating economy, and the effect on our society is very negative. A new mother should not have to choose between staying home so that she can breastfeed her baby versus being able to save her milk while at work. She may be a single mother, or her husband may be facing a layoff, so she probably cannot afford to lose her job. Her need to bond with her baby by breastfeeding is real and very reasonable for an employer to accommodate. Please help these mothers out.

For large employers, it does not take a lot to provide a private room with a sink and refrigerator. For very small employers, just provide a refrigerator and a safe place to keep it. Your employees are your greatest strength, and happy and motivated employees will help you navigate through these difficult times.

Chapter 5: Discrimination and harassment at work

I received the largest number of questions from employees on discrimination and harassment in the workplace. In my answers, my stating of the public policy against discrimination and harassment (Title VII of the 1964 Civil Rights Act) may be repetitive in various answers, but it was necessary for each answer to be complete.

Woman stripper bringing singing telegram

Question: I work in an office. Last week, some men bought a singing telegram for a male colleague's birthday. The girl was very sexily dressed. While singing, she performed a striptease until she was scantily clothed. The men were making profane comments and sounds. Some women also got into the act. I felt so embarrassed. What recourse do I have?

- *Julie*

Answer: Sexual harassment in the workplace is illegal. It can take the form of individual harassment by a boss or a colleague. Or it can take place when the company allows a sexually charged environment to occur that makes others feel uncomfortable. Such striptease acts have no place in a professional work environment. So, what is your recourse?

It depends on what outcome you are looking for. If you want to hold the company liable for damage, I will not recommend that approach in the first incidence. Your complaint will be viewed as monetarily motivated, and your company will put up all sorts of legal defenses.

Your goal should be to stop such behavior from recurring. You should meet with your director of Human Resources and inform him/her of what happened. He/she will most likely find this unacceptable as well. Ask for a workplace dress policy to be established. However, remember that you will be opening a Pandora's Box. Even some of your female colleagues may not agree with you. The debate will be regarding where to draw the line. Which of these are acceptable—low-cut blouses, short skirts, bare midriff sections and tank tops for women, and muscle shirts for men? Everyone has a different definition of what is acceptable, and that can vary from an office environment to a night club to a casino. But every employee has the right to a fair dress policy and a professional work environment that is free from harassment. So, hold your ground.

Once the policy has been established, any visitors like singing-telegrams must comply with the policy, otherwise they should not be allowed in the building. Do not settle for comments like, "Hey loosen up. What is the big deal? What is wrong with a little spice?"

Creating an environment that promotes sexual harassment is a big deal. Ask the men to take the birthday boy to a strip club or a private home where you have a choice not to go. But you should first try to create an environment that means you don't have to ask.

Relationship with boss

Question: I am a single female. I made the mistake of getting romantically involved with my boss. After knowing the other side of him, I am no longer interested in him. But I do not know how to break it off because I am worried about my job.

-Anonymous, Scottsdale

Answer: It was a serious error in judgment to get involved with your direct boss at work. Romantic relationships with co-workers—especially bosses—rarely work out. And they create an uncomfortable environment when they end. That is why many companies have policies against managers dating their subordinates.

You should meet with your company's director of Human Resources (HR). Tell him/her that you made a mistake in getting involved with your boss and now want to end the relationship. You should come clean and not make up a story; and certainly, do not accuse your boss of pressure for dates or harassment if it is not true. The truth usually comes out in these matters, and it will be very bad for you if you lie. So, tell the truth and then ask HR for help. If your company has a policy against such relationships, then put yourself at the mercy of HR and ask for forgiveness. Additionally, you may ask to be transferred to another department.

The director of HR is then likely to meet with your boss. If the boss violated a policy, then serious disciplinary action should be taken against him. The boss, being the senior person, has a higher burden in the violation of the policy. If you come forward first, your punishment is likely to be less severe.

If your company has no such policy, then the director of HR may not do anything. However, you have now put your meeting with him/her on record. After meeting with HR, you should meet with your boss and break off the relationship. You should also tell him that your HR department is aware of it. That way, your boss is not likely to take any action against you.

Being the first to come forward may save you from any fallout. At Microchip, we do have a policy against such relationships. I do not want to scare you, but the last time I uncovered one such relationship in which neither party came forward, I fired them both.

Supervisor cannot exert religious pressure on a subordinate

Question: I read your column regarding relationships with bosses, and it stirred a pack of sleeping dogs within me. 28 years ago, I worked at a defense contractor as a clerk. The supervisor assigned me to his secretary, who proceeded to mercilessly harass me in an attempt at conversion to her brand of Christianity.

I did not report this activity to the supervisor because I suspected he was somehow complicit in it. I instead went to HR. However, the HR rep immediately began screaming at me. I left with my tail between my legs. I realized what I was up against and discovered that the purpose of HR was not to promote any naïve concept of a harmonious labor-management environment, but to control costs.

I strongly considered filing a grievance with the EEOC but did not. God only knows to what extent management were prepared to go to distort, obfuscate and lie. Had I pursued the grievance, it would have been a losing battle and a disaster for me.

HR departments are generally not benign, compassionate and well-meaning entities, although things may have improved over the years.

-Nate

Answer: I am so sorry to hear your story. What happened to you was a direct violation of Title VII of the 1964 Civil Rights Act, which prohibits discrimination based on religion in any non-governmental organization with fifteen or more employees.

There are misguided people in many positions of authority. There are bad bosses, CEOs, HR departments, senators, presidents, judges, and police officers. That is why our system is built on checks and balances. The rights of the individual and the rights of employees have been strengthened significantly in the last 28 years. However, what happened to you 28 years ago could still happen to anyone today. My retired VP of HR and I co-authored a book called "Driving Excellence," published by Wiley in 2006. Please read it and see how far the HR discipline has come. But I have to agree that there are plenty of bad HR departments, even now.

That is why we have the U.S Department of Labor and the EEOC. An employee being discriminated against should go to HR first, and then to the EEOC; and you should have gone to EEOC back then. I understand your hesitancy to go to the EEOC as a new and young employee who was afraid to take on your company. Through your decision, your boss, his secretary, and the HR department got off without a trial or a penalty; and they probably continued to inflict pain on many others in their careers. However, you absolutely had no legal obligation to stick your neck out and correct the injustice. Still, a lot of bad bosses, judges, police officers, HR departments and even criminals go free because people do not want to get involved.

Your experience brings to mind the lines of the movie "Tears of the Sun":

"Evil gets its best chance to prevail, when a lot of well-meaning people choose to do nothing."

Custody battle between owners' stresses employees

Question: I work for a wonderful small company that has one of the best reputations in its market. I like my work, my coworkers, and my clients. The problem is the toxic custody battle going on between the once-married owners of the company, and the other woman (who still works for the company in a managerial job created for her).

Each player habitually spills details about their lives and business plans to rank-and-file employees, and then tries to get those employees to disclose what the other two have already said. Each player has threatened those employees' jobs, should they say anything.

The situation is bad enough that customers have witnessed shouting matches between the owners, and some employees have already left because of the strain.

Short of sticking our fingers in our ears and saying "La la la" whenever a boss starts talking about personal issues, what can we do? Writing a letter about the hostile work environment merely resulted in more shouting matches, as each person blamed the other for causing the problem. Despite everything, I would like to stick around because I feel that the company has a great future.

-Sandra, Flagstaff

Answer: I feel very sorry for you and your fellow employees, and I have struggled to provide a good answer for you.

Ordinarily, if someone creates a hostile work environment, then the employees are protected by the Title VII of the Civil Rights Act of 1964. However, this protection does not apply here, because the shouting and hostility is not directed at you. If you can prove that the owners have threatened your job, via witnesses or recordings, you may have a claim. However, I think that you just want the situation to improve so that the company can pursue a good future.

My sense is that this situation is untenable because the people in charge, who can make a change for the better, are the root cause of the situation! Under these circumstances, whatever great future the company has is at risk because the leadership situation has degenerated from doing the right thing for the company to doing the right thing for each of the three people involved in this saga. And the poor employees are caught in the crossfire.

This situation is unlikely to get better and has a high likelihood of getting worse. I would recommend that you start looking for other jobs and jump ship as soon as you find one that is suitable. Life is too short to put up with personal BS created by the leaders of a company.

Want wife to dress sexy

Question: My wife and I own a small company with twenty-seven employees. I would like my wife to wear sexy clothes at work, with low-cut blouses and short skirts. This should encourage other female employees to do the same. And it could dress up the workplace. But my wife refuses to wear such clothes. She should do it if she loves me enough.

-Paul, Scottsdale

Answer: This is one of the most ridiculous questions I have ever received. It has nothing to do with seeking business advice. This question should be better put to the radio host Dr. Laura or the TV host Dr. Phil.

I have no idea whether your wife loves you. You do not seem to be making it easy for her to do so. As a company with over fifteen employees, your employees are covered under Title VII of the Civil rights act of 1964, which prohibits discrimination based on gender. If your request were to any other female employee besides your wife, she would have a sexual harassment claim against you.

As an owner of the company, you are supposed to create a work environment that is free of sexual innuendo and harassment. Your company is a place of business, and the focus should be on work output, efficiency and service to your clients and customers. Instead, you want your wife to role model wearing sexy clothes to dress up the workplace.

If your desire were for your wife to wear sexy clothes for you in private, on a dinner out, or at a night club or casino, it would be understandable. However, even that would be her choice—not yours. Your desire to have your wife wear low-cut blouses and short skirts at work has nothing to do with her love for you. It has everything to do with your demeaning attitude toward women.

You should be proud of having built a company with twenty-seven employees, but apparently, it is not enough. You are trying to stroke your ego and flaunt your masculinity with a babe hanging on your arm. And for that, you get booed, not applauded.

Trumped by a young blonde

Question: I am a 45-year-old trade show representative for our company. For several years, I have arranged booths at trade shows. After two kids and age, I have gained some weight, and my young looks are gone. Last year, the company hired a young, 24-year-old blonde with impressive hardware to help at trade shows. Slowly, she has taken over and I have been relegated to office duties and behind-the-scenes arrangements. The company claims that she produces better results at the trade shows in attracting customers to the booth. I feel hurt and upset. What should I do?

-Carrie, Phoenix

Answer: A very controversial topic, indeed!

It is disconcerting to learn that a company wants to sell and showcase its product through "booth babes," and not on the product's merits. On the other hand, it is not uncommon to see this at trade shows. It is even more common in Europe, where I have seen men almost run into poles while walking with their eyes glued on the scantily clothed women in the booths.

The question is, what should you do? I will not assume that your younger colleague is the culprit. She has not done anything wrong. She may be just as diligent as you were when you were that age.

You should look at the situation objectively. Is she producing better results at the booth? And I do not mean by "selling" anything else. Is she attracting better traffic to the booth, while dressed professionally, and creating more new contacts and potential customers for your company? It is a very competitive marketplace. Your company cannot afford to lose potential clients to the competition. In the end, clients will buy based on the value embedded in the products and services of your company. But they first need to be courted and given a chance to hear the pitch.

Take the time to listen closely to what your colleague is saying to attract customers to the booth. She may have a compelling business story to tell. After too much time in the trenches, people making the first customer contact needs to refresh their approach. Search for what your customers need to solve their problems now, then better position your booth introduction in that direction. Regardless of the physical attributes of the person asking, an intelligent inquiry to a person coming by the booth will be more effective than just another "booth babe" with empty-headed dialog.

The second thing to look at is whether the company has reduced your salary, benefits, and opportunities. I would guess that it has not. It is possible that the job is just split differently, where you do the organizing, and she does the booth duty. If this is the case, then there is no harm and no foul.

But, if the company has simply removed you from your job because of your age, weight and looks, then this amounts to discrimination. What you should do if this is the case depends on the answers to several questions that your letter does not address. If you believe that you have been discriminated against, then you should begin with your ~HR representative; then escalate as needed, including consulting a lawyer. However, it is very difficult to prove, and the process is quite grueling as opposed to just finding another company that will appreciate your skills.

Gender biased work environment

Question: I am a male human resources manager working in a department and a profession that is largely made up of females. Our department manager, a female, goes on outings with the other female workers, such as ladies' nights out, spa treatments, baking & houseware sales, and even male strippers. Business is not conducted at these outings, but I feel left out of the chance to know my boss and bond with co-workers. It is not sexual harassment, but it is a gender biased environment. What should I do?

-Adam, Phoenix

Answer: Your department manager should re-enroll in HR 101. She should be a role model for others in creating gender-neutral equality. Instead, she is creating a gender-biased environment.

The problem is not uncommon, though. Let us reverse the roles and look at a situation with a male boss who has several male subordinates and one female subordinate. It seems to be perfectly all right for the male boss to play tennis with a male subordinate, followed by showering in the locker room and a lunch or dinner. But the moment a male boss attempts to do the same activity with the female subordinate, all eyebrows go up. Is she kissing the boss? Or, worse yet, is she sleeping with the boss? Is it fair to the woman? Is it fair to the boss to not be able to do outside activities with male subordinates?

These are very tough questions, because of the fears and stereotypes in our society. All a boss can do is to withdraw from socializing with subordinates—not an ideal option. That is why I often say that it is very lonely at the top.

Your department manager seems to have gone well beyond what is normal. She could easily choose activities that could include you: a department dinner instead of a ladies' night out; a shopping trip versus a baking & housewares sale; department tennis or golf instead of spa treatments; and cut out the male stripper altogether.

You could speak to her about it. Or you could go to her boss who could be the division VP or the CEO. Depending upon the culture of the company, it may help, or it may expose you to some risk or ridicule.

Female engineer feels excluded

Question: I am a female engineer working in a department full of men. Our boss arranges department outings from which I feel excluded. Examples include dance clubs and even strip clubs where I feel uncomfortable, and golf (I do not like playing golf). Why doesn't he pick simple activities where everyone can be included, such as hiking, shopping, and bowling?

-Karen, Phoenix

Answer: I answered a very similar question above "Ladies' nights demoralizing male staffer." In that column, a male staffer felt excluded in a department full of females. With your question, the shoe is on the other foot.

I sympathize with your position because the male boss could easily choose activities that are more inclusive, such as a department dinner or bowling, instead of dancing and strip clubs.

However, I stop short of completely agreeing with you. You gave examples of three activities—hiking, shopping, and bowling—that you describe as simple activities where everyone can be included. But you reject golf because you do not like it. And that is where the problem lies.

A boss will usually organize activities around what he likes. It is better to do it by consultation, so everyone likes the activity somewhat. But a boss is unlikely to organize an activity that he dislikes. Well! Some men do not like shopping. Some may like bowling, but others do not. The problem surfaces when you become self-righteous around the activity that you like.

I am not a golfer. But there have been occasions when I joined a golf game to feel included. I simply played the best ball of our foursome continuously, which ensured that I got plenty of "pars," a few "bogeys" and even a "birdie." Golf is a very popular sport in Phoenix, and you cannot blame someone for not including you because you do not like golf.

So, I would criticize your boss for choosing dancing and strip clubs. But I would also ask you to be more accommodating in accepting golf.

You should speak to your boss about it. Propose joining the department for golf and suggest other activities like bowling. Maybe you will all find an activity that makes everyone feel included and promotes team harmony.

Harassment by a client

Question: I have read several columns that you have written about various kinds of harassment. But none of those apply to my situation. I am a female receptionist in a law office. Our office is in the midst of a very major deal. Our client is a young male CEO. Every time he comes into the lobby, he would make sexual remarks, stand too close to the desk, and look down and shake my hand and then squeeze it inappropriately. He has asked me out which I have refused, but he continues to make me feel very uncomfortable. He is a very large client, and the lawyers will choose him over me. What should I do?

-Anonymous, Phoenix

Answer: I sympathize with your situation. It will take some skill, courage, and determination to solve this problem. Sexual harassment very often is more about the misuse of power than about sex. The client CEO knows his importance to the law firm, and he is misusing his power to take advantage of you.

The law requires employers to stop sexual harassment when they learn of it; even it is a customer or vendor who is causing the problem. When a supervisor or co-worker is committing improper comments or conduct, it is easier for the employer to stop the harassment because the person is directly under the control of the employer. Nevertheless, your law firm needs to handle the situation, even though it involves an important client. The law firm, more than anyone else, will be very knowledgeable about their responsibility and liability here.

You should check your employer's policy against harassment and report the matter in accordance with the policy without delay. If the law firm does not have a policy, report it to your supervisor. You may also want to check first with coworkers to see if anyone has witnessed the conduct so you can report that to the law firm.

Alternatively, have a coworker present in the lobby at his scheduled arrival, so that you will have a witness.

You could suggest to your supervisors that they ask the client to stop his conduct that is making you uncomfortable. If they do not want to do that, they could arrange for you to take a break during the times that the client is expected to be in the reception area.

It is not an excuse for the man involved, but in a position such as yours, it will help avoid unwelcome comments if you make sure that you are dressing professionally and conservatively at work.

The law prohibits your employer from retaliating against you because you reported unwelcome, offensive conduct. You should make notes of how the law firm reacts to your request that they protect you from inappropriate comments or conduct.

(I want to thank the law firm of Ballard Spahr Andrews & Ingersoll for their help on this question.)

Sexual harassment by female boss

Question: I am a customer-service representative with a female boss. I am happily married and do not want to be involved with my boss. However, she will not take no for an answer. She is constantly pressuring me for dates, and recently tried to get me to go with her to a sales conference. (She tried to disguise it as a work assignment.) She dresses provocatively and puts me in compromising positions. What can I do?

-Neil, Scottsdale

Answer: You have a clear case of sexual harassment. Harassment from a female boss to a male subordinate is less common, but it does happen. Sexual harassment is illegal and can get the harasser and her company in trouble. But it is difficult to prove, and the deck is often stacked against the accuser. This exact scenario was played out in a 1994 movie called "Disclosure," with Michael Douglas and Demi Moore. When Douglas's character reports the harassment, he is labeled as incompetent in his job.

The laws, case histories, and sensitivity about sexual harassment have come a long way since that 1994 movie. But some of the basic issues remain. It is one person's word against the others. Sexual harassment often does not have much to do with sex. It has everything to do with power. The boss enjoys the misuse of his or her power over the subordinate in carrying out the sexual harassment.

You should begin by lodging a written complaint to your company's HR department. Keep a diary of all the incidents and acts of harassment by date, time, and place. It will come in handy someday. HR will speak to your boss. She will likely deny everything and blame you for being incompetent and using harassment to get cover from being fired. It gets messy and unpredictable after this. Unless the boss has a rash of past complaints against her, she is not likely to be fired. She may just get a warning or get her hand slapped. But now your life has become miserable.

It is not that you cannot ultimately prevail in your case. (Michael Douglas's character prevailed in the 1994 movie.) But it is often a lot easier to get another job in a different department of your company, or another company. It may sound like I am suggesting a cop out. However, based on my life experience, I am just being practical. You need to decide whether your goal is to preserve your career or destroy hers. Getting another job will preserve your career. However, if you believe that you want to fight for the principle of it and destroy her career, I am with you on that path, too.

Boss having an affair

Question: I am a secretary for the vice president of our company. I recently learned that my boss, a married woman, is having an affair with another man. My boss's husband and my husband are friends and often play tennis together. Should I tell my husband? He will surely tell my boss's husband. Is my job in jeopardy if my boss finds out that I was the one to expose her affair?

-Wendy, Phoenix

Answer: The obligations of your work and your personal life have become entangled. Let me untangle your work obligations.

You are an employee of your company first, and your current assignment happens to be working for your boss. Your company pays you to handle the administrative duties so that your boss can be efficient and concentrate on making her company successful. Among many other requirements of your job, one of the highest expectations in working for an officer of a company is to maintain strict confidentiality and exercise discretion.

Let us say that you glanced at a layoff list on your boss's desk and it happened to have your cousin's name on it. Can you tip off your cousin? Absolutely not! This is company confidential information and may not be disclosed to anyone.

Similarly, let us say you type a letter for your boss in which she is going to cancel a major contract with a supplier, and your mother works for that supplier. Can you tip her off? Absolutely not!

So, you learned that your boss is having an affair. Should you tip her husband off? Absolutely not! Telling your husband amounts to the same thing. You will be violating your obligation of confidentiality to her. What she does in her own time is none of your business unless she chooses to share it with you. Even then, without her permission, you are required to maintain her confidentiality.

What about your relationship with your husband and your husband's friendship with your boss's husband? They are social relationships outside of work. You cannot tangle those social obligations with your moral and legal obligation to maintain confidentiality on what you learn at work.

You may be struggling with your own moral beliefs on extra-marital affairs. What your boss is doing is immoral, not illegal. The case would be different if you discovered that your boss was acting illegally in a business-related context, or she was having an affair with another employee in violation of the company policy—if the company has such a policy. Then, you are supposed to let someone know—her boss, human resources, or corporate legal counsel. In such an event, "whistle blower" laws or anti-retaliation laws may protect you from reprisal. But the same laws may not protect you if you violate the confidentiality that you are paid to uphold.

If you cannot work under the pressure that is part of working for the officer of a company, then you should seek other employment and remove yourself from this stressful situation.

Moral reform should start at the top

My column regarding the boss having an affair and keeping the workplace brought several confidential responses from readers.

Question: The topic of your column this morning is unfortunately too common. I would have difficulty deciding what to do, especially if I were a close friend of the affected spouse. In this case, I do not doubt that your advice was appropriate.

However, I disagree with one item in your analysis, "What your boss is doing is immoral, not illegal." A married spouse who has an affair is committing adultery. In Arizona, adultery is a Class 3 misdemeanor, punishable by up to 30 days in jail and a fine of five hundred dollars. A.R.S. Section 13-1408.

-Saul

Question: As an officer of the company, the vice president's personal affairs are representative of her character in dealing with business affairs.

The fact that an executive assistant comes to know that her boss is having an affair has nothing in common with "glancing at a layoff list," or "the associated impact of a canceled contract on an external third party." Your association of legitimate business decisions and their related impacts has nothing in common with the moral decision of adultery, and I personally find it offensive that you co-mingle the two concepts.

The fact is that the affair is wrong and Wendy the administrative assistant is now involved. Telling her to keep the secret is as bad as the secret itself. She has an obligation to God and to herself to bring healing, and to approach her boss with the insight she has gained and the moral wrong that is being performed. What happens next is a matter between these two individuals but let us be sure to keep our moral compass clearly pointed. Our corporate world has too much controversy already…being ambivalent to personal moral weakness is something that should not be promoted.

-John

There were others who posted on my AZCentral blog and talked about the moral compass.

Answer: I knew that by selecting the original question from Wendy, I would open Pandora's Box. Everyone has an opinion on Wendy's situation. I had my own administrative assistant; my director of human resources; and my corporate lawyer (all women) review my response before I posted it. After a barrage of emails for or against my advice, I would not change it.

My responses in this column tend to be guided by what is the most practical solution in a business environment. I stand educated on the illegality of adultery. I do not know the laws of Washington D.C., but did we not elect a President who committed adultery in the oval office? I do not condone adultery, but I think that A.R.S. Section 13-1408 does not deter anyone.

Regarding John's comments, we need to keep one goal in check. We are trying to advise Wendy regarding what would be best for her. If the question posed to me was how to correct the moral compass of American business, then I would have dealt with that question. But to put the burden of that moral compass on poor Wendy by threatening her job, if she divulges the secret, would be incorrect advice.

I do think that the moral compass is pointed incorrectly today. But we should start at the top with presidents, governors, congresspeople, and priests—not with administrative assistants like Wendy.

Racism in the workplace

Question: What should an individual do when confronted with overt racism in the workplace, and what is the protocol for presenting the issue to upper management? Most corporations have large funds and prestigious law firms while the employee must place their career on the line. Rarely does the employee stand a chance at stopping the racist behavior.

-Fred

Answer: While federal law prohibits racial discrimination, most responsible organizations of significant size have a written policy that directly addresses racial discrimination and harassment in the workplace. Accordingly, the appropriate response for an employee who is the target of racist conduct is to report it immediately to the person identified in the policy. If your employer does not have a written policy, you should still immediately report it to your supervisor, your supervisor's supervisor and the company's HR department. Reporting the conduct immediately will allow the employer to investigate and respond to the complaint quickly and effectively.

I disagree that there is no way to stop racist conduct in the workplace. Management should, and I think generally would, respond quickly to a complaint by conducting a thorough investigation. Where racist conduct is discovered, it can and should be addressed immediately and in a manner that is likely to correct the situation, including in some cases termination of the employee who engaged in such conduct.

It is important to remember, however, that allegations of racism and the resulting investigations give rise to a host of concerns, and the rights of everyone involved must be considered. Such investigations are generally confidential and conducted with respect for all employees' privacy, and information is shared within the company only to the extent necessary to conduct an effective investigation. Remember, there are two sides to every story and the employee who brings the charge in most cases will not be privy to all that is done. Accordingly, it is sometimes difficult for the employee who brings the charge to trust that the investigation has been done and been done right.

If you are not satisfied with the actions of your company, you can seek help from the Equal Employment Opportunity Commission (EEOC). If they find enough cause, they can represent the individual and provide the legal backbone to help them against a company.

What is my race? Check "Other"

Question: I am 16 years old, and my father was filling out the 2010 Census form, which created a discussion in our house regarding 'what is my race?' My father is half Cuban and half American. My mother is half Filipino and half Mexican. So, who am I? I will soon be filling out a lot of college forms and will come across this question over and over. How do you see it?

-Natalie, Phoenix

Answer: This question hits so close to home for my children that I have chosen to take an essay that my daughter Christie wrote in 2003, which I publish here with her permission.

"During my years of growing up, every time I filled out an application, I encountered a section called ethnic background; and every time I wondered, "Who am I?" Not fitting any of the choices given, I always checked "Other." I am Christie Sanghi, born in Sacramento, California.

My mom is from Nicaragua; she came to the U.S. in the middle of a civil war in Nicaragua in 1979. Her first language is Spanish. She speaks English well, but I find myself correcting her English to this day. My dad is from India and is the CEO of a successful public company.

My mom was born and raised as a Christian, whereas my dad was raised as a Hindu and converted to Christianity before he married my mom. My mom does not speak Hindi, and my dad does not speak Spanish. Therefore, they speak English—my first language. I grew up in this household influenced by these two cultures, learning to live with the differences, celebrating the similarities, learning the values from both, and yet forming my own identity.

I have learned to embrace the values, lessons, and traditions that each of my parents has taught me and try to apply them to my everyday life. From my mom, I have learned conservative values, high morals, and a sense of self-worth. From my dad, I have learned the value of hard work, honesty, career success and the drive to make this world a better place to live.

I have been to Nicaragua with my mom and to India with my parents, and I have known the extended families on both sides. Both sides have some admirable qualities and have worked hard to make their cultures a major part of my life. I respect them completely and appreciate their commitment and everything they have taught me, which has so strongly impacted my life.

As I leave home after 18 years, I leave with a sense of curiosity to explore the big world ahead of me. I also leave home with a sense of confidence that I have the values, courage, honesty, and commitment to deal with the challenges I face ahead. I am from a Spanish heritage with the values I have learned from my mother, and an East Indian heritage with the values I have learned from my father. I am American from what I have learned from my parents and friends, and from eighteen years in the U.S. So, who am I? After some profound thought, I still check the same box- “Other.”

-Christie (Sanghi) Wieger

Follow up from layoff dilemma

Question: I read your column “Solving Layoff dilemmas”. I do not understand the problem in letting an employee go—one of the 16—regardless of which one.

I thought Arizona was an “at will” state, and that anyone could be fired. What am I missing?

-Charlene

Question: Race and gender come into play in layoff lawsuits. This question would not be asked if the business owner had sixteen white male employees, nor would he have a problem. It is the double-edged sword of keeping a diversified work force, then having to worry about downsizing.

-Desert Ghost (from the Ask Steve blog)

Answer: These questions could go into the layoff chapter. But I chose to cover it here because it deals with discrimination. Title VII of the civil right act of 1964 prohibits discrimination based on gender, race, or national origin in any non-governmental organization with fifteen or more employees.

You can fire a Caucasian male under forty without disabilities at will. Your reason could be anything and, he would have no recourse under Title VII of the Civil Rights Act of 1964. Everyone else has rights. And, if they can claim discrimination in their selection to be laid off, then they have some recourse.

They have no recourse if they work for a governmental organization, because Title VII does not apply to governmental organizations. So, Congress does not inflict the same burden and pain on governmental organizations, or on itself, but it requires all private companies with fifteen or more employees to bear this burden. Come on members of Congress—what is good for the goose is also good for the gander!

Desert Ghost writes that if the employer had sixteen white males, then he would not have a problem. First, if he kept rejecting every non-white male, then he would have been sued by now for discrimination in hiring. And he would deprive his business of the significantly diversified talent base that exists. One can also make the argument that if he only employs white males; then all other groups should not do business with him. If that happened, he would deprive his business of many customers. White males are a minority, when you consider that over 50% of the populace are women and non-white males.

The question really is whether Title VII is fair. I am sure that in 1964, it was fair. But after 60 years, today, it hardly seems fair. Should a non-white male from a rich family have more protection than a white male from a poor family? I think not. I believe that Title VII should be repealed. You cannot build a colorblind society by discriminating against white males.

Now, how is that for opening Pandora's Box?

Offensive words in the workplace

Question: I was called a monkey at work by my boss—I am black, and he is white. It was said in a joking way, but it was offensive, and I advised him that it was. He blew it off. I reported this to the owner and all that was done was a talk, as far I know. What are my options? I was humiliated, as this was done in front of others.

-Nicole

Answer: There is no doubt that being called a monkey would be very humiliating for anyone. Therefore, I am not sure whether race played any part in this, unless there is a history of racial slurs being used by your boss.

If there is such a history of racial slurs, or intimidation or discrimination, then you have all the protection offered by Title VII of the Civil Rights Act of 1964. For such protection, you must work for a non-government employer with fifteen or more employees. You should see your human resources manager and ask that such treatment be stopped. You could ask to be moved to a different department. If nothing is done, then you could go to the Equal Employment Opportunity Commission (EEOC) and file a claim against the company and your boss. You can also sue for discrimination.

If you find that there is no such history of racial slurs and discrimination, then it was just a one-time incident. If your boss had a bad moment on a bad day and said something totally ridiculous and offensive, then you need to find a way to put this behind you.

You reported this incident to the owner, and you said that your boss was talked to. So, please ask yourself what else you are looking for. If you want an apology from your boss, you are entitled to one. Ask your boss, and you may get an apology. If you want an apology in front of others, you may get that, too.

If your manager has not repeated such behavior, then he probably has gotten the message. At that point, you may choose to put this issue behind you.

I have found that many times, a manager in a bad moment may say something stupid, but not realize or not be sensitive enough to the fact that someone has been hurt. He or she gets busy with the other pressing issues of the day and may not take the time to come back and apologize. Or they may simply believe that you did not mind too much, and it was OK to move on.

So, bring it to his attention and—especially if you found the remark to be racial—then he should apologize.

Do not call women girls in the office

Question: I am a customer-service representative and work in an office with other women, men, and a male boss. Our boss often refers to the women as girls: "Come on girls! Hey girl, pick up line 2! What did you girls do over the holidays?" Some women are in their twenties, but others are in their 30s and 40s. I find it offensive to be called a girl. What can we do?

-Annette, Phoenix

Answer: Some words, when used in the workplace, can be very offensive. While other words can be interpreted by some as offensive and others as affectionate. "Girl" is such a word. I have often heard it used by women on other women, as in "come on girl, we are late to the meeting." Suze Orman uses it all the time on her TV program. When used in an affectionate and caring manner, it does not come across as demeaning. But, when used all the time by a male chauvinist boss, it can come across as very offensive.

In the end, the meaning of the word must be judged not by the one who says it, but by the one who it is said to. If the way it is said is offensive to you, then you are in the right and your boss should stop. But how do you go about achieving this result?

I would recommend a very soft and anonymous approach. Just type up a letter and say that you do not like to be called girls. And, that you prefer to be called by your first names, individually, and collectively as women or ladies, not girls.

If he is considerate, he will stop using the word. You should overlook his occasional missteps as he tries to change the habit. But, if he makes no attempt, you may need a second and stronger reminder.

Or you might try a humorous approach. The next time he says, "Girl, pick up line two." You can respond, "OK, boy-I mean, sir."

Age discrimination

Question: I know that it is illegal to ask an employee for their age in a job interview or application, and then discriminate based on age.

When I decided to go back to professional work, I had to deal with the standard request for the date of my graduation from high school and college. I do not see it as relevant whether my M.A. degree was earned 3 years ago or 20 years ago. I certainly do not see the job relevance of one's high school graduation date for a seasoned professional. Yet, these questions are routinely asked. And, with the prevalence of online applications, one cannot continue with the application unless all required boxes are filled in.

Once I give the date of my high school graduation and my undergraduate degree, the recruiter knows within a year what my age is. The employer can then use whatever excuse is handy to not interview/hire the applicant. I have a strong suspicion that this is what happened to me in cases in which I applied for positions within the education industry. Why is it legal and allowable to ask for this information?

-John Thaxton

Answer: You are correct that it is illegal to ask an employee for their age in a job interview or application. However, it is legal and appropriate to assess applicants based on their years of experience. So, in that respect, it does matter whether the degree was completed 3 years ago or 20 years ago.

Let us compare two potential candidates. One, after completing high school, went to work in a factory as a machine operator, and the second went to college to get an undergraduate degree. The latter candidate then worked his way up in various professional jobs for 10 years. The machine operator was in the same job for 10 years and then received an undergraduate degree later in life. When considering both of these candidates for a position, the recruiter will see that the first has machine-operator experience prior to the degree while the second has experience as a professional after the degree. This information matters.

For the selection process to be efficient, it is preferable to have all relevant information ahead of time. The employer is going to guess your age at the time of the interview, and through the analysis of your experience. Hiding your year of graduation is not going to bring you much benefit.

Just as with age, it is illegal to ask about race, color, religion, or national origin. But do you not think that those things are easily decoded while looking at the application and during the interviewing process (except, perhaps, for religion)?

What is important is that age, race, color, gender, religion, and national origin are not criteria for hiring. Merely having knowledge of these things does not create discrimination. If you can prove that one of these was a criterion in your case, then you have a valid complaint. The mere suspicion that it happened does not meet the test.

Random security checks in company lobbies discriminatory?

Question: I represent my company at the customer site of a local corporation. I am subject to searches of my lunch box, computer bag and toolbox prior to entry. I understand the need for such security measures with all the terrible worksite violence, not to mention theft and IP risks.

My question has to do with the equitable treatment of all individuals entering the building. Currently, only contractors and vendors are routinely asked to open their belongings for inspection. Regular full-time employees are never searched at any time for any reason. A sign at the entrance clearly states that all individuals are subject to search prior to entry, as well as defining the materials prohibited on the site.

This practice of focusing on non-employees is personally offensive, but I am not sure how to address the issue or if I would be within my rights to complain. My feeling is that this practice fosters a non-trusting working relationship and should be stopped. I would be interested to read your opinion.

-Brian

Answer: The company that you work for is not the only company that handles security the way that you describe. You are really asking if it is fair for employees of a company to be treated differently than contractors or vendors that work at the same location. It is common for employees to be treated differently than contractors or vendors at the same location.

The employees of the company come there every day and are usually known to the security officers. The employees sign documents at the time of hire, which bind them to confidentiality, IP protection, company policies, and termination for breach of contract. The contractors and vendors coming into the building are not always bound by similar policies and documents. An employer may qualify its workers through references and background checks before hiring, but that company likely does not do such checks for its contractors. Therefore, it is not unreasonable for a company to treat its own employees differently.

If the issue were that only certain contractors are having their bags checked or if there were only certain individuals that have their bags checked, then I think there would be a reason to be concerned about equitable treatment. Trust me, I have had my own computer bag checked and driver license and passport copied before I was allowed to enter certain customers' premises. Does it irk me? Yes. But they are the customer, and the customer is always right. No one forced me to call on that customer. I wanted to do so. So, I accepted the search.

If the sign says that all individuals are subject to search and there was a known threat, then the company would also search its employees. If the bag check is done professionally and there is no hint or even perception of harassment, then I think the policy as you have stated it is reasonable.

Political affiliation

Question: I work for a small private company. Our president is a staunch member of one mainstream political party and openly displays his views in the workplace. Recently, an associate friend of mine, a registered member of an opposing political party got into a political argument with the president of the company. A couple of weeks later, the employee got fired. Does my friend have recourse?

-Donald, Chandler

Question: During the last election, I supported one major candidate, while my boss (the department manager) supported the other. We had several lively debates leading up to the election. When my candidate won, my boss was really upset and has held a grudge against me since. Later, because of an uncertain economy, our company had a layoff, and I was one of those laid off by my boss. I am very sure that my boss was politically motivated in selecting me. Do I have recourse against my boss and the company?

-Ray

Answer: I am not entirely sure Ray that your selection for layoff was politically motivated. Selecting employees for layoffs is a very difficult process, and I have written about it in several past columns. Despite the best efforts and practices deployed, it always leaves certain employees with the belief that they were unfairly targeted. The dirty laundry from the past comes into play and the affected employee blames that for their selection. The fact is, in a layoff, many good-performing employees must be let go because of a downturn in business.

I am not a lawyer, but from what I know, I do not have good news for you. First, I would like to say that political views should be kept out of the workplace. If they are discussed in informal sessions, such as lunchbreaks, everyone's views should be respected. For your boss to hold a grudge against you is unreasonable. If I accept your account of what happened, then taking the action of firing you because of your political beliefs is reprehensible.

However, recourse is an entirely different matter. Federal law states that non-governmental employers of more than fifteen persons cannot fire or discriminate against an employee because of his or her race, color, gender, or national origin (Title VII of the Civil Rights Act of 1964). Unfortunately, political affiliation is not a protected class under the Civil Rights Act or under Arizona employment law, and employees can be discriminated against on this basis unless doing so violates the company's own written policy. I know that this does not seem right, but employers have the right to select employees based on political affiliation. However, I recommend that you check into whether your company has a written policy against political discrimination.

Changing this law will require congressional action. Good luck with that. Meanwhile, the best policy is, "Do not ask and do not tell your political affiliation".

Chapter 6: Dealing with employees

Managerial work would not be as difficult if it were not for employees. Dealing with employees is hard work. Dealing with underperformers in the workplace is even harder whether you are dealing with it as the boss or co-worker. Also difficult is dealing with troublemakers like workplace bullies.

Question: I am a middle-level manager. I have an employee who just will not do the job. We have trained him, but he does not follow instructions and is very stubborn when asked to change. I am ready to fire him, but I feel bad and want to know if there is another way.

-Justin, Mesa

Answer: When an employee is not doing a job, I usually ask, "Is it that the employee cannot do the job, or that he or she would not do the job?"

If the answer is that he cannot do the job, then he has not been properly trained. It might be that job-specific training is needed, or it could be something bigger. Maybe he just does not have the prerequisite education required to comprehend and apply the training you have provided. You could provide him with more job-specific training. However, if he lacks the minimum education for the job, then this was a hiring mistake.

If the answer is that he will not do the job, then he is not motivated. There are six managerial powers that can be exercised to motivate employees: the power of fear; the power to reward; legitimate power; referent power; expert power; and connection power. The powers of fear and reward are well understood and should be used sparingly. Legitimate power is when subordinates follow strict authority—as in the military. Referent power is when subordinates work for the boss because they like him or her. Expert power is when subordinates work for the boss because they respect him or her as an expert. Connection power is when subordinates work for the boss because he or she has high connections that could be helpful to them.

Different powers are applicable in different situations. Excessive use of any one power is usually wrong. And a good manager uses a mixture of these powers to motivate and manage employees. However, it seems that the most appropriate powers to be used in the case of your employee are the powers of fear and reward.

If you cannot motivate him with either fear or reward and he is just too stubborn, then your only recourse is to fire him.

Only praise when deserved

Question: I promoted an employee to a supervisor position last year. He was an excellent employee who knew the job the best. Since then, he has not met my expectations. He does not demand enough of his subordinates, who were his coworkers. He now thinks that I do not appreciate him enough. Should I give him some praise in front of his subordinates to build him up?

-Nancy, Mesa

Answer: Giving him praise in front of his subordinates in this case is probably the worst thing you could do. In management, this is called "phony praise". And, if you give such phony praise in front of his subordinates, then it will validate his behavior in his own mind as well as in the minds of his subordinates. That is the exact opposite of the result that you desire.

First, just because he knew the job the best is not a good enough reason for you to have promoted him. Promotional considerations should also involve the person's aptitude and ability to change from an individual contributor role into a supervisory role.

Second, after promoting an individual contributor to a supervisory role, you should provide him with some training and familiarize him with the management skills he needs to acquire. This is best done in the form of sitting down with him and developing some objectives and key results that he needs to achieve in a specified period of time (six months or a year are good timelines). If he needs formal training in certain areas, that should be part of the key results.

The most important thing that you need to do is to have a heart-to-heart talk with him regarding matching of expectations. It is quite clear that your expectations of him are different than his expectations of himself. This is not uncommon, especially after a role change for an individual who is in a supervisory role for the first time.

You should write down your expectations for him, and then ask him to do the same for his own role. Compare the two documents in front of him and you will find the answer to why you are having problems. Then, merge the two documents into a single document, which will become the blueprint by which his performance will be judged. Delete the expectations from his list that you do not believe belong there. Be flexible yourself, to ensure that your expectations from a first-time supervisor are not unreasonable.

After this, you should periodically meet with him to review his progress. Remember that it is easy for him to slip back into the role with which he is comfortable. So, keep the pressure on for making the changes that you desire.

Only after an employee has made significant progress towards their new objectives, should you praise them in front of their subordinates. This praise will be coming from your heart, and it will be seen as both genuine and deserved. Additionally, it will validate the new desired behavior that you have been trying to teach.

Desired characteristics of an employee

Question: You have written several columns on management, supervision, and leadership, including your column "Desired Characteristics of a Manager." As a manager, I am often asked by my employees what characteristics I would like to see in them. I give them general answers. Do you have a comprehensive list of the desired characteristics of an employee?

-Larry, Scottsdale

Answer: I love it when I can answer a question right out of my book "Driving Excellence," published by Wiley in April 2006. The answer to your question is on page 238.

Ordinarily, it is difficult to develop a list of the desired characteristics of an employee because the list is usually very job specific. The characteristics needed for an airline pilot are very different than those for an engineer working in an electronics company. Therefore, use my list only as a guideline and then choose the characteristics that are applicable for the specific job.

You can use the list for recruiting or performance-appraisal purposes but be careful in its application. For recruiting purposes, select a smaller list of applicable characteristics on which to quiz the candidate. If you use it for performance-appraisal purposes, then select a couple of areas for your employee to focus on during the coming year. If you bombard him or her with eighteen desired characteristics, you are likely to turn the employee off.

With that said, here is a list of the desired characteristics for employees:

1. Practices the company culture
2. Achieves the desired results and meets commitments
3. Produces quality work, takes the job seriously and displays good work habits
4. Strives to make improvements to the operation
5. Seeks to satisfy customers (internal or external customers)
6. Is bright and displays good common sense and technical competence in his or her field
7. Can handle empowerment and desires to be involved and engaged
8. Is a team player with good interpersonal interactions
9. Demonstrates good effort, perseverance, and dependability
10. Shows initiative, creativity, and resourcefulness
11. Has good communication skills—verbal and written
12. Listens actively and considers others' input and feedback
13. Displays good judgment, is well organized and operates with limited ego
14. Is a continuous learner, and desires to enhance his or her skills and knowledge
15. Uses good analytical and problem-solving skills
16. Shows flexibility and adaptability and responds well to change
17. Acts safely, ethically, and honestly
18. Is frugal (not a frivolous spender) and sensitive to profit and loss

Performance reviews that promote teamwork

Question: What are your thoughts on the following analogy?

Depending on business results, each department can only have so many average performers, exceeding performers, and far exceeding performers. Management uses the analogy that the annual review process is like a horse race and not everyone can win. So, it is a matter of making yourself stand out amongst your peers.

I find this analogy to be more derogatory than motivating because it pits the team members against each other, instead of promoting teamwork. For those that live and die by their reviews, they will go to great lengths to make themselves look good and others look bad.

-Lorie-Glendale

Answer: Your question relates to a practice known as "Ranking and Rating."

In this practice, a manager is given a budget for annual merit increases. He or she is asked to rate the employees in his or her group as "Meeting Requirements, Exceeding Requirements or Far Exceeding Requirements". There is usually a range of merit increases tied to each class of performance. The higher the performance rating, the higher the merit budget for that employee. The actual ranges may vary based on the company's overall budget.

The manager is usually given an approximate percentage of employees that can be rated in each category. This serves two purposes. First, the manager must set a standard of excellence and do the hard work to rate people in each category. Without that, it is much easier for a manager to give "Exceeding Requirements" to everyone.

Secondly, it allows the manager to live within his or her budget. If everyone is "Exceeding Requirements" and everyone is given an increase for that rating, then the manager exceeds the budget, which is usually not allowed.

So, you can see how setting some parameters for percentages of people in each category helps the process of rating performance, as well as allocating the increases.

If not managed well, the process can pit the team members against each other instead of promoting teamwork. Good companies build a culture and deploy tools to cope with this.

I wrote a book several years ago titled "Driving Excellence," which was published by Wiley. There is a complete chapter in it on Performance Appraisals.

At Microchip, employees are judged on five dimensions: Quality of Work; Quantity of Work; Improvement to the Operation; Teamwork; and Customer Satisfaction. By judging teamwork, the non-team players do not get ahead. Customer satisfaction is judged via a 360-degree feedback process in which, once again, making others look bad does not get one ahead.

Supervisors are also evaluated on additional factors—Employee Development; Empowerment; Communication; Planning & Organizing; and other such traits.

By deploying a multidimensional performance review process, you get the best of both worlds—employees strive to excel and work as a team. The performance of each team member improves which, in turn, improves the performance of the entire team.

Yearly performance review is a must

Question: When I was hired one year ago by a small company, I was given an employee policy manual. It states, among other things, that employees will receive a yearly evaluation. I recently passed the one-year mark, and I expected a good review, a better title, and some discussion of future goals and responsibilities. When I tried to ask about getting my review arranged, however, I was refused and reminded that I could be fired at any time. In the meantime, I have discovered that no one ever has a performance review at this workplace. I have also never had a job description. I have nothing to prove I ever performed certain functions or was a satisfactory employee. Is there any recourse? I am afraid it will take a very long time to find another job.

-Tamara

Answer: Your expectation of receiving a yearly evaluation along with some discussion of future goals and responsibilities is a very reasonable one.

First, it is not uncommon for companies to disregard their own policy manuals. And there are plenty of companies that do not have a regular process of formal yearly performance appraisals—policy or not. The question is, do you want to work for such a company?

In my view, a yearly performance appraisal is very important. It is time for the supervisor to formally write an appraisal and then sit down with the employee to go over it. The appraisal should cover the job definition and key responsibilities, accomplishments during the year, and any missed goals. The supervisor should rate the employee on the quality and quantity of their work, and other factors such as improvement to the operation, teamwork, and customer satisfaction. And the appraisal would not be complete without giving the employee some guidance about areas for improvement, some future goals and responsibilities, and any change in title and/or compensation.

Obviously, none of this happened in your case. However, many companies choose to delay performance appraisal schedules by six months to a year. This can help keep the focus on current tasks to survive in a difficult economy. It can also be the case that a company is in no financial position to increase anyone's compensation. So, if your company has decided to delay the yearly appraisal process for these reasons, that is reasonable; but the caveat is that they should clearly communicate those plans and their reasoning to the employees. If your company has never done any employee appraisals, then there is a bigger problem.

In terms of documenting that you have performed certain functions, this problem should not be as significant. I have never seen a prospective employer ask for performance appraisals from your prior job. If you would like to document your accomplishments, I suggest that you write a self-appraisal and document your job description, responsibilities, accomplishments, missed goals, and areas of improvement. You should then ask your HR department to put a copy of this document in your file and give a copy to your supervisor.

Bad performance appraisal

Question: I just received my performance appraisal, and I was stunned to find out that my supervisor did not know what I did last year. He did not list most of my accomplishments and was generally critical of me without giving any facts. I did not sign the review. To that, he said there may be further consequences. What are my options?

-Paolo, Phoenix

Answer: Performance appraisals are very complicated and need to be built into a process rather than be a yearly event. Very few companies have a good performance-appraisal process.

There needs to be year-round, periodic meetings between the supervisor and the employee, often called one-on-one meetings. In these meetings, the supervisor and the subordinate need to discuss the description of the job, objectives, key results, accomplishments, missed goals, challenges, obstacles, and career planning.

Then, prior to the formal performance appraisal, the employee should write a self-assessment and give it to his supervisor. In the self-assessment, the employee should list his accomplishments, missed goals, any environmental factors affecting the job, strengths, weaknesses, and career goals. Only then should the supervisor write the performance appraisal. The performance appraisal merely documents what has been discussed throughout the year and should not be a surprise to the employee. Unfortunately, when a bad process is followed, there can be an unwelcome surprise when the review is not good. So, what should you do now?

First, not signing a review probably would not accomplish anything. Like a traffic ticket, signing generally acknowledges that you have received it, not necessarily that you agree with it. You can even write in it that you did not agree with the review and then sign it. Not signing it makes you look like you are not taking any ownership and are not showing any commitment to resolving the issues.

You should write a self-assessment now and give it to your supervisor. Then, ask for a periodic one-on-one. In those meetings, you should share your quarterly goals with the supervisor, discuss resource or technical challenges, discuss progress on projects, and ask for coaching on areas for improvement and commit to improving them. With such an approach, you should be able to quickly get back in the supervisor's good graces and get a good follow-up review.

On the other hand, if your relationship with your supervisor is so destroyed that you cannot bring yourself to ask for help to improve your performance, then simply resisting your company's system and your boss will not get you anywhere. You might as well start to look for another job.

Fudging data could land engineer in jail

Question: I am a test engineer in a large electronics company. I know another engineer in our department who fudges characterization data to complete his work on schedule. Whenever he runs into any trouble, he just makes up data in the expected range without conducting the experiments. I have spoken to him, but he says that actual processes never drift in those corners where the management is asking for the data to be taken. So, there is no harm. I feel that our company is exposed. How should I handle this?

-Randy, Mesa

Answer: The actual processes in the real world do not often drift into remote corners, except when they do. And when they do drift into those corners, your products can have unexpected failures. This can cause serious jeopardy in customers' end products, potentially including loss of life if the defective product goes into military hardware that crashes or a medical device that fails. Then your company would be in a very hot seat, and someone could make a criminal case against the engineer—potentially landing him in jail.

You cannot ignore this problem. You should immediately take it to your supervisor. A person in your position is often worried about exposing himself or herself and then having negative consequences. In this situation, whistle-blower laws will protect you. You are essentially blowing the whistle on something that your company is doing seriously wrong. You may also want to send a copy of your complaint to your company's HR director, general counsel and even the chairperson of the audit committee of the board of directors.

I cannot imagine that any company would endorse the practices of your coworker. Instead, I believe that your company would immediately investigate this issue. I do not know if you have any proof of his fudging data. For example, there may be a tester log available that shows it was testing a different product when this engineer claims to have done the work. There may be other documentation available. Even if it comes down to just your word against his, the company is likely to put a procedure in place to avoid this problem. And the company may order the re-characterization of certain products that may have been affected.

You may be able to report this anonymously. However, since you have already spoken to the engineer, your name may be decoded when the investigation begins. So, in reporting this, you would certainly take a chance and expose yourself to some dislike or ridicule by the other engineers. But you also give yourself an opportunity to make an outstanding contribution to the company by saving it from a huge and potentially expensive embarrassment, not to mention the potential harm that could befall end users.

Office size for my grade level

Question: Our company has open cubicles for its employees to create an open and collaborative workplace, so they say. But the cubicles do anything but that. First, the cubicles are very small. Second, the sizes are by grade. So, a higher grade gets a larger cubicle. Last year I got promoted, but the company did not give me a larger cubicle. The company claimed a lack of funds to rearrange or build new cubicles. I waited so many years and finally got my promotion. But I am still in the same office.

The cubicles also do not block out the noise. You are interrupted too frequently, and productivity and morale suffer.

-Unhappy in Scottsdale

Answer: If you are unhappy, then my answer is not likely to make you happy. You are quite incredible. You are not grateful that your company promoted you just before the business started to deteriorate. You are unhappy that you did not get a bigger office.

Did your company lay off employees during this downturn? In February, I responded to a question from an engineer whose promotion was withheld due to the bad economy. He was not very happy and felt entitled to his promotion. You have certainly topped that. You would like your company to build you a new and larger cubicle instead of laying off one less employee. How reasonable is that?

Regarding the disturbances and interruptions, I have worked in open cubicles for large parts of my career without the issues that you are mentioning. Working in an open cubicle environment requires the company to adopt some "cubicle etiquette" standards. Examples include not allowing music or loud hallway conversations; taking meetings to conference rooms; turning down phone ring volumes; no speakerphones; and respecting privacy by not entering others' cubicles without permission.

If you can lead your company to develop such healthy "cubicle etiquette" practices, then you will have added to your happiness. And, in the process, you would be making a valuable contribution to the culture of your company.

Dealing with difficult people

Question: I want to know how to deal with difficult people at work, in my neighborhood, in the government, and in the community. I have a difficult colleague whose goal in life is to make trouble. One of my neighbors has loud parties and is insensitive to others. There is a difficult person in city hall with whom I often must deal. And there is a parent of a bully at my kid's school who is a poor role model for his bully kid. How do you deal with such difficult people all around you?

-Ron, Mesa

Answer: You have identified four separate difficult people from various facets of your life. In this limited space and without much information, it is hard for me to give you an answer that deals with these four different individuals. So, let me take up the question in general.

My answer centers on the two rules of dealing with pigs that I have followed for a long time. If someone's goal is to just make trouble, then I describe them as a pig. A troublesome and insensitive neighbor, a government employee who relishes the power that requires you to go through him to get something done, and a parent who role models being a bully to his kid are all examples of people who I will describe as pigs.

Now, it is useless to lecture a pig. It is not the first time they have been lectured to or cursed at. They know it. But they derive pleasure from being difficult to deal with. If you lecture or say something that is not nice to a power-mongering city employee, you are likely to upset them and get even less service.

Another tendency that some people have in dealing with pigs is to fire back by doing something bad to them. This could be taking the air out of your colleague's tires; doing some damage to your neighbor's property; or arranging to have the bully kid beaten up. Unfortunately, this tactic often backfires. Pigs are looking for a fight and enjoy it when they draw you in. They have an uncanny ability to twist the facts. Just like Murphy's Law, someone will see you doing damage to their car or property and the pig will take legal action against you. It will make you look bad, and the pig will smile and gain visceral satisfaction out of the whole altercation.

I always remember the following two rules. It is not that I never violate them. But, whenever I do, things usually go wrong; thus, reminding me of the rules. Here they are:

1. Never try to teach a pig how to sing. It wastes your time and annoys the pig.
2. Never get drawn into a cursing or wrestling match with a pig. First, you get dirty. Second, the pig likes it.

Dealing with workplace bullies

Question: I am an engineer at a medium-size company. I am having a problem dealing with a bully in our department. It almost reminds me of high school, where bullies got on other students' nerves. He continuously challenges everything I say and do. He unplugs my lab equipment, misplaces papers or car keys from my desk and just hounds me. How do I deal with this bully?

-Ron, Mesa

Answer: Dealing with bullies is difficult and tricky. The bullies from high school graduate and often become workplace bullies. Many times, you do not have a choice of going to a different school. This is not so at work. You have a choice of companies, and you have a choice of departments within the same company. But this should not be your first option. If you like your job, your department, and your company, then your first option should be to deal with the bully.

Start by documenting every negative action of the bully, with dates, times, locations, and the specific act. If there are any witnesses, note that down too. Then, you should see your HR director or employee-relations specialist. Bullying other employees is an act of harassment and should be dealt with accordingly. Most likely, your employee-relations specialist will investigate, speak to your boss, his boss, and then take some action.

In high school, students worry about their physical safety from bullies, and therefore, put up with a lot to avoid physical abuse. In the workplace, adult bullies very rarely get physical, because a physical assault is quite visible and could get them fired or even put in jail. Therefore, workplace bullies are more prone to causing emotional damage, which is harder to prove.

If your employee-relations specialist and your boss cannot bring relief, then you have a choice to make. One undesirable choice is to seek another job. Another is to stay put and fight by escalating the issue to your boss's boss or the Equal Employment Opportunity Commission, your union representative (if you have a union) or even the police if you can document an illegal act (e.g., he takes air out of your tire or steals something from your office).

There is a lot of reading material out there about bullies. Why do they do it? Emotional issues, low self-esteem, etc. A bully wants to engage you in his weird world. He commits a bullying act, and he expects that you will do something back. Then, he will ratchet up his behavior until he has you engaged. When you do not engage with a bully, it drives them crazy.

Therefore, whatever you do, do not engage a bully by committing acts yourself—such as disturbing their office or lab equipment, or scratching their car.

Chapter 7: Navigating company mergers

I received many questions from employees whose companies are being merged into other companies. I also received questions from owners of the companies selling their companies. Here's what I told them.

Evaluate risks & rewards before following boss to new job

Question: I am a middle-level manager in a company that recently got acquired by its larger competitor. My former boss and many of my former colleagues left the company soon after the merger. We were very resource constrained in the smaller company. As you recently wrote, the merger may give us the opportunity to provide the complete solution. Because of my skills, my job seems safe. But my old boss wants to rehire me at his new company. I am afraid that we will face the same constrained environment that we just came out of. Please help me evaluate whether I should stay or leave.

-Phil, Scottsdale

Question: My company was just acquired by a larger company. The new company has let some senior people go, including my boss. I feel that because of my skills, my job is safe. But I also have the option of following my boss to his new opportunity. Can you help me figure out whether to stick with the acquiring company or follow my old boss?

-Mark, Phoenix

Answer: This question is very timely. My own company, Microchip Technology, acquired another company. A lot of our newly acquired employees were likely asking themselves the same question. So, thanks for allowing me the opportunity to provide some perspective.

When a company is acquired, the combined company usually has some duplication of resources. The acquirer has paid a premium to acquire the other company. So, some rationalization of resources, and hence, redundancies, is very likely. However, if you have critical skills and feel that your job is safe, then you are in a very good position.

The biggest problem that I often see in a merger is that the employees of the acquired company continue to march in the direction they were marching before. However, the acquiring company could have better technology in certain areas. So, certain developmental pipelines for the acquired company may have to be modified or, in some cases, terminated.

In many cases, the acquiring company has achieved a higher level of efficiency and profitability through its operating model, culture, business systems, and technology. The acquiring company will then instill such disciplines into the acquired company to bring it to an equivalent level of efficiency and profitability. This involves substantial change for the acquired employees and often adds to the stress of uncertainty about their jobs and benefits. But it also enables the employees to gain new skills and operate and contribute at a much higher level.

The employees of acquired companies may wear the new company's badge on their shirt pocket, but they really need to be wearing the badge in their heart. They always need to think of the right answer for the new company (and not for their old company).

If you can utilize your skills in advancing the agenda of the new company and wear their badge in your heart, then you will be very successful, and you should stay there. You should also evaluate the culture of your new company and your opportunities there. Do they promote from within? How have the people from prior acquisitions done with this company?

Beware of the offer from your old boss. Is your old boss giving you a more senior position than you had before, and thus providing an opportunity to grow? If you work for the same boss for a very long time, I believe that you amass less skills overall. Your strengths remain your strengths, and your weaknesses remain your weaknesses. Working for different bosses gives you a broader perspective, and you can professionally grow to take on more challenging tasks. I have always managed and led my employees to build their loyalty for the company, and not for me. Therefore, my advice is that you should throw your loyalty in with your new company and not with your old boss.

Dealing with new boss after merger

Question: Our company recently merged with a larger company. After the merger, my boss was let go and our department was combined with a similar department of the acquiring company. Now I have a new boss. The other company has different ways of doing things. That would not be a problem if a proper training program were to be implemented. Instead, we have just been thrown into the situation. When I have a question, my boss answers it rather quickly without much explanation. If I do not get it and ask again, he puts me down and makes me feel stupid and vulnerable to another layoff.

-Mark, Phoenix

Answer: Mergers and acquisitions cause some of the largest organizational upheavals and turmoil in business. During the process of conducting due diligence, the acquiring company looks at the acquired company's business plan, profit and loss statement, balance sheet, cash-flow statements, products, markets, competition, intellectual property, risks, and opportunities. These are all important items. But the most important items are the culture and employees in the company. They often get overlooked.

It is difficult to talk to many employees lower than the top management, because the due diligence is done in secrecy. The talk of a merger in public can very much reduce the chances of a merger taking place at all by tipping the competitors and/or spike the stock price of the company being acquired (if public). Therefore, due diligence is often conducted at fairly high levels of the organization. Unfortunately, this deprives the companies from being able to assess each other's culture and ways of doing things.

Many mergers in corporate America fail because of the dramatic difference in culture, which is not uncovered until well after the merger has been completed. Good companies put together a comprehensive integration and training plan. But many companies that are inexperienced in mergers skip this very important step. Then, when the companies are merged, the differences in ways of doing things show up in spades, as is in your case. If the managers are not sensitive enough and do not take the time to explain, it makes things even worse.

My best suggestion to you is to hang in there and have patience. The ways of doing things are probably second nature to your boss. And he is likely upset by anyone who does not see it as natural. Over time, you will learn the ways of the new company and the new boss. Meanwhile, try asking some of your fellow employees and not repeatedly asking your boss. Soon, their ways of working will become second nature to you; hopefully before any new layoffs.

Post-acquisition culture clash

Question: Our company, an electronics distributor, acquired a smaller distributor. As a trainer, I continuously see bad attitudes from the salespeople of the acquired company. How can you get the employees of an acquired company to adopt the culture and the attitude of the acquiring company?

-Frank, Phoenix

Answer: Your question recalls a relevant example that I experienced many years ago at US Airways. Several years ago, America West bought US Air and then renamed the merged company US Airways. I was on a US Airways flight from San Jose, CA to Phoenix. One of the flight attendants recognized me and said, “Mr. Sanghi, I really enjoy your columns.” I thanked her for the compliment. And then, to advance the conversation, I asked, “Did you come from the America West side of the merger, or US Air?” She said, “Can’t you tell?” Then it dawned on me, and I said, “Of course, you are from the America West side.” She acknowledged and then said, “We are nicer.” To that I agreed, and then we proceeded to share stories about our respective experiences and comparisons between the service providers of America West versus the former US Air.

During the prior month, I was at Logan International airport in Boston. I had a lifetime club membership card for America West. So, I went to the US Airways club at Logan. The service attendant would not let me in. She said that she has never seen that card and they do not accept it, and who is America West? To that I replied that America West was their owner. After some haggling, she called the supervisor who was no better. Eventually, she reluctantly searched my name by my frequent flyer number, found my name as a member and let me in.

While leaving the club, I asked the woman how long she had been with US Airways. She said that she joined US Air five years ago. She had to have known about America West acquiring them and must have been trained in America West's policies and procedures. But did she care? I guess not. I had flown with US Airways on twenty-six round trips that year. Why would they let a poor attitude risk losing such a good customer?

So, coming back to your question, how can you get the employees of the acquired company to adopt the culture and attitude of the acquiring company? The US Airways example tells us that it is not easy. But the management needs to continue to try to engage the employees of the acquired company to adopt the policies and procedures of the new owner. It is easy to get the employees of the acquired company to wear the new company badge on their shirt pocket, which is on their heart. It is much harder to get them to wear the badge "in" their heart. That involves acknowledgement of the change in ownership, and training on its policies, procedures, culture, attitude, goals alignment, and engagement.

Our experience at Microchip Technology shows that, over time, many acquired employees will make the change and become indistinguishable from our existing employees. Others will never make the change and will either leave or must be let go.

Does management have an indecision problem?

Question: My company was acquired by a larger one, and we are seeing indecision by the new management. We have been told that the new company will be re-evaluating R&D projects, realigning the compensation and titles of the employees to its own pay scales, combining the benefits of both companies, etc. But decisions continue to be delayed. Is this type of indecision common after an acquisition?

-Anonymous, Austin, Texas

Answer: I am receiving a flood of questions about the impacts of acquisitions on employees, yet I do not see any spike in acquisition activity. Since our company, Microchip Technology, recently closed a large acquisition, it is safe to assume that many of our new employees are using this "Ask Steve" column to ask questions that are important to them. Subject to the editorial discretion of the Arizona Republic, I will answer some of their questions, since they have broad applicability to many acquisition scenarios.

After an acquisition, the new management team has a very large amount of activity on its plate. The acquirer paid a large premium to buy the acquired company, so, it must implement financial improvements to make the company worth the price. One of the main goals is to make the acquired company more efficient. This often requires the consolidation of finance, IT, business, and manufacturing systems. This consolidation effort usually requires a combination of various disciplines, such as purchasing, planning, audit, tax, internal-control, warehouse, and CAD systems.

Combining two companies also requires the integration of two sales forces, who were often calling on common customers. With access to the contractual terms and conditions from both companies, customers often attempt to negotiate the "best of both worlds" for themselves. In some cases, they even try to renegotiate contracts that have already been finalized.

At the same time, a public company has to abide by the U.S. Securities and Exchange Commission (SEC) calendar, which requires that financial results be reported within 40 days of the end of the quarter. Reporting such results in the very first quarter requires the revaluation of the acquired company's inventory and assets, and the allocation of the purchase price to various businesses, assets, inventory, intellectual property, and customer relationships.

During that same timeframe, the acquired employees are nervous about their jobs, benefits, future compensation, and career goals. So, the company management has all of this on its plate. They need to juggle all these priorities to ensure that the deadline-driven items get done. Consequently, items that are not deadline driven must wait.

This is where I explain the difference between 'indecision' and a 'delayed decision'. Indecision is when management is incapacitated. After all the data has been gathered, senior management still does not know which way to go. An indecisive management team has a significantly negative impact on both the company's employees and its results.

However, do not confuse indecision with a delayed decision. The priorities that a company sets for many of its integration issues are driven by financial reporting requirements. Namely, the SEC deadlines by which it must make those decisions. There is no such regulatory mandate for R&D rationalization, employee compensation, benefits, or titles. Therefore, the company most likely has not yet gathered all the data regarding those items and has not done a comparison and realignment. Additionally, these comparisons are often complicated by the existence of international sites and the cost-of-living differences among domestic sites. That is why those unregulated decisions are delayed.

If there is no timeline provided for low-priority decisions, then this could seem like indecision to those who are impacted. I recommend that managers develop and communicate timelines for those low-priority decisions, to avoid the appearance of indecision. A six-month timeline for lower-priority items is quite reasonable.

Should I sell my business now?

Question: I am president/owner of a staffing firm with stable revenue stream; earnings before interest, taxes, depreciation, and amortization (EBITDA) at 16.8% of revenue; no debt; self-funded; excellent management; no legal issues; etc. I have been trying to sell the firm via a broker but most of the offers are low-ball, in my opinion. I recently received an offer from a large national staffing firm who wants to aggressively grow, and we are strategically and culturally a good fit. They offered a reasonable total price, but only want to pay 55% down and will pay the rest in an earn out over two years. I keep the cash and accounts receivable on the balance sheet.

The broker says it is a great deal, but it is less than what I asked for, and who knows if I will ever see the earn-out?

Should I hold firm, or should I cave in and sell?

-Anonymous

Answer: In this column, I will cover the general advice and what to look for in structuring the deal for an earn-out.

You have been trying to sell the business though a broker, but most of the offers have been low-ball offers. You finally got an offer that is in the ballpark of what you were looking for but is still lower than what you were willing to accept. There is an earn-out payment over two years, but you are not convinced there will actually be an earn-out.

In my view, the offer that you are getting for upfront money seems reasonable given the backdrop you describe of the economy. My questions are more around how the earn-out will be structured.

First, are you going to stay with the company for two years during earn-out? If you are going to stay and manage the company during that period, then I would be more interested in structuring an earn-out and take the upfront offer that you are getting. You also need to ensure that the new owners do not have the right to remove you until the earn-out period is complete. Or if they remove you, you have a severance arrangement or that the target earn-out is accelerated and paid. You also need to negotiate the rules of engagement, i.e., who will make the pricing decisions, and will you have autonomy or shared control? You also need to negotiate whether you will have to relocate if they decide to move the company.

However, if the new owners want you out, and they are the ones who will manage the company, your earn-out could be in jeopardy. You do not know their preferences or other obligations and combining your business with their other assets dilutes your chances of getting an earn-out. In that case, I will hold out and negotiate for a higher offer close to what you were looking for.

(The column was originally withheld pending the closure of the deal. The seller was able to negotiate a higher upfront amount and satisfactorily structure earn-out for a win-win.)

Should I sell my small company?

Question: I am the CEO of a small technology company. We have an innovative new product that is getting good reviews in the marketplace. However, it takes a long time for customers to evaluate the product, and some customers are hesitant to commit to a small company. I wish that we were a larger company so that the task would become easier. Should we merge with one of our larger competitors?

-Pat, Phoenix

Answer: Your question does not have a yes or no answer. There are usually several reasons why a small company would consider selling itself to a larger competitor.

Sometimes, a small company needs strong sales and marketing channels to get their product to market. At other times, a small company may need adjacent technologies to win their customers. They may not have the resources to develop the adjacent technologies, and a merger with a larger company may bring the complete solution to the market.

Other times, investors become impatient and want liquidity—particularly when a near-term Initial Public Offering does not look likely. Therefore, a merger becomes a viable alternative. Yet, other times the investors may not become impatient, but may not want to further add to their investment. Therefore, the company would lack the funding to wait out the incubation period for its customers.

This is only a subset of the reasons, and many special circumstances exist. It would be best for you to engage with an investment banker who has a good reputation in your industry. The investment banker should help you navigate through the strategic alternatives for your situation.

While there can be many good reasons to merge your company with a larger competitor, the task of making it easier and faster for customers to evaluate your product is not one of them. Small company CEOs tell me all the time that they think larger companies have an easier time. Let me tell you from experience, this is not so.

As you become larger, you must find larger and larger dollar revenues each year to maintain your growth rate. Your stakeholders multiply with public investors; financial analysts; employees; communities; governments; public company auditors; the Security and Exchange Commission; regulations like Sarbanes-Oxley; the board of directors; audit committees; competitors; customers; security class action law firms; and on and on.

At more than six billion dollars in annual sales, our company—Microchip Technology—could be considered a large company. I do not remember the end of a single quarter when I said, "Oh, that was easy." So, I will leave you with this final thought…

Every morning when a gazelle wakes up, it knows that it must outrun the fastest lion to survive. When a lion wakes up, it must outrun or out-maneuver the slowest gazelle in order to not starve. So, it does not matter whether you are a gazelle or a lion. When the sun comes up, you better be running.

Company acquired by private equity

Question: My company was acquired by private equity firms about a year ago. Since then, the financial condition of the company has worsened. We are not told a whole lot in the trenches, but rumor has it that the company is having trouble because of the large debt load. The company is laying off people indiscriminately. There seems to be no long-term vision. The morale in the company is very bad. Can you weigh in on these private-equity deals?

-Brian, Phoenix

Answer: Private-equity partners are like venture capitalists. Traditional venture capitalists tend to invest money in creating new businesses and funding innovations. Private-equity partners tend to buy existing businesses, which they believe they can improve and then resell for profits.

What creates an opportunity for a private-equity deal? When the public stock market does not realize the potential of a company and undervalues it in the public market, the opportunity arises for private equity to step in. Private-equity partners are not always right in choosing their company. They occasionally make mistakes, and sometimes deal fever can bid up prices to the point where they pay more than the real economic value of an enterprise.

I do not know which industry you are in, so I will take two examples from the semiconductor industry. Several years ago, the same private equity firm bought two companies—Zilog and ON Semiconductor. Both were bought with a small down payment, and the companies were saddled with a large debt. A few years later, Zilog (based in San Jose, California) filed for bankruptcy—wiping out the private equity investment. ON Semiconductor (based in Phoenix) has flourished after some initially difficult times.

While private equity owners have done a few good things, they are in general very harsh on a company. They often siphon off the entire cash flow of the company to pay off debt, their own management fees, and dividends. If at the same time the purchased company runs into hard economic times, the private-equity owners tend to cut costs indiscriminately to keep the cash flowing. This, in turn, can compromise the long-term future of a company, which is what seems to be happening in your case.

I am sure that various private-equity partners reading this may disagree with my analysis.

If you are an employee in the trenches, there is not much you can do. Try to ignore the rumors and focus on serving your internal and external customers and hope that the storm will pass. If things get worse, find another job before you become the victim of the next layoff.

Do right by employees when selling a company

Question: I am about to sell my company to my top competitor. The offer is too good to let it pass—it is over three times the current value of my company. I have learned (by accident) that they intend to shut my company down immediately after the acquisition and lay off the workers.

I have 17 full-time workers (software developers) on the payroll and have worked with most of these people for more than 10 years. And the revenue has been stable in recent years. How ethical would it be to sell the company under these circumstances?

I understand that there could be good arguments made for either option, but what would you do?

-Jack

Answer: To fully answer your question, I would need more background information on your situation, including your age with respect to nearing retirement and some other factors. So, I will deal with a couple of scenarios by making some assumptions.

First, I will assume that you are at a stage where instant money from the deal will set you up for retirement and assure that you can continue your standard of living. And, therefore, you feel the deal is too good to pass up.

You should ask the acquiring company what they plan to do with the employees. Then, you should negotiate some sort of severance agreement, should any of your employees be laid off by the acquirer. This can be done by either the acquirer offering them a contract at closing, or by you offering them a contract now that the acquirer assumes upon closing.

The second thing you should do is to share the equity you receive upon closing with your long-term employees that have made the company what it is, and worth purchasing at three times its current value. These two steps will absolve you of your ethical dilemma.

If my assumption is incorrect and you are not nearing retirement, then you should also explore the prospects of your company remaining standalone. If the revenue has been stable in recent years, can it grow in future years through the hiring of more software developers? Could your company then fetch an even higher price a few years down the line?

In either case, you should share some of the equity with your long-term employees and, when you are ready to sell, ensure that the buyer will either maintain their jobs or provide a reasonable severance upon involuntary termination.

Chapter 8: Dress code at work

Dress code at work is always a controversial topic. Employees, especially young ones, are sometimes not able to distinguish the clothes they wear outside work hanging out with their friends from the clothes they need to wear to dress professionally at work.

Dress professionally at work

Question: I am a sales representative for an electronics distributor. I visit customer sites to make account calls and meet with purchasing and engineering departments that consist of mostly men.

I am young, beautiful, and blonde, and I dress like most women my age. But I have this problem with men that they are talking to my breasts instead of talking to my face.

My mother says that my dress is too low cut and I dress trashy, but my mother has always felt that way. She is just too conservative. I would like your opinion. How would you set up behavior guidelines in your company to address this problem? And what can I do to deal with these men, with whom I must work to keep my job and grow in my company?

-Megan, Phoenix

Answer: I chose to answer this question reluctantly. Either your question is not serious, or you already know the answer, but you are not willing to implement the solution. Instead of taking ownership, you want to divert the blame to men in your business—whose behavior I do not condone, either. My answer is likely to draw fire from both sides, but I welcome opposing views.

I am not young, beautiful, or blonde, so I really do not know how someone in that position should dress outside of work. But it is clear to me how everyone should dress at work.

Every company should have a dress policy; as does our company, Microchip. We prohibit provocative clothing, such as low-cut blouses, short skirts, bare midriff sections and tank tops for women, and muscle shirts for men. We also prohibit visiting contractors, vendors, or sales representatives from violating this policy, even if their own company does not have one.

I am not making any excuses for the behavior of the men that you described. But in this case, it would be very difficult to implement any kind of policy across all your customers, at their many sites and departments. So, you must take the responsibility to solve this problem by looking at yourself in the mirror. There should not be even a hint of your selling anything other than the value embedded in the products and services of your company.

I can tell you that dressing provocatively will hinder your climb up the corporate ladder. If you do not believe me, just look at successful women in business and government, and the female vice presidents at Microchip. They all dress professionally and conservatively at work.

I invite other young, professional women to write with advice for this situation. Depending on the number and quality of your responses, I plan to publish a follow-up column compiling some of this advice.

Follow up on dressing professionally at work

My column regarding Megan's question on dressing provocatively at work brought a record number of responses containing advice from women. Here is a sampling of their responses:

You only have one chance to make a first impression. A stranger will judge you by the way you present yourself. In the corporate environment, if you desire to be taken seriously, dressing as upper management would like to present itself to prospective clients goes a long way toward solid employment. Assemble your wardrobe accordingly.

-Betsy Ross

This young woman sounds like she has the maturity of a high-school teen. If she feels that men are talking to her breasts, then surely, they are "talking" back. Please continue to stress proper business attire to all, just as you did in this article.

-Name withheld upon request

If you get dressed, look in the mirror and think, "Wow, this will look nice to wear to the club," then you need to change clothes.

I simply feel that work is not the place to show off my body—I save that for the beach, pool, and clubs.

-Ann Van Kerkwyk

I am not young, beautiful, or blond, but I was 20 years ago! And the rules of dressing for success have not changed since I was in Megan's age group. It does not matter what type of product she is selling. The bottom line is, if her typical business attire is provocative, revealing and 'trashy', that is how she will be perceived; regardless of how great her selling skills are. It is hard to move up the corporate ladder when you are perceived as 'trashy'.

-Bobbie

I have to agree with Megan's mom; conservative is the name of the game in the workplace. It does not matter how attractive you are, hanging the 'sisters' out in any work environment is not acceptable at any age. If Megan thinks the guys are looking, she needs to realize that so are the women; and none of us appreciate having to try to keep our eyes focused off her chest. I have sent many young women home to change tops because their attire was unacceptable for a professional environment.

-Andrea

The problem with cleavage is that it begs you to look. Megan needs to put on a top that covers well. If she likes she can change it after work to go out with her friends.

-Stephanie

Three words: Wear a jacket. (A knee-length skirt would not hurt, either.) Additionally, perhaps watching about 12 or more episodes of "What Not to Wear" would not hurt her, either.

-Ann R. Werries

When I was growing up, my mother on occasion said to me or my sister, "You do not think you are going to leave the house that way?" Megan needs to listen to her mother.

-Annette Donelson

I once worked with a successful professional who said the best advice was, "Ask yourself what your mother would say." When making important decisions, this never fails. Dressing for professional work is far different than dressing like "most women my age."

-Mary Janecek

This is one time Megan should listen to her mother. This young woman seems to be full of herself and wants the world to march to her drummer. If any part of her breasts or cleavage shows above her dress, whether standing or bending over, then the dress is too low cut and unprofessional.

-Jane Linville

Megan needs to take responsibility for her choices. She must decide what is most important to her—sexual validation or being taken seriously as a professional. I am a CPA, and I know how I want to be viewed and dress appropriately in order to be taken seriously for my brainpower and skills. I am also single. When I feel the need for sexual validation, I dress accordingly and go out.

-Jamie

Like Megan, I was a young female sales representative who called on mostly male customers. I was very aware that my looks could skew the perception that people had of me, and always dressed and acted conservatively and professionally at work.

My advice to Megan is to cover up and stop showing off her sexuality on the job. She needs to realize that she is a party to the 'behavior problems' she thinks the other companies need to address.

-Been There

I suggest to Megan that she save the cleavage for after 5 p.m. Dressing professionally is always good to do and will never invite criticism. In fact, bosses often remember those that have some class to their attire.

-Diana

Dressing professionally for men

Question: I liked your columns on dressing professionally for women. I am a customer-service representative in a large branch of a bank. I have seen some of my male associates not dressed well for work. They show up in cut-off jeans or an un-collared shirt. It does not make a good impression on our customers.

Can you please provide advice on dressing for success for men?

-John, Phoenix

Answer: Dressing for success for men is generally less controversial than it is for women. Very often, the problem with a man's appearance at work is either improper grooming or clothes.

The simplest rule is that your clothes and grooming should be suitable to both the environment in which you work and your role. Cut-off, faded jeans with holes may be OK for a non-office environment, such as gardening, plumbing, lumberyards, long-haul trucking, loading docks, warehouses, etc. But the same clothes are not suitable in a bank environment, in a law office, an accountant's office, etc. Can you imagine a lawyer showing up in court to represent you wearing cut-off, faded jeans with holes? How much confidence is he likely to project for you?

My sense is that most intelligent employees, who are not trying to make a scene or be difficult, can easily figure out the right attire for their role and the environment. Problems occur when one employee wants to test the limits of the system by violating the dress code.

In that case, the management must enforce the dress code. Do you want your customer-service employees to wear neck ties? May they wear T-shirts, or must they wear a collared shirt? May they wear sneakers or sandals?

Like I said in the beginning, the problem with men can often be their grooming. Here, it is easier to draw controversy. Let us say that your new financial advisor shows up with long hair, a ponytail, an unshaven face, pierced earrings, and tattoos showing on his hands and neck. Would you want him to manage your hard-earned money? You may not admit this to avoid getting some flack, but it would at least be unsettling. However, I do not have the same reaction when a plumber, gardener, or garbage collector shows up at my house looking like that.

In your case, your branch manager should set up a dress code. I would include a collared dress shirt, dress pants and dress shoes, with necktie optional in the summer; either a clean-shaven face or a beard (not an unshaven face for four days) and a businessman's hair cut; and no visible piercings.

Chapter 9: Functioning of a team

Disagree and commit

Question: I work for a technology company. I was on a cross-functional team to develop its networking strategy. Unfortunately, I believe that the team has made an incorrect decision. My boss is ready to make a proposal to the vice president. How do I voice my disagreement?

-Greg, Scottsdale

Answer: The time to voice your disagreement was during deliberations and before the cross-functional team made its decision. There are always multiple solutions to a problem. A good cross-functional team will usually make 90% of the decisions correctly. It is impossible to know which 10% of the decisions are wrong. Therefore, there are three choices after the decision has been made:

1. Everyone agrees and commits to the decision
2. Some team members disagree, but commit to the decision
3. Some team members disagree and do not commit to the decision

The first two choices are the only ones that should be allowed. If the third option is allowed and individual team members who disagreed do not commit to doing their part, then chaos will reign, and all decisions may fail. This is because someone disagrees with every decision.

On the other hand, if everyone commits to the decision and does their part, then 90% of the decisions made will be successful. I will take a 90% success rate any time. In the 10% of cases where the team made an incorrect decision, a good, vigilant cross-functional team will get more information in due time, discover the mistake, and course correct.

Therefore, even if you disagree, you should commit and support the decision made by the team. However, your boss should include the dissenting team members' objections in the proposal as risk factors, to provide a balanced view to the VP.

Confrontational hot shot employee

Question: I manage a group of twenty-five employees. One of our new employees is relatively harsh in group settings. He confronts and criticizes others very aggressively. He is very knowledgeable and most times he is correct. But he is disliked for his style. Can you offer some advice?

-Phil, Scottsdale

Answer: You have a hotshot employee who does not value the team. Public criticism and confrontation put employees down and foster a bad team environment. It draws a strong defensive response from the one who is being confronted and is not always productive. Some companies call this 'constructive confrontation'. In my experience, it is almost never constructive for the one who is being confronted.

You should guide your group's culture toward respect for the individual and the team. Consider the following equation that I described on page 239 of my book "Driving Excellence", published by Wiley.

Output = Individual Expertise + (Rate of Improvement x Contribution to the Environment)

Your hotshot employee only focuses on his individual expertise. When you measure his total output, he gets negative scores because he is lacking in 'Contribution to the Environment'.

It will be best to teach this employee to look at the second half of the equation. He needs to control his aggressiveness in group settings. That does not mean that he cannot ask good and even tough questions. But he needs to focus on the task—not the individual. If he has criticism of the individual, it would be much better to talk to the presenter after the meeting and offer criticism privately. This is less likely to draw a defensive response and should be more productive.

Successful group dynamics is very critical to a team's success. No one individual should be allowed to affect it negatively. This does not mean that you sweep the problem under the rug. It means you work it privately to preserve individual dignity and team harmony. A team in harmony will get better results than the one in confrontation.

Therefore, the best policy is to praise in public and criticize in private.

Team choosing a strategy that boss will veto

Question: I am an executive with a technology company. I have given my organization a task to develop the strategy for a project. I gave them wide latitude regarding the strategic options. Now, I am hearing that they are choosing a strategy that I will veto, but I do not want to discourage the team. How should I manage this situation?

-Eric, Scottsdale

Answer: This type of problem happens when you assign a task to a team without defining the boundaries in which they must operate. Most empowering cultures still have boundaries. You should have defined the team's boundaries, which could have included cost, timeline, resource constraints, capital constraints, and specific goals and objectives for the strategy being created.

If you are concerned that you will veto a given strategy, then you should spell out the strategies to be avoided from the start. However, if you think that you will be open to listening to the arguments for the strategy your team has developed, then you should tell them that you do not like that strategy but are open to changing your mind based on the arguments presented. This preserves the team's enthusiasm, teamwork, and empowerment. And it still gives you the chance to either veto their strategy or change your mind.

At this stage, you should call a team meeting and do what you should have done in the first place. Tell them that you have heard where the team is headed. Inform them of your reservations about that strategy. If you are firm, then tell the team to give you an alternative strategy. If you are flexible, then tell the team that you are biased, but you are still open minded.

Trust me—your team will appreciate it. If they still come up with the same strategy, they will look at it much more carefully before they recommend it to you. And, they will likely have a back-up plan if you veto it.

CEO Condemns everyone

Question: The CEO of our company gave the employees a 'pep talk'. Key points were:

- Each person can be replaced by five Chinese workers; so, to keep your job, you need to work five times harder.
- You no longer work at the parent company, since this was a spin-off; things have changed.
- Get off your lazy rears. This is our worst performing plant in the company.
- You complain too much; if you do not like it, leave.

Most talented people began leaving, and the remaining employees were totally demoralized. The management cannot figure out who is not contributing, so they condemned everyone.

I am puzzled by this speech; would you please shed some light on this?

-Ed

Answer: I refer you to two books: "Good to Great" by Jim Collins and my own book "Driving Excellence" from Wiley. Jim Collins breaks leadership into five levels. The highest "Level-5 CEO" looks out the window and praises his/her subordinates when things are going well, and he/she looks into a mirror and takes responsibility when things go poorly. Clearly, your CEO is far from a Level-5 leader.

In my book, I state that, "Every system is perfectly designed to get the results it is getting." Employees work IN the system and, therefore, the management should work ON the system. Your CEO needs to be involved and lead the plant, to modify the system for better results.

It is true that Chinese workers are producing excellent output with 1/5th the pay. In a global economy it is putting tremendous pressure on U.S. workers. Your CEO is frustrated, but the approach of saying, "You all suck," has simply de-motivated everyone and does not create any engagement to right the ship.

A better approach would be to praise the people for the good work they have done, and then highlight areas for improvement. Then, he needs to personally commit to work with you to provide the tools, training, and resources to achieve the needed improvements. The Chinese worker issue needs to be presented positively by saying, "Globalization is already here. Let us focus on changing what we have personal control over, such as constantly improving our own skills so that we can do higher-level tasks in this high-cost country." Watch the use of a term that implies "we vs. you". The CEO needs to consider himself included in the quest for improvement and must then provide the necessary motivational leadership to enlist the employees' commitment to the mission. On the other hand, if the CEO continues to preach that it is 'your' problem, and to suggest, "If you do not like it, leave" perhaps that is exactly what you should be considering. Life is too short to tolerate a tyrant CEO.

The importance of an "open door" policy

Question: Our management has come up with a new initiative called the open -door policy. This is apparently in response to a series of employee lawsuits regarding harassment and discrimination. Management now wants to listen to and provide access for employees. How do you define an open-door policy, and will it work?

-Lance, Phoenix

Answer: The real definition of the open-door policy for your company can only come from your management or HR. Its success will depend on how it is defined and implemented, as well as whether it is believed by the employees.

An "open-door" policy is a company-wide policy that allows employees to bring any issue to anyone in their management chain, or to HR. Employees are encouraged to escalate the issue up the organizational hierarchy, within their management chain of command, until the issue is addressed. For example, if an employee were in manufacturing and could not find a satisfactory resolution to an issue, that employee would eventually get an audience with the VP of Manufacturing, VP of HR or even the CEO. If an employee felt uncomfortable bringing an issue to anyone but the VP of HR or the CEO, he or she could have direct access to either party. This would apply to issues such as sexual harassment or inappropriate conduct within the employee's management hierarchy.

When implementing this policy, some managers feel apprehensive at first—just as you are feeling. They worry that the employees may abuse the policy, taking all of their issues directly to senior management and bypassing them. This concern is understandable. However, my experience is that this concern is unfounded. Rarely do employees want to bring their issues to senior management if it is not required. The benefits of maintaining the desired culture clearly outweigh the occasional abuse. HR is there to ensure the proper escalation process through the management hierarchy. If management truly embraces this policy, it will strongly reinforce the company's commitment to communication. It will also give a voice to those employees who would not otherwise be heard.

I would like to point out an important cautionary note for employees. There is a difference between management hearing a complainant versus agreeing with it. This policy ensures that the employee will be heard, but it does not guarantee that senior management will agree. With an open-door policy, the answers employees receive may not be what they want to hear. Regardless, employees typically appreciate that management cared enough to listen. This type of open access to management builds a great deal of goodwill with employees. It can also help the company avoid legal problems by correcting potential violations.

I have had many employees use the open-door policy to seek a meeting with me. In one case, I ordered the reinstatement of an employee who was terminated. In many other cases, I did not agree with the complainants, and the facts and investigations led to denying their requests.

Should close relatives work at the same company?

Question: My mother operates a furniture store for a national chain. My sister and brother work at the same store, but I do not. My sister and mother bring home their problems from work. My sister does not like my mother's management style and is always arguing with my mother on behalf of the employees. My brother often tries to mediate, but passions run high, and he is largely unsuccessful. I just watch the drama spoil many of our family meals and evenings together.

Should there not be a law against family members working at the same store?

-Jessica A., Scottsdale

Answer: Your question highlights a problem that occurs when family members work together at a business. Over the years, I have seen similar problems between parents and their offspring, problems between siblings, and the most common problems between a husband and a wife. Could you imagine if a husband had to write a performance review for his wife? Any negative comments would surely put him in the doghouse at home. Problems of various magnitudes crop up with other relationships at work.

There is no law in any state that I am aware of that prevents relatives from working at the same business. Many businesses form their own policy to deal with such situations. The most common policy I am aware of is that a relative cannot directly report to another relative but can work in a different department. This rule minimizes most of the problems by creating distance between the two relatives in terms of reporting relationships. And, I have seen it work fairly well over the years.

In your case, the company seems to have no such policy. As a result, your sister and your brother have a reporting relationship with your mother—the store manager. The only way to make such relationships function at work and at home is to keep the two relationships distinctly separate. At work, your siblings are your mother's employees, and they should not have any more rights than any of the other, non-relative employees. At home, your siblings should have a distinctly different relationship. This should be a normal family relationship, not encumbered by the stresses of work.

This is all much easier to say than to do. Since you have taken the initiative to ask me about it, I am asking you to insert yourself and not be a silent observer of the drama. You need to do some shuttle diplomacy. Start with your mother and have a heart-to-heart talk with her regarding the impact it is having on the family. Advise her to keep the two relationships separate. Then, have similar talks with your sister and your brother, separately. Get each person's commitment to leave the work arguments at work, and to have a loving relationship at home.

For this to work, the most important person is likely your mother. She is the boss at work and should lay down the ground rules for operation. If her children will not take orders from her at work, she should be willing to ask them to seek employment elsewhere; just like she would do with any other employee. At home, she is the mother and should set the tone and not answer any work questions at home.

My own son worked for our company as a summer intern for three years while he was in high school and at university. After he graduated with his bachelor's degree in electrical engineering, he received an offer for a permanent job from our company. He declined and decided to find a job that is independent from where his dad is the CEO. He currently works for an internet marketing company in California. When I asked him why, he told me that at Microchip, he would always be known as Steve Sanghi's son. That is a pretty good principle to follow.

Choosing what to delegate

Question: I am a senior manager in a technology company. I often face a dilemma when I have a lot of work to do and I am trying to decide what I should do myself and what I should delegate? Is it reasonable to do myself what I like to do and delegate what I do not like to do?

-Ron, Mesa

Answer: A manager is always juggling between several activities and often comes across this dilemma of what to delegate and what to do themself. When I come across this same dilemma, I choose the opposite of what you are suggesting.

I usually choose to delegate what I like to do. And I try to do myself what I do not like to do. I find that I am often very familiar with and good at what I like to do. And I am often less familiar with and not as good at what I do not like to do. So, which activity should I delegate?

The answer lies in understanding the role of the manager in delegating. Delegating is not abdicating. Proper delegation requires helping set the objectives and key results for the activity, frequently meeting for one-on-ones with the delegate and monitoring the results.

So, which one am I more capable of monitoring with the least amount of time spent by me? It is obviously the activity that I am more familiar with. On the other hand, it would be more difficult for me to monitor an activity that I am less familiar with, and I am not as good at doing. Besides, I am not likely to learn anything new by doing what I already do well. I am likely to learn something new by doing something I am less familiar with.

For all these reasons, whenever I face such a dilemma, I choose to delegate what I can do myself very well. I must admit that there is temptation to do what you are suggesting. And a vast number of managers will choose to do what they like to do. But that is why a vast number of managers reach a plateau in their careers, because it is hard work and commitment to learn what you do not like.

I was faced with such a dilemma when our company Microchip Technology acquired Silicon Storage Technology (SST) headquartered in Sunnyvale, California. It was clear that the integration activities and the transformation of the culture of SST would require a significant amount of face time in Sunnyvale. I could have my Chief Operating Officer do the job at SST while I continued to run Microchip Technology. That would be very easy for me since I had run Microchip for the prior 20 years. However, I chose to do the SST job myself and delegated Microchip to the COO. It is because it is much easier for me to monitor Microchip from a distance. I would be able to sense any trouble at Microchip from a distance. I was not likely to be as good at detecting the same trouble at SST from a distance if I had delegated the SST job to the COO.

Managing a multi-location team

Question: Our company recently acquired another company. Following the reorganization, I now have employees on two different remote sites. One of the sites is in California and the second one is in Bengaluru, India. How do I communicate with and manage those remote employees?

-Jack, Phoenix

Answer: In the age of globalization, management of remote employees is becoming a very necessary skill to acquire for anyone looking for upward mobility in an organization. If all your employees are in the same location, it is easy to get a meeting together to discuss goals, objectives, opportunities and risks, and then monitor performance.

When employees are scattered in remote locations, the task becomes harder. At the beginning of every quarter, start by getting everyone together on a conference call. Define the organization's mission, objectives, and specific key results that need to be achieved during the quarter. Define the roles and responsibilities clearly. This is easier via video conferencing but can be accomplished through audio conferencing. Also, be sure to post pictures of all team members at every location.

Make sure that each remote site has a local supervisor who manages the employees on a day-to-day basis. You should then set up a weekly call with each local supervisor to review progress and issues.

You should also set up periodic project reviews, where employees from all sites working on the same project join a conference call to review progress and plans. Do not penalize one site with off-hour calls; instead, spread the burden around. Your company's Intranet site might allow setting up a workgroup, such as "SharePoint," where everyone can post information to stay coordinated. Also, establish Key Process Indicators (KPIs) to help measure global work performance.

You should periodically travel to each of the remote sites. During your visit, you should hold an all-employee communication meeting to cover goals, progress, and issues. You should also discuss any changes in benefits, bonuses, and stock plans. And you should take employee questions.

You should also set up a regular exchange program, where one or two employees from each remote site spend a week to two weeks at your site. And one or two employees from your site should do the same at remote sites. This is very important to cross pollinate the culture, develop best practices, and learn from one another.

When you have sites in other countries, you have one more issue. English words and gestures do not mean the same things in every country. Employees in different countries react differently to situations. Asians tend to be more reserved and do not ask too many questions. Therefore, at Microchip, we have developed training programs such as "How to work with Americans" and "How to work with Indians".

Remember, these recommendations should not be treated as isolated events. Rather, this is a comprehensive process that must become a way of life.

Employee communication meetings even more important during downturn

Question: I work for a large technology company. Our company used to have employee communication meetings from time to time. A senior executive or the CEO would present some useful information in these meetings, and I always looked forward to them. For the last nine months, my company has chosen to stop doing communication meetings. The reasons given have been that management is busy, executives are traveling, and the economy is bad. We are asked to just focus on the job and not ask any questions. Does this seem right to you?

-Melinda, Mesa

Answer: I believe that the CEO's quarterly communication meeting is the single most powerful vehicle for communication, and for instilling and maintaining the company culture. I wrote about this in my book "Driving Excellence".

Communication meetings have several functions. They allow employees to hear how the company is doing, directly from the top. In addition, there is usually time set aside to answer employees' questions. Typically, this meeting should focus on the company's overall business, market conditions, quarterly P&L results, major initiatives, and current challenges.

When the company faces difficult periods, such meetings are effective forums to discuss the situation. If the company needs to take an undesirable action, such as a factory shutdown or layoff, then the CEO can explain these actions. This may scare some CEOs and management teams. But, having done these more difficult communication meetings a few times, I can attest to their advantages. If the CEO is open and forthright, the employees understand the economic environment and the company's associated actions.

These meetings also reinforce that communication is valued. I often hear employees say after these meetings, "With such a hectic schedule, is it not great that the CEO takes the time to communicate with us directly?" This is the CEO's opportunity to reach people and inspire them to achieve future goals, or to prepare them to begin adapting to difficult business conditions.

The scenario you describe is quite common, wherein many CEOs will initiate these meetings with a sincere desire to improve communication. However, due to time pressures, a meeting can be postponed. If the economic environment turns negative, the CEO may not know which way the business is headed. The CEO then avoids facing the employees and cancels another quarterly communication meeting. By now, six to nine months may have gone by, and regular communication meetings have become a thing of the past.

Conducting regular communication meetings requires a steadfast commitment from the CEO. At Microchip, I have not missed a quarterly communication meeting since 1990.

Pets do not belong at work

Question: I have worked for my company for three years and never before had this problem. One of my coworkers started bringing his dog to the office a few months ago. I do not like dogs. I am annoyed by the dog, his slobbering, and the smell from the food dish. Copying him, some of my other coworkers have begun occasionally bringing their dogs or cats to work.

I have complained to my coworkers. But, so far, they have laughed me off by calling me a pet hater. My coworkers say that our progressive company should be commended for allowing their pets in. When I joined this company, I did not sign up for this. How should I address this problem?

-Samantha, Phoenix

Answer: This is a problem that is becoming more common these days. Many Silicon Valley startup firms allow employees to bring their pets to work. So, let us look at an analogy.

Suppose a coworker brings his 8-month-old child to work and puts him in a crib in his office. Would that be acceptable to your company? Suppose another coworker brings his chicken, rooster, pigeon, rat, snake, or turtle to work, would that be acceptable? The question is, where do you draw the line?

Some might argue that dogs are loving pets, and most people love them. Well, children are also loving. And there are people who happen to love roosters. In a free country, you cannot deny one's right to keep a rooster as a pet unless disallowed by specific community laws. So, if it is OK for a dog, it should also be acceptable for a rooster.

So, you see my point. Except for seeing-eye dogs to assist the blind, I have never seen pets allowed in any workplace—especially not an office environment. It may be different when a job is in a lumberyard or an outdoor environment. However, as a compromise, your company could hold a "bring your pets to work day" once a year, and you could reasonably be expected to accommodate that. This would be comparable to having a "bring your child to work day". This event should accommodate all reasonably sized, domesticated pets—including roosters.

This whole thing is quite silly. I think that you should see your director of human resources. If your company has an open-door policy, then you might also meet with your division's vice president. Then, you could help to craft a policy that would prohibit pets from the company premises, at least during normal business hours.

If your company will not put such a policy in place, then you have two options. First, you can find another job. Or you can try protesting by bringing a rooster to work and demanding equal rights—claiming discrimination if denied such rights. If a rooster does not provoke the desired response, escalate it to a pig. Your company will get the message.

My response is indeed silly here. Bringing a rooster or a pig to work in retaliation for someone bringing the dog will likely get you fired. So, do not do that. I don't believe that the gap between dog lovers and the ones who do not like dogs is bridgeable.

Dog lovers are likely to win every time.

Chapter 10: Coping with management shortfalls

Manager in a comfort zone

Question: How do you feel about a middle manager who is in his comfort zone and is able to fire employees, such as my wife (a registered nurse of 52 years) and me (in a selling capacity for the same time)?

We were revered by our co-workers, customers, patients, and the sales managers who recognized our hard work and dedication. Supervisors like these use the power of their desk to control and create an ideological discipline. You become either a threat or a thorn in their side, and they demand control of you.

CEOs will side with their managers, when in reality that individual is the weak link. Standing up to our mis-managers was their grounds for our dismissal.

-Norman, Casa Grande

Answer: I am sorry to hear about you and your wife's situation. The problem you describe is not uncommon. There are a lot of middle managers who are in their comfort zones and in their jobs for a very long time. They are not growing themselves, and they become a barrier for others below them who have innovative ideas and fresh thinking. These newcomers can become a threat, because they are pushing the manager to change and improve the work processes. This gets the manager out of his comfort zone, and hence he feels threatened for his job security, power, and control. It is common to see such managers trying to control and discipline newcomers. It is rare to see someone get fired in these scenarios, and extremely coincidental to see both you and your wife fired for the same reason. I will assume that nothing else is in play here, such as attitudes, work habits, family versus work obligations, etc.

What you do about it depends very much on the culture of the company. In a progressive, well-managed and employee-empowered company, you can talk to human resources. Or you can just ask for a transfer to another department to get away from this abusive manager.

Since you said that the CEO sides with the managers, it is a sign of an organization that is not necessarily committed to continuous improvement. It has a "top down" culture, where managers feel like its "my way or the highway".

In such a culture, you are out of luck. You should not waste your time seeking a long-term career there. You are better off finding a more vibrant place to work, where it is motivating to go to work every day. But, before you leave, please get a copy of my book "Driving Excellence," place a bookmark on Chapter 8 "How Managers Become Barriers," and place it on your old manager's chair.

Manager versus leader

Question: I am a middle manager for a medium-size company. I am trying to continuously improve my managerial skills to grow in the company. I continuously come across the words "Manager" and "Leader" used interchangeably. How would you describe the difference between a manager and a leader?

-Charles, Chandler

Answer: Congratulations for committing yourself to continuous improvement and thank you for asking this very thoughtful question. There are very significant differences between a manager and a leader.

A manager can be assigned or appointed to head up a department or an organization. But a leader has to be chosen by the followers. A leader is not a leader without followers. A manager can follow a cookie-cutter process to manage a department or a franchised store. But a leader is a lot more than just the person in charge.

A leader provides long-term vision for the organization. They set priorities; grab hold of tough problems; set standards of excellence; impart a sense of urgency; have exuberant commitment; keep the big picture in view; provide the ability to deal with failures; and are tough but fair with people. A leader is someone followers look to for guidance, problem resolution, comfort, support, and help.

Both managers and leaders have some power over their subordinates. There is a column about the powers of a manager later in this book. Leaders tend to make use of "Referent power" a lot more than managers do.

Leadership is a dynamic relationship between leader and follower based on mutual influence and common purpose. In a successful relationship, both leaders and followers benefit in achieving a higher level of motivation and moral development as they affect real and intended change.

Management can be turned into a science by developing methods, processes, and rules to manage. But leadership is more art than science and can change significantly with the culture of the organization and the task-relevant maturity of the followers.

So, as you can see, while a manager can be appointed just to head up a group, it takes vision, hard work, courage, and skill to become an effective leader. Leadership can be fragile and easily lost if you let down your followers. A leader must occasionally look behind to see that someone is following.

The late General and United States Secretary of State Colin Powell summed this up the best: "Leadership is the art of accomplishing more than the science of management says is possible."

Director who considers organizational chart confidential from the team

Question: The director of our organization considers the organizational chart confidential and does not reveal the chart to anyone. If you were really determined, you could just talk to a lot of people in the organization and find out this way, so why hide it from your employees? I was always, maybe naively, under the impression that a clearly structured and communicated organization encourages interaction and cross-organizational communication. Whereas this behavior just festers mistrust. Do you have any explanation for this behavior?

-Dirk

Answer: I have absolutely no explanation for such a behavior by the director of your organization. The only thing I can think of is that he is afraid that the organization chart will get out and his people could be targeted for recruiting by headhunters.

I believe that an organization chart should be well communicated so that everyone's role and responsibility is understood. As you said, it encourages interaction and cross-organizational communication. The benefits of everyone understanding their roles will increase the efficiency of work. In general, productive employees will be happier employees and less vulnerable to headhunter attacks.

The behavior of your director will create mistrust in the organization. If the company cannot trust its employees, then the employees are not likely to trust the company.

I believe that your director should go much further beyond just sharing the organization chart. On a quarterly basis, he or she should write down the objectives for the quarter and some key results to be achieved to support each of the objectives. The names of individuals responsible for achieving those objectives should also be written down. Then those objectives and key results should be presented to the organization.

This way, everyone will know which way the ship is heading. Everyone can tweak their bearings to align themselves with the direction of the company or the division. Without such communication, everyone will choose their own direction. In some cases, one part of the organization may be working against the interests of the other part of the organization. Chaos is likely to result from such lack of communication.

In my first book "Driving Excellence," chapter 17, "Human Systems: Backbone of the Culture", I talk a lot about a comprehensive communication system. You should pick up a copy of this book and place it discreetly on your director's chair.

Replacing a leader

Question: Is it harder to replace a good leader or a bad leader?

-Tom Baumbach, Chandler

Answer: I consider my forty-six years of business experience in which I have replaced good as well as bad leaders. It is hard to replace any leader, but after much deliberation, I believe that it is harder to replace a bad leader.

A good leader leaves the organization in good shape with a good strategic plan, annual plan, and cultural values. With well-defined goals, teamwork, an execution-oriented culture, and employee empowerment, an organization under a good leader is often on semi-autopilot. Subordinates respect a good leader. They have proven themselves and the style of the leader has been well established, with respect to the task-relevant maturity of the subordinates.

When this good leader leaves or retires and a new leader comes in, it upsets the applecart. It leaves the subordinates unsure of where they stand. It also raises questions about the strategic direction of the company. A new leader often wants to put their stamp on the direction of the company. Established projects, plans, and budgets can be reopened and asked to be re-justified. This anxiety is what makes it hard to replace a good leader.

A new leader replacing a good leader should ease into his or her new position and not come in with guns blazing. The new leader should sit back, listen, learn, and absorb. Then, they should slowly make changes as a part of normal review processes, annual plans, or strategic reviews. This will be less threatening, and the momentum is more likely to continue.

Now, what about replacing a bad leader? A bad leader is likely to leave the organization in shambles, without a good strategic or annual plan. The cultural values are often screwed up. The organization lacks teamwork, empowerment, or an execution-oriented culture. Employees in such organizations are often backstabbing while trying to watch their own backs.

When such a leader leaves, the organization breathes a sigh of relief. But the new leader is unknown, so the organization keeps marching to the old tune. Some managers in favor of the old leader, because of their misguided views or because the old leader promoted them, will resist the new leader and the changes he or she wants to make. These employees are often very mistrusting and do not easily respond to the good cultural values being promoted by the new leader. This is what makes the job of replacing a bad leader very difficult.

As opposed to a good leader replacing a good incumbent, a new leader who replaces a bad one needs to come in with the guns blazing. That's because such organizations usually have a low task-relevant maturity. So, the new leader's initial style needs to be very directive. Some managers will probably need to be replaced. Then, the leader needs to simultaneously work on a new strategic plan, annual plan, review projects and budgets, institute a new culture, and work on the company's system in aggregate.

In the final analysis, it is much more difficult to repair a broken organization than to ease into a functioning one; but neither is a simple task.

Executive employment contracts

Question: Do employment contracts for senior management make sense in an uncertain economy? What items should be addressed in the contract? Does it depend on the industry?

I expect to be offered the Chief Financial Officer position for a start-up company within the next month. First-year revenues are expected to be in the range of $9-10 million.

-Marsha

Answer: Employment contracts for executives, although very common, do not make sense in any economy, in my view. A lot of the criticism of executive pay is because of lucrative employment contracts. Often, an underperforming executive gets fired from a company and yet walks away with tens of millions in severance pay.

The seed for this problem is sown when an executive is hired and given a lucrative contract. The board of directors does not think about firing an executive when they are trying to hire one. The executive is often chosen after a significant search-and-selection process. The focus is on hiring and retaining the executive, not firing them. This lack of focus on the severance package during the hiring process comes home to roost later if the executive does not work out.

None of the executives at Microchip have an employment contract, including me. An executive should prove their worth all the time. Their job should be vulnerable to underperformance or recession, just like any other employee. That only seems fair. There are exceptions, however, so let me go over those:

1. It is fair for a senior executive to have a "change in control" agreement. When a company is acquired, its senior management is immediately vulnerable to losing their jobs. This is because the acquiring company often wants to build the new company around its own culture and around the senior management it knows. Therefore, executives of the company being acquired will often be uncooperative and unwilling to champion the new company. A change-in-control agreement guarantees certain severance benefits to executives if their jobs are eliminated following an acquisition. If the severance benefits are reasonable, this exception passes the test, in my view.

2. When an executive is asked to relocate overseas for an assignment for a specific period, the executive assumes extra hardships in relocating the family. If he or she is then terminated without cause, the executive has additional hardships in relocating the family back to the originating country and finding a job, when some of his or her contacts may have dwindled because of living overseas. An employment contract is reasonable under such circumstances.

3. Others may argue that an employment contract is also reasonable when an executive is asked for any relocation, even within the United States. I disagree, but in special circumstances involving a

coast-to-coast relocation, certain considerations may be reasonable.

While employment-contract standards should not depend on the industry, it may be necessary to consider comparable agreements that come from a specific industry. Employment contracts usually cover a severance payment that includes salary, bonus, stock options, and health benefits. In exchange, it is customary for the company to get a non-compete clause for the duration of the severance benefit period. However, non-compete clauses are increasingly not enforceable in many states.

Develop your career—with or without the boss's help

Question: My manager is always very busy and never takes the time to coach me or any of his other subordinates. He is not interested in our development and thinks that we should go to training sessions elsewhere to learn. Do you agree with this manager?

-Lori, Phoenix

Answer: This management style reflects managers who cannot or will not spend the time necessary to grow their employees because they often do not believe that it is their job. That is why your manager says that you should go to a training session elsewhere.

I am not sure about your case, but in some cases such managers may be threatened by hiring or developing high performers. They operate out of fear that, as their employees become more valuable, the manager becomes less valuable. Therefore, they may hire mediocre performers and not spend much time coaching them.

It is true that in today's flat organizational structures, and with the incredible demands placed on managers, it can be very difficult to find the time to coach employees. However, coaching and developing employees are essential tasks. Training is one of the foundational elements for maintaining a company's continuous-improvement culture.

You should ask for a routine one-on-one meeting with your manager. Then, develop an agenda for each of these meetings. The agenda should have four sections. The first section is for personal items. Here, you can discuss your performance, career aspirations, and training and coaching needs. The second section should be a status report wherein you update your manager on the progress of various projects. The third section can be for work-related issues. And the fourth section can be a general discussion on improvement ideas and some "outside the box" thoughts by you and your manager.

You will find that with this structured meeting format, you almost force your manager to give you feedback, coach you on your ideas, and provide his ideas, all of which you can use toward your development.

Do not rely solely on your manager to be responsible for your development. You should also assume responsibility by utilizing other resources such as your human resources group, your training group, peer mentors, and outside training classes.

I have also found that if you can get someone higher up in your company (not your manager) to be your mentor, it offers tremendous advantages. Such mentorships are very valuable because, unlike your manager, the discussions with your mentor do not get easily sidetracked by issues related to your current projects and schedules.

The bottom line is that the ownership for your development lies with you and not your manager. But your manager should be a better resource than he is. So, take control of the situation and develop broader developmental resources to realize your full potential.

Boss with volatile temper

Question: I have a problem with my boss; he has a volatile temper. The other day, he blew up at me for no reason. After things calmed down, he seemed to have no memory of the episode. But it left me feeling vulnerable and wondering where I stand with him. What would you suggest?

-Richard, Scottsdale

Answer: I do not know whether you are a new employee working under this boss. There are certain managers who have a volatile temper, and they will unleash it on anyone who happens to be present at the time. If you have worked for this boss for a while and have not seen this before, you should ignore it as a one-time occurrence since your boss seems to have no memory of it anyway.

If you are a new employee working under this boss and you have heard about his bad temper, then you have a bigger problem. His bad temper has probably been there for a long time, but this was probably just the first time that you became a victim of it.

I remember an Intel Corporation senior executive back in the 1980s who had a bad temper that he would unleash for no reason. After he unwound, he would suddenly become very friendly. He meant no harm, but only if you knew him. The first time you saw that behavior, however, you would be worried about your job.

So, my advice is to persevere in your job. Observe over the coming months whether he blows up at you again, or if it was a one-time occurrence. If he blows up again, try to make an appointment with him when he is calm. Try to talk to him about the impact he is having on you. My sense is that he will agree that he was unable to control his temper. The relationship may improve for a while, but my sense is that the episodes may continue; albeit less frequently.

If he is not rating you badly, and your performance appraisals and merit increases are satisfactory, then you are just dealing with an annoying temper that you are probably not going to get him to control. In that case, you have a decision to make. You can either ignore his temper, like everyone did with that Intel executive, or you can find another job inside or outside the company.

Dishonest purchasing manager

Question: I have a difficult dilemma. I own a small company that distributes construction supplies to large builders. One of my clients has a purchasing manager who asked me for an all-expenses-paid vacation. Otherwise, he will award the contract to my competitor. If I try to expose him, he will simply deny it and I may lose the contract. What would you suggest?

-Charlie, Phoenix

Answer: You do have a difficult dilemma. To find an answer to your question, you must go to the guiding values of your company. Does your company have guiding values? Are they written and practiced, or are they just understood (or so you think)?

At Microchip, our guiding values are written, taught, practiced, and measured. One of our guiding values is "Professional ethics are practiced." In a survey of employees last year, the employees were asked how well our guiding values are practiced. Overall, employees scored 90% on this value (a high score). And the most frequent answer was 100%. This tells me that this guiding value is believed and widely practiced.

Perhaps it would give you some perspective to review Microchip's purchasing policies. First, we send a letter to our suppliers every year, reminding them that all we expect from them is excellent service at competitive prices. The letter also emphasizes that suppliers are not to give any gifts of monetary value to our employees. We exempt minor things, such as lunches, which are essential in business for relationship building. In your case, the company you are dealing with either has no such policy or the purchasing manager is violating it.

You should not look at this dilemma as a decision regarding a single transaction. This is a trend-setting decision that will be watched by your employees and then used as an example in the future. If you bow to the purchasing manager's ultimatum and pay for his vacation, what will you be communicating to your own employees? You may be signaling to your purchasing manager that it is OK for him to accept a personal bribe. So, the overall cost to your business in future from that single, trend-setting decision will be too high.

I would not accept this purchasing manager's ultimatum. I would approach his manager and present the situation in a way that makes it plain that you realize that you are likely to lose their business, but you feel compelled to speak. Who knows? Maybe his manager already has an inkling that his employee's activities are not ethical, and this is the piece of data that is the final straw.

If the purchasing manager is terminated, you may find yourself the exclusive supplier to the resulting organization. Or it could get ugly, and you may lose their business. Either way, you will have established a fundamental guiding value for your company—that professional ethics are never compromised.

Chapter 11: Marketing, selling and financial analysts

Advertise to the right audience

Question: I work for a semiconductor company other than Microchip. I have seen that our company does not advertise in our community, nor does Microchip. I do not see any signs in any of the ballparks or public places. Why do semiconductor companies not advertise their brands in our community?

-Raul

Answer: You ask a very important question that goes to the heart of how marketing and philanthropy sometimes overlap.

Every company falls into one of two broad categories. The first category consists of companies that sell products or services directly to consumers. Examples include Motorola (smart phones), Lexus (cars), McDonalds (food) and General Electric (appliances). When these companies advertise in our community, they are asking you to choose their brand for a product or service.

The second broad category comprises companies that sell products or services to other businesses. Your company and Microchip belong to a sub-category of this class consisting of companies that sell their products to original equipment manufacturers. Consumers buy Motorola smart phones, Lexus cars or GE appliances because of their individual brand preferences, not whether these products may have a Microchip Technology microcontroller in them. A consumer most likely cannot buy anything from Microchip or your company.

When it comes to advertising in their communities, companies have two major budget categories. One is the philanthropic budget, and the other is the marketing budget. The marketing budget is usually orders of magnitude bigger than the philanthropic budget. However, companies that sell their products directly to consumers typically see their philanthropic and marketing budgets as somewhat intertwined. When they sponsor a charity ball, they are also advertising their brand name to the attendees. That is why consumer companies have a much larger reach in terms of community advertising. When they advertise in ballparks, they reach a very large and concentrated group of their customers.

On the other hand, companies like yours and Microchip spend their marketing budgets advertising in trade magazines, at trade shows, and on technical web sites. 75 percent of Microchip's business is international, and only 2 percent of our revenue comes from Arizona. The community activities of these companies become limited to small philanthropic budgets. There is also some small benefit in recruiting from local advertising but, even then, Microchip hires most engineers from a national pool. Most often, it is factory and administrative level positions that are hired locally. So, advertising in ballparks does not provide much payback for Microchip.

One notable exception to this thesis is Intel. With the "Intel Inside" campaign launched in 1991, Intel established a connection with consumers—particularly with PC owners. With microprocessors playing such a key role in PC systems, this was truly an exception. A microcontroller from Microchip does not play as large a role in a car or a refrigerator; hence, these products are sold based on the manufacturer's brand name.

Companies that sell their products to consumers, therefore, have an advantage in terms of name recognition, brand advertisement, and presence in the community. However, this does not mean that companies like Microchip and yours do not care about the community. Microchip cares a great deal and supports various philanthropic programs. But we cannot match the visibility of consumer companies.

Correct amount to spend on ads

Question: I am a marketing engineer in an electronics company. Our company does not spend enough on the advertising of its products and brand name. I am continuously arguing with the division manager that we need to spend more to promote our products. But he always says that the corporation does not have a budget for it. How is the corporation's budget established? And what is the right amount to spend on advertisements as a percentage of revenue?

-Richard, Mesa

Answer: The fact is that the dollars spent on advertising are never enough. Whatever a company spends, it must be allocated among various divisions, product ads, corporate programs, corporate brand-building ads, marketing literature, website maintenance, lead generation, trade shows, etc. I have never been told that the budget was sufficient, because there is always more that can be done.

The second problem lies in trying to create accountability for the advertising dollars spent. Companies usually do not have a good way to demonstrate the return on certain ad spending. It is easier to prove on the extremes. If you spend nothing, then the product may fail because no one will know about it. If you spend too much, then at some point in time you are getting no return for the incremental dollars spent. The problem lies in the middle. How do you prove that, if you are given $250K more, the results will improve by a certain amount; let us say $10M? That would be a 40 to 1 return, which is good. But how do you know that the last $250K was needed to get that result?

So, companies usually set the budget as a percentage of revenue. This percentage can vary based on whether you market to consumers or industry, and whether you sell locally, nationwide, or globally. Companies tend to set a budget that is affordable in their P&L models. Then they ask the divisions and marketing groups to live within that budget and prioritize their activities. Many times, when a different CEO is hired, the budget percentage may change based on his or her biases about the return on marketing spending, so it is a bit more arbitrary than you think.

My advice is that marketing engineers should build a mechanism to show return on investment. Track web hits or leads generated from an ad. Then track the number of those leads that eventually turn into revenue; hence demonstrating the return on the ad spending. If you build a database of past ads and their returns, you may then have a greater chance of convincing management about incremental spending on the next product.

Question based selling

Question: I have a business plan that sounds too good to be true to most people. I have uncovered a way to use a certain kind of equipment in an unconventional manner, which will meet a great market need. But the equipment owners do not use the equipment for this job, and the companies with the need are not aware of this solution. What is the best way to get my foot in the door with a large company?

-Glen

Answer: It seems like you have an innovative idea and a business plan. However, your plan threatens the status quo of the equipment industry and the companies currently utilizing this equipment—and you cannot get them to see it your way. Every large company has "guardians" who are the self-appointed defenders of the status quo. A new idea from the outside can appear threatening to the people doing the job, as they are often fearful that these fresh ideas will make them look bad.

The best resource I can suggest for overcoming these barriers is the book "Secrets of Question Based Selling" by Tom Freese. This book suggests practical methods for selling and convincing the customer through asking questions that lead to your solution. Most salespeople lead with their pitch (the solution). Freese suggests leading with several questions about the customer's problems. This enables you to analyze the problems with the customer, which then leads to your solution in a more natural and customer-centric fashion. I know it works because I have tested it hundreds of times.

Ask the customer this question, "What is it that you cannot do today, but would love to, if you knew that it could be done." The customer will tell you everything about their problems. If you have the solution, you will have a captive audience.

Sales process redefined

Question: I am a sales manager with a technology company. I am looking for a good book to help redefine the sales process at our company. Our sales process seems to be very old fashioned, where salespeople look at the customer as a target and try to win the business at all costs—not always resulting in the best option for the customer.

-Walter, San Jose, CA

Answer: I have a lot of ideas in this area, and we have implemented a progressive sales process at Microchip. In fact, our retired Sales VP, Mitch Little, once wrote the following letter to his sales force on this topic:

"Most people look at the world of sales incorrectly. They think that the job of the salesperson is to get customers to do things that they do not want to do. Today, the job is all about learning what customers want to do and helping them do that. The biggest error in thinking is that 'Sales' is about 'getting' something from people. The very best salespeople know the truth...sales are all about giving. Giving your time, support, advice, knowledge, empathy, and value. Our efforts should be aimed at creating value in the eyes of the customer, by helping them solve problems in their world.

"Many years ago, the average industrial salesperson was the key to obtaining and learning about the products his company sold—data books, samples, and pricing. Relationships were important, but mainly he was the king of information. Now, in the age of the internet, the average customer knows a lot more about the products. The internet has completely changed the role of the most effective salespeople. Today, the best salespeople are those that create the most 'value,' as seen by the customer.

"Let us look at a leisure sports analogy with hunting and fishing. There are critical differences in these two activities that directly relate to sales.

"Hunting is what we are traditionally told that salespeople should do. We should hunt down and get business. We are told that we should track down our prey (the customer) and close that order, no matter what it takes. This is kind of like tracking down a 600 lb. grizzly bear and confronting it up close and personal. Your chance of closing the order with a hunting mindset is low.

"Fishing more closely resembles the art of sales as it has become today. First, you have to study the fishing grounds, the environment, and what the fish are feeding on. You need to clearly understand your equipment and make critical choices about the type of bait that you are going to use to attract fish. You do not 'go get a fish'. You attract the fish by your choice of bait and how it is presented. In sales terms, you facilitate the buying process.

"The definition of salespeople as hunters is out of date. They are now more fisherman and facilitators than anything else. You have to shift your focus from 'getting,' to 'giving.' Give to create value. Create value to differentiate yourself."

I could not have said it better. If you follow the advice in Mitch's letter, you will be on the right track toward redefining your company's sales process. Good luck.

Bad article about my company

Question: I am the CEO of an emerging technology company. The business reporter of a trade publication recently wrote a very bad assessment and cited incorrect facts about my company. I am very upset and want to blast him. But he is an influential reporter. What do you suggest?

-Tony, Phoenix

Answer: Please calm down. Blasting the reporter will not accomplish anything and likely make things worse.

An assessment of a company is usually subjective. Some figures like revenue and profits are facts. But even facts can be confusing with numbers that have GAAP, non-GAAP, pro-forma, acquisition accounting, and stock-option expensing. Other things, such as the market potential of your products, competitive positioning, leadership, and corporate image are assessments, not facts. A reporter may not agree with your assessment. Once published, he is not going to back down and recant his story. Believe me, it never happens.

You need to work on systematically repairing the image of your company. The two books I recommend are "The Regis Touch" and

"Relationship Marketing"—both by my marketing mentor Regis McKenna.

You need to develop a statement and story of how you would like your company to be seen. Be realistic, because the marketplace is harsh, and the truth will come out. There is nothing wrong with being #2. Remember the Avis story, "We're #2. We try harder." Then, you need to tell that story to your infrastructure—manufacturing partners, software and hardware suppliers, industry luminaries, dealers/distributors, financial analysts, industry analysts, and customers. Also, get some testimonials from your key customers.

Armed with an infrastructure that will back up your story, you should meet with various trade publications, including the editor in question. In that meeting, do not drag in the old article. Tell your story with data, facts, and testimonials; and give the editor some references.

Some publications will publish your story. But this editor may be skeptical. So, repeat the meeting in a few months when you have more good news. Consider offering an exclusive. If your facts are correct and your story is good, then, with persistence, you will win the editor over. Trust me, I've been there.

Whatever you do, remember what Regis McKenna taught me (and wrote in his book The Regis Touch), "Never pick a fight with someone who buys ink by the barrel."

Dealing with financial analysts

Question: I am the CEO of a newly public company. I am struggling to deal with the financial analysts and commentators that cover our company. I seem to think that most of the analysts have never run a business, and they tend to make worthless critical comments. I get plenty of advice from my board, but I will value your opinion.

-Don, San Jose, CA

Answer: You are dealing with a challenge that is faced by the CEO of every public company. I have seen some very good financial analysts in the business. But I would agree that many of them fit your description. And dealing with them can be a frustrating exercise at best.

Analysts and commentators can be like score keepers. I remember from my high school days that students who did not make the team became score keepers, commentators, and assistant coaches. They made critical comments about the players and pushed them around.

Financial analysts and commentators can be similar. I am not saying that they are all washed out people from business. But many of them do not have any business experience, so their commentary and research reports can sometimes be annoying, especially if you know they are wrong.

I know a financial commentator on one of the Phoenix business radio stations who never applauds any CEO. I have heard him criticize such prominent technology CEOs as John Chambers of Cisco and the late Steve Jobs of Apple. If a company beats the earnings guidance, he criticizes the CEO for being a sandbagger. And, if the company misses the earnings guidance, he criticizes and accuses the CEO of lying in his prior conference call when he provided the guidance. Obviously, he has never run a business, and he does not understand the uncertainty involved in closing a business deal.

So, what can you do about it? Financial analysts and commentators are a necessary part of business. As a newly public company CEO, you may not appreciate it yet, but you do need them for telling your story to a broad investor base and the wider community. So, ignore the short-term criticism and develop a thicker skin. If you continue to post strong financial results, they will come to appreciate you. One more thing you can do is to take your story directly to your large investors by visiting them in what is called a "non-deal road show". Trust me, it works.

Whatever you do, try to contain your anger and emotions, and do not confront the analyst to the point of pissing him or her off.

Providing financial guidance to analysts or not

Question: I am the CEO of a technology company that went public within the last few years. We have a tremendous debate on our board of directors as to whether we should provide quarterly financial guidance to the investors and analysts. There are obvious pros and cons for doing so. Your company has been public for many years, and you have seen the public market through various ups and downs. What is your opinion about providing financial guidance?

-Michael, San Jose, CA

Answer:

Most financial analysts and investors tend to have limited original thinking. When you provide financial guidance for revenue and earnings, most investors and analysts build their models around the guidance provided by you. Some of them may not completely believe what you say and may model it more aggressively or conservatively; but the models usually bracket the guidance provided by the company. There is very little fundamental financial research done these days.

Financial analysts are also mostly reporters of information. They keep good scores regarding how many times you have met your financial guidance, missed it, or beaten it. Therefore, it usually helps to provide a range for your sales and earnings guidance, and to keep the midpoint of that guidance conservative.

If you do not provide any financial guidance, investors and analysts may find that to be a difficult situation for them because they could be left in the dark. There is a relatively high turnover rate in the analyst community, so most analysts cannot figure out a good financial model from just the tone of the business guidance. In addition, the seasonality of businesses varies, and there are further effects of new products, competition, pricing, and the economic environment. If you do not provide any financial guidance, the price-to-earnings multiple (PE ratio) for your stock is likely to take a hit compared to your competitors.

There are perils in providing financial guidance, too. If you miss your financial guidance, you get beaten up by Wall Street. You, your management team, and your board also assume some legal liabilities in providing the guidance. There are ways to avoid such liabilities: (1) by staying conservative in the guidance; and (2) by providing a safe-harbor statement that says the guidance and forward-looking statements involve some risks and uncertainties, and the investors and analysts should review all the risk factors associated with the company; (3) you should state all of the risk factors associated with your company in your earnings release, as well as your various filings with the Securities and Exchange Commission.

In the final analysis, I come down on the side of providing financial guidance and have always done so with our company.

Chapter12: Resources to finance and grow your business

I received several questions from entrepreneurs looking for resources to finance and grow their businesses.

Take the investment from a customer or VC

Question: I started my company with my own money and some funding from angel investors. Now, I need $3M in equity financing for the next phase of growth. I have interest from one of my customers and a professional venture capital firm (VC). My investment banker has a conflict of interest because of commission from the VC deal. Which option is best?

-James, Arizona

Answer: First, I want to congratulate you for starting a company that has now grown to attract interest from your customers as well as a VC.

When customers invest in a company, their interest is not just getting a return on their investment through capital appreciation. Customers are usually interested in shoring up a weak supplier, first right of refusal to acquire, technology license, preferred pricing, ability to influence the product, technology roadmap, etc. Not all these factors are present in every deal, but some are. Therefore, customers often place higher valuations on the company. The company also benefits from stronger commitment and strategic alignment with its customers, as well as benefiting from the endorsement of its technology and intellectual property.

Professional VCs, on the other hand, only invest to get the highest return on their investment. Therefore, VCs are a lot tougher and stingier on the company valuation. However, VCs can bring business and customer contacts and can also bring management talent to the often-shallow management bench of a start-up company. VCs also tend to exert significant, and often excessive, control and influence on the company, which is something that you may not be prepared to accept. When opinions differ, you are no longer the sole decision maker—which could lead to significant conflict.

For its long-term success, a company will need its customers, VCs, and investment bankers. The best option is to get everyone in on the deal, even if you have to increase the total funding amount. If that is not possible and you cannot split a small deal, then I would say that if you can get the equity funding from your customer without giving away too much of your intellectual property, that is the preferred route. A CEO is always raising money to grow the company. Eventually, you will have to bring in VCs. Meanwhile, enjoy your independence without VCs breathing down your neck.

Tax incentives in Arizona

Question: I am considering investing in an Arizona technology company. Are there any Arizona income-tax credits for investors in Arizona technology companies? If so, how do they work?

-Bob, Phoenix

Answer: Yes, it is called the Arizona Small Business Capital Investment Incentive Program (also called the Angel Investment Program). Led by the Arizona Governor's Council for Innovation and Technology, it was passed by the Arizona legislature and went into effect on July 1, 2006, and recently extended until June 30, 2031. The main purpose of the program is to encourage capital investments in small, early-stage Arizona businesses. The program accomplishes its goal by providing state tax credits to investors who make qualified capital investments in small businesses certified by the Arizona Department of Commerce (DOC).

For a complete review of the "Angel Investment Program" and various other incentives, please visit www.AZcommerce.com.

Small private school suffering from bad economy

Question: We are a small private school that goes from kindergarten to eighth grade. Our school is suffering, like many small businesses. Our principal had to cut back, and unfortunately, laid off some teachers. Our enrollment is low, and we are barely surviving. Can you suggest how to improve this situation?

We would also like to seek your help. The tax credit would be a great way to help. Is there a corporate tax credit allotment?

-Prabha Nair, Mesa

Answer: I am sorry to hear that your school is suffering. You are correct that a private school is like any other small business and is not immune from the effects of the economy. Here are some ideas.

As you mentioned, there is the "Private School Tuition tax credit." Arizona tax code allows an individual to donate $731 ($1459 for a married couple) and receive dollar-for-dollar credit on the Arizona tax return. This does not cost an individual anything and helps our schools.

You should make the same pitch to all the parents and grandparents of your students and ex-students. Many parents do not make tax credit donations after their children graduate from high school. Reach out to them one-on-one and make the appeal.

There is no such thing as a corporate tax credit for charitable donations. But certain corporations will match any donation made by their employees. Seek out these corporations and find a way to solicit donations from their employees, who may be parents, relatives, or friends of your students.

In such difficult times, just like any business, it is important for your school to differentiate your product from that of any other similar school. All private schools provide the basic education to prepare students. Private schools are expensive for a family. In times of economic crisis, parents are more willing to send their children to public schools. You need to make your product even more appealing than ever before.

One idea is to provide babysitting for the younger siblings of your students. This will allow certain families to have both parents go to work. Additionally, providing babysitting for students and their siblings beyond the normal school hours would allow both parents to have full-time jobs.

Another idea is to bundle your products for better pricing. For example, you could provide a rebate if a family were to enroll a child and pay the tuition for the entire year. This would simply be pulling some revenue ahead and is no different than a business providing a discounted price on higher volume. This will help your current cash flow. Hopefully, the economy will improve, and you may have higher enrollment then.

To go public or not

Question: I was visiting Phoenix and enjoyed your column. I am the Chief Financial Officer of a fast-growing company in Austin. Venture capitalists (VCs) own 30% of my company, with the balance owned by the management team. Given the difficult requirements of Sarbanes-Oxley legislation, we are debating whether to take the company public. If you had to do it again, would you take Microchip Technology public?

-Major Horton, Austin, Texas

Answer: Whether to take a company public or keep it private is a very complex matter and depends on several factors. The first and foremost is whether the company has enough access to capital for growth. Most businesses do not generate enough cash from operations to fund growth. Access to bank loans can be limited unless you have enough collateral. So, getting access to public capital becomes the primary reason to take a company public. Such was the case with Microchip Technology in 1993.

The second reason to take the company public is to create liquidity, also commonly known as an "Exit Strategy". VCs eventually need liquidity to pay their investors. This is accomplished either by taking a company public or selling it. Management loses complete control of selling the company, so going public is often the preferred route.

The third reason is for the owners to gain liquidity for themselves. Owners have usually worked very hard up to the pre-IPO point, often having mortgaged their houses and invested their savings in the company. They deserve some fruits for their labor and sacrifice by cashing in a portion of their stock ownership. Here again, a public offering becomes the preferred route.

The fourth reason is employee morale and retention. Public companies can offer stock options and restricted stock units to employees. This can increase the employees' commitment to the company, boost their long-term compensation, and create employee retention.

There are also negatives to going public, because the profitability and strategy of the company becomes known to competitors and customers. On the other hand, public companies are better known, thus gaining some free advertising and attracting more customers.

So, despite the complexity, the requirements of Sarbanes-Oxley legislation and some loss of management control in taking the company public, most fast-growing companies with VC funding have no option but to go public. If I had to do it all over again, I would take Microchip public.

Why do public companies go private?

Question: I understand why private companies would go public, but sometimes a public firm will go private again. What is the advantage of this?

-Andy Barrett, Peoria, AZ

Answer: In the previous question, I discussed why a company would go public. The first and foremost reason is to get access to capital for growth. Most businesses do not generate enough cash from operations to fund growth. Likewise, access to bank loans can be limited, unless you have enough collateral. So, getting access to public capital becomes the primary reason to take a company public. I listed a few smaller reasons in the answer above.

Now, why do some public companies go private? First, very few companies do so. A small number that goes private do it because the reasons why they went public are no longer valid. The VCs and many of the original founders and owners are usually long gone. The company may have become profitable to the point where it is generating sufficient cash to fund its operations and its growth. So, the need for additional capital is no longer there. And, regarding employee morale and retention, being public may now be hurting rather than helping. The stock options could bc at a price where employees do not make enough money from the growth of the stock. As a result, they may be more attracted to go to smaller start-up companies and get low-price, start-up stock options.

In addition, some of the negatives of going public may be at play. For example, the company may want to do a substantial strategy shift, which it does not want to tell the world—including its competitors and customers. It is easier to perform surgery on a private company and away from the public eyes of investors, analysts, the Securities and Exchange Commission, etc. And there are great savings in avoiding significant public-company costs.

So, the bottom line is that when none of the benefits of being public are valid and some of the negatives are in play, then the company may consider going private again. To accomplish this, all the public stockholders need to be paid, often at premiums. This will, in almost all cases, require significant outside capital. This capital either comes from VCs who want to buy distressed assets, fix them, and then take them public again; or it comes from significant bank loans.

Networking to grow your business

Question: I am a life-insurance salesperson and started this profession just a few years ago with a very reputable and large life insurance firm. A life-insurance practice is built by references and networking. Where should I go to meet successful executives?

-Laurence

Answer: You are correct that you will require networking and references to build a life-insurance practice. There are several networking organizations that you should join. My favorite one is the "Association for Corporate Growth" (www.acg.org/arizona). Their primary product is a monthly gathering where a prominent local business executive presents the story of their company. The audience consists of business executives, entrepreneurs, and service providers like you. There is an hour of networking followed by dinner and a presentation.

Just enter “Arizona Association” into Google. You will get a large list of associations in all kinds of fields—realty, medical, software, mechanical engineering, etc. Make your selections based on how you relate to the membership.

Once you have decided which groups to target, you need to find a way to distinguish yourself. One way is to sponsor some part of the event—the cocktail hour, dinner, or venue rental. Then, as a sponsor, you will be given the opportunity to introduce yourself and say a few words about your service.

You are probably aware that people often have a negative initial reaction to a salesperson. Rather than pitching everyone right away, try to develop a softer approach where you meet people and collect some business cards. Refrain from selling life insurance until you have known the person for some time and you understand their needs and family situation.

Recommended business books

Question: Over the holidays, I read several of the books that you listed in your prior “Tips for Improving Your Staff's Customer Service”. I am a general manager of a medium-size business. I have read plenty of good books that talk about successful companies. Do you know of any books that discuss unsuccessful companies? It would be good to learn what mistakes not to make.

-Brent, Scottsdale

Answer: That is a great and thoughtful question. I read two excellent books on this subject last year. The first was “How the Mighty Fall” by Jim Collins, who is the author of two other great books: “Built to Last” and “Good to Great.” “How the Mighty Fall” addresses two related questions: Why do good companies fail, and how does management respond once a company gets into trouble? Collins introduces a five-stage model to answer these questions, where steps one and two address the roots of corporate failure and steps three through five outline management's response.

The second book, which I read over the holidays, was "Will Your Next Mistake be Fatal: Avoiding the Chain of Mistakes That Can Destroy Your Organization" by Robert Mittelstaedt. The book includes thirty-eight insights that summarize the main teachings and help the reader focus on making the necessary changes for success. These insights are easy to remember and should quickly bring you back to a proper attitude for running a successful and thriving organization. Once you start to implement a systematic approach to managing multiple mistakes, you will not guarantee that your company will never make an error or misstep again, but you will be assured of not letting things get totally out of control.

Since you are reading a lot of business books, I should give you one caution from experience. I read a few books every year, too, but find that I am only able to implement ideas from one book at a time; and it takes three years or so to make a difference in an organization. Reading for fun is fine, but real value is added by implementing, not just reading. Implementation requires all the senior executives in an organization to read the same book, create a discussion, develop training material for the organization, and diligently monitor the implementation for effective results.

After implementing "Good to Great" for several years, we added "Performance Without Compromise" by Charles Knight. It was a great book to implement. If I were to select new books for you, "How the Mighty Fall" and "Will Your Next Mistake be Fatal?" are good candidates.

The tradeoffs of start-up employment

Question: I recently joined a three-year-old start-up company. I like my job, the opportunities, and the challenges. But I am having real trouble with the look and décor of our company's facilities. The company is in an old building where the walls are not painted well, the carpet is worn out, the furniture is really old and everything else about the company just looks cheap. I worked for a large firm before with excellent facilities, and I felt proud to go in and work. Is my current company being too cheap and not making the correct impression?

-Brandon, Phoenix

Answer: First, I would say, "Welcome to the wonderful world of startups." You could have been talking about our company, Microchip Technology, in the early 1990s.

Most start-up companies are formed by bootstrapping capital from various sources. Many times, it is from the personal savings of the founders. Other times, it is from borrowed capital, such as credit cards and mortgaged houses. It could also be risk capital from angel investors or venture-capital investors. In all these cases, risk capital is very scarce.

Therefore, start-up companies focus on deploying capital towards their business plans, such as product development, manufacturing infrastructure, market development, sales, and distribution. Wise start-up companies do not spend their precious capital on the look and feel and décor of their premises.

When you interviewed with your company, you were able to glance at the buildings and the work environment. You took the job because you liked the challenge and the opportunities this company provided. The company has not changed—your priorities have changed. Therefore, I would suggest two things…

First, you should review your own priorities regarding the challenges and opportunities provided by your company, versus the look and feel of a larger company's décor. Your company may be in this mode for a while, and you should not be distracted from its mission. So, you should accept the working environment until the company has either gone public or has otherwise become successful.

The second thing that you can do is to get together with some of your coworkers and offer to paint the building and clean up the facility during weekends or holidays. This makes you look like a "can do" self-starter, rather than a complainer. However, after the building has been painted, do not be surprised to hear a rumor in your company that sounds something like, "They painted the building and the lobby. They are probably going to sell the company." I have been there, too.

Chapter 13: 401K savings plan, IRAs, and pensions

I received many questions on 401k savings plan, IRAs, and pensions that I will cover in this chapter.

401(k) savings plans

Question: My wife and I are both twenty-nine and make about $70K per year, jointly. Neither of us has signed up for our respective companies' 401(k) plans because we have been dealing with a lot of expenses setting up our household and paying student and other loans. We now want to start saving in our 401(k) plans. Are there some very simple rules of thumb?

-Rob and Kathie, Phoenix

Answer: Financial advice usually has some personal bias involved. That is why you should get financial advice from your own financial advisor, whom you can trust over time. Every time I offer personal-finance advice, readers from the financial-advisor profession take issue with it and I get rebuttals. Having said that, the following are my simple rules of thumb…

Most companies have some sort of 401(k) match, which is like free money. These companies typically offer matching funds up to a certain percentage of each employee's contributions. For example, if you withhold 7% of your income in the 401(k) plan, your company's policy could be to match the first 4% of your contributions with fifty cents to every dollar. In that case, you should first make the contribution of 4% to take advantage of the maximum free match. Find out your company's match and invest up to that amount. If your company offers a Roth 401(k), invest in that because your earnings will grow tax free.

Next, you should investigate your broader financial picture. Do you have credit-card loans with high interest rates of 18% or above? Do you own a home or are you saving for a home? Is your car paid off? I would pay off some of the high interest credit-card loans and get to the point where you do not carry any credit-card balances. You should always pay off your entire monthly credit-card bill, if possible. Use the credit card only for convenience, consolidating bills, and earning airline miles, not to accumulate high-interest loans.

If you have any discretionary income left, you have two options. The first is to increase contributions to your Roth 401(k) plan, up to the limit, even if you do not get company match on the additional amount. The second option is to save in a Roth Individual Retirement Account (Roth IRA). I recommend the Roth IRA because you have much broader investment options than with the company's 401(k) plan. However, if you do not have much investment experience, then you may want to opt for the additional 401(k) contributions, where the core mutual-fund choices are managed by your company's 401(k) administrative committee. They have a fiduciary responsibility, and in most cases will do a reasonable job of providing good investment options.

Are my 401K funds safe?

Question: I work for a mid-size public company. The company is going through financial difficulties, and I am concerned about the safety of my 401(k). Taking money out will cause a 10% penalty. Please help.

-Stacy, Mesa

Answer: In general, your 401(k) will be safe from your company's financial difficulties, but there are exceptions. Government regulations require that 401(k) money be kept separate from the company's treasury. Your company cannot borrow money from the 401(k), nor can it raid the 401(k) in case of financial need. Then why did employees of Enron lose their 401(k) money? The reason is that their 401(k) assets were invested in Enron stock, which plummeted with its bankruptcy filing. It is a bad idea to put your job and your family's life savings all at risk with your company. It does not matter how good your company is, your 401(k) should not be invested in your company's stock. In certain cases, when companies provide a matching contribution, they do so with the company's stock to save cash. If this happens, sell your company's stock from your 401(k) plan.

Your 401(k) should be invested in well-respected mutual funds and diversified across asset classes—large cap and small cap funds; growth and value funds; bond funds; and international funds. The ideal asset mix depends on your years to retirement and your other, non-commodity assets—an independent financial advisor can help you achieve the best portfolio. Your company's 401(k) committee should provide several good fund choices across asset classes.

It is also important to know who manages your 401(k) funds. If your 401(k) is managed by a reputable firm like Fidelity, Vanguard, or Merrill Lynch, you have nothing to worry about. However, if your 401(k) is managed by a small firm run by your CFO's brother-in-law, then you have a lot more to worry about than the 10% early withdrawal penalty.

Is my pension safe?

Question: I found your Sunday column on 401(k)s to be very informative regarding the requirement for companies to leave that money untouched even if they have financial need. Is there any similar requirement for companies to leave the money that is set aside for retirees' pension plans to also remain untouched, even if they have financial need?

-Bob & Jenny, Prescott

Answer: Just like a 401(k)'s, assets that are held in a defined benefit plan (commonly referred to as "pension") are held in trusts that are legally separate from the Company's assets. The company is prohibited from withdrawing funds already contributed to the plan's trust, even in times of need.

If the company goes into bankruptcy, the participant's benefit in a pension plan would be unaffected -- their vested account balance would remain their benefit. However, the participant's benefit in an under-funded pension plan would likely be affected if the company became insolvent and terminated the plan.

The assets of a pension plan are not allocated to individual participants, as in a 401(k) plan. Instead, assets of a terminated pension plan are distributed based on the priority of benefits (retirees receiving benefits, vested, and active participants). Depending on the extent of the under-funded status and whether the plan is turned over to the Pension Benefit Guaranty Corporation (PBGC), benefits are likely to be significantly reduced. If the PBGC has control of the plan, there will also be limits on the maximum benefits allowed to be paid to each participant.

Participants in a pension plan always have the risk that the plan sponsor may either freeze their benefit at any time or terminate the plan, even if it is over-funded. A frozen benefit and a terminated benefit will be lower than what the participant would have received, had the plan continued. If the plan is overfunded and terminated, any excess plan assets may be distributed back to the company or to another qualified benefit plan sponsored by the company.

I know that all of this sounds very complicated. I like a plan where I can check what I have anytime on the internet and make the decision where it is invested. That is why I like my retirement funds in a 401(k) or an Individual Retirement Plan (IRA).

Rebuttal from readers on 401K plan and pensions

The April 15 column regarding pensions got a huge response from the readers…

Question: You should not endorse a 401(k) or IRA instead of a pension. While your 401(k) may have great matching money and a good list of investment options, others would see things differently. Most 401(k) participants are not financially qualified and are unlikely to have either an IRA or the services of a financial professional. Consequently, many fail to realize the financial gains possible through prudent and qualified investing. Defined pension plans are not the end-all, but those people who are not offered a 401(k) are now receiving defined pension benefits.

-Omer, Goodyear

Question: I enjoyed your article on 401(k) vs. company pensions. While I receive a small company pension, it would be nice to know it will continue. We can request copies of the information on "the plan," but they are difficult to understand. What do we look for to determine if a pension fund is underfunded?

-Pat

Question: I am a student of defined-benefit plans and a retired enrolled actuary under ERISA. The major problem in large defined-benefit plans is the potential and actual manipulation of assumptions. This results from management's pressure on actuaries to legally bend the assumptions and permit very small, if any, contributions during the good years.

Assumptions, such as employee turnover, actuarial longevity studies, and assumed interest rate can be manipulated in any given year. If you change them to lower or omit contributions in good years, you can be woefully short sighted with requirements in later years.

-Robert

Answer: I thank all my readers for their views.

Robert has really answered the questions of Omer and Pat. Pension plans are very complicated and are subject to a great deal of meddling by management. That is why you occasionally hear that a company is $1 billion dollars short of its pension obligations.

We live in a brutally competitive global market. Companies have no guarantee of being around for 50 years anymore. Factors like longevity, interest rates, and inflation are unpredictable, and can change over 50 years. I believe that pensions give employees a false sense of security. Many find this out in their later years when pension plans go awry and it is too late to do much about it.

I like employees taking personal responsibility for their retirement and systematically saving for their future. Companies should take the money that they would reserve in a pension plan and instead distribute it to the employees as matching funds in their 401(k)s. This way, employees have control, and they know exactly what they have.

However, I should add that I believe employees should never invest their 401(k)s in their company's stock—a cardinal sin. Besides, what would have happened to Enron's pension plan?

Regarding employees being financially illiterate, Microchip spends a great deal of time educating our employees to save through a 401(k), including its investment choices and the availability of a very low-cost financial advisor. Employees should educate themselves and take control of their retirement.

401K upon job change

Question: I know that you are a fan of 401 (k) plans. I just changed jobs and want to know what to do with my 401(k) with the old employer. I am getting conflicting advice from others.

-Matt, Scottsdale

Question: I have recently switched jobs. My new employer is a very small startup company and has not set up a 401(k) plan yet. My old employer has sent me a check for my entire balance. Can I cash that check?

-Stephanie, Peoria

Answer: Although this column was set up to give business advice, I have selectively answered a few financial advice questions. The response from the readers has been good. They see my advice as independent and without any conflict of interest. So, I will occasionally answer financial advice questions wherever I see my expertise as applicable. First, I am in no competition with hundreds of very qualified financial advisors. Second, please consult your own financial advisor before you take any action.

Yes, I am a fan of 401(k) plans. I see 401(k) plans along with Individual Retirement Accounts (IRAs) as the only viable vehicle for millions of Americans to save for their retirement while deferring taxes. So, what should you do with your 401(k) when you change jobs?

You have two options. The easiest one is to roll the funds into the 401(k) at your new employer. Your new employer should have a form that you can fill out where this transfer can happen without money coming into your hands. Most employees changing jobs use this option and that is what Matt from Scottsdale should do.

It is quite likely that the choices of investments in 401(k) are different at the two employers. Therefore, the funds will be transferred to your new 401(k) in cash. You will have to invest those funds by making choices amongst the funds provided in your new 401(k) plan.

A second option is to roll the 401(k) funds into a "Rollover IRA." Any of the major investment management firms like Fidelity, Vanguard, Charles Schwab, E-Trade, and others can help you set up a "Rollover IRA". In a Rollover IRA, you have broader investment choices because you are not limited to the choices given in your new employer's 401(k) plan.

Since Stephanie's employer does not offer a 401(k) plan; "Rollover IRA" is her only choice. She has 60 days from the time she received funds from her old employer to roll those funds into a Rollover IRA without incurring regular taxes on those funds and a 10% early withdrawal penalty.

IRA money protected from creditors

Question: I am 66 years old and retired. I recently caused a three-car accident. The liability limit that I carried on my insurance was $15K for each person and $30K for each accident. It is reasonably clear that the liabilities from the accident will exceed the limits of my insurance coverage. My biggest concern is my Individual Retirement Account, which I have worked on all my life to save and grow. A friend tells me that IRAs are protected from creditors. Is this true?

-Gregory, Mesa

Answer: First, I am sorry to hear about your accident. In this day and age, liability coverage of only $15K/$30K is not sufficient. If you have any assets to protect, every driver should carry higher liability limits, such as $100K/$300K. It would be very sad to see a young person saddled with a huge liability judgment and then have to work for years to pay it off. Similarly, it would be very sad to see a retired person get a huge judgment and then lose his life savings.

It is always advisable to carry higher liability limits. In addition, it is prudent to get an umbrella policy with liability limits of $1M or even $5M. Umbrella insurance covers the liability on your cars and your home, over and above the limits of your policies on those items. If you kill someone in an accident, in your home or in your car, then $15K/30K liability limits will be nothing. Umbrella policies are also less expensive than the higher limits would be on individual policies.

In your case, your friend is right. Your IRA account is protected from creditors for up to $1,512,350 due to the Banking Abuse Prevention Act. But you must file for bankruptcy to seek this creditor protection. Congress, in enacting this legislation, was trying to prevent someone—who lived by the rules, saved his entire life, and built up a nest-egg in IRAs—from losing it all due to one negligent act. The same credit protection is available to funds in other qualified plans, including 401(k), 403(b), Roth IRA, SEP IRA, etc.

A couple of things you need to know. First, if you have a $2M IRA and a judgment of $100K, the creditors will get their money because the protection only covers up to $1,512,350. Second, federal creditor protection of IRA assets only applies to the owner of the IRA—not the beneficiary. So, if your IRA was inherited, you are out of luck.

The same protection is not available to you on the funds that you hold outside of your qualified retirement plans. So, on the IRA funds, consider yourself lucky; but please do follow up on increasing the liability limits of your policy and potentially getting an umbrella policy. And, as always, please use my advice only as a starting point. Do consult an attorney, as the laws are complicated and keep changing.

Chapter 14: Investing your money

Giving investment advice was not the original purpose of the Ask Steve column. However, I received too many questions on investments to ignore them. In many cases, readers just wanted a second opinion from a successful CEO. Reluctantly, I answered some of those questions. My caveat is that I am not a certified financial professional. Readers should consult their own investment advisor before they act on any of my advice.

How should a busy executive invest?

Question: I am a senior executive in Phoenix and busy traveling like you. I would like to ask you a personal question. How do you manage your money? Do you use a financial advisor, or do you do it yourself? If you do it yourself, how do you invest?

-Dan, Scottsdale

Answer: While this is a personal question, fellow executives often ask about my investment strategy—so I believe that it is worth answering. However, I will answer it in general terms. I have managed my money myself for the last 40 years. I have taught myself over the years, sometimes through making mistakes.

My experience with financial advisors who manage money in discretionary accounts has been largely negative. In side-by-side investing, I have achieved superior results in several tests over the years. That may incite hundreds of excellent financial advisors to want to contact me for a rematch. Please don't.

I used a simple approach for most of the last 40 years. After keeping some money for short-term obligations and an emergency fund, I take the rest of the money and divide it among four portfolios of mutual funds. My first portfolio is an Aggressive-Growth portfolio, comprising 75% growth funds, 15% international (emerging markets & Europe), and 10% sector funds (energy and industrial materials).

My second portfolio is a Growth portfolio, with 20% growth funds (large & small cap), 45% value funds (large & small cap), 10% international funds, and 25% high-yield bond funds. My third portfolio is a Growth and Income portfolio, comprising 15% growth funds (large & small cap), 35% balanced funds, 45% bond funds (TIPS & high yield) and 5% international. My fourth portfolio consists entirely of index funds and enhanced index funds.

I am currently out of real estate. For a busy executive, you would have to be insane to own a rental. A real-estate investment trust may be a better option, but not right now.

I could probably achieve all my objectives through a single portfolio, but I like to separate them based on how far into the future I am able to access the funds. I may access Growth & Income portfolio funds in five years and Growth portfolio funds in over 10 years. The other two portfolios are inaccessible for much longer terms. I do not trade often, except to occasionally rebalance or reposition portfolios to address major turns in the economy and stages of my life. I ignore trend following, moving averages, candlestick charts, option hedging, and other trading tools since I do not have time for them.

One more twist—I have found that it is better to keep income-producing funds in tax-deferred accounts (401k/IRA) and growth funds in taxable investment accounts to get lower taxes on capital gains.

Your personal situation, available funds, risk tolerance, and investment objectives may be entirely different. Please check with your financial advisor before you follow any of my strategies.

Home ownership accelerator

Question: Like many homeowners who bought with adjustable-rate mortgages, I am now stuck with a mortgage that is going up in interest rate. At the same time, my paycheck is going in my bank account and earning a pathetic 1 to 2% interest while I spend the money through the month. Is there a way I can get a higher interest rate on my short-term cash?

-Tom, Phoenix

Answer: This column is about business advice, not financial advice. However, your question is quite compelling and is one being asked by millions of homeowners today. Therefore, I am choosing to answer it.

There are a couple of ways to make your money go farther while it is sitting in your checking account for monthly expenses. The simplest way is to have it in a Money Markct Account rather than a bank checking account. Money Market Rates today are around 5%. However, there is a minimum deposit amount needed which is usually $2500. Be aware that it may not completely replace the convenience of a checking account.

The other way I have found is through a new revolutionary loan program called the "Home Ownership Accelerator." With your current mortgage, much of your earnings are flowing through a low interest checking account, while you spread your expenses through the month.

With the Home Ownership Accelerator, you deposit your entire paycheck into this innovative loan instead of your checking account, dramatically reducing the principal balance. Since interest is compounded on your daily balance, you start saving interest immediately.

You pay all your expenses in the month out of the Accelerator. Until you need the money, it stays in your account, keeping your loan balance lower and saving 6 to 7% in interest costs, versus earning 1 to 2% in your checking account.

Paying less interest means that more of your money can go towards principal reduction. If you are a borrower with good cash flow, you could pay off your loan in half the time – with no change in spending habits.

For your everyday expenses, you have checks, ATM/Visa card and electronic bill pay, just like your checking account.

Please consult with your financial advisor before you take any action.

Should I cancel my HELOC?

Question: I read your column and find it very enlightening. Congratulations on your recent anniversary of the column. I know you claim not to be a financial advisor, but I was hoping you could answer a question for us.

Last year, we took out a Home Equity Line of Credit (HELOC) for $200K in the event we would need it as a bridge loan between finding a house and selling a house. Since then, we decided to sell first and not risk carrying two mortgages. We no longer need or want this loan, which we have not touched. I just received an annual maintenance fee of $35 which is prompting me to decide. I want to call the lender to cancel the HELOC, but I am told that it will harm our credit rating/FICO score which is quite high.

I do not like having this over our heads. Knowing we will not use it; can we cancel it without any harm?

-Anne Marie

Answer: Thanks for your comments on my column.

You seem to be quite astute about making financial decisions. Getting a home equity line of credit to bridge between buying and selling a house was smart. Then as the market deteriorated, you concluded that you did not want to risk having two mortgages and decided to sell the house first. That was an even smarter idea. You seem to be able to reason well under these scenarios and make intelligent decisions.

Now you have another decision to make. I am not sure whether canceling the HELOC will lower your FICO score. That question should probably be put to a financial advisor. But for a mere $35 annual maintenance fee, you should not cancel the $200K HELOC. There is no place today where you can secure a $200K credit at HELOC interest rates for a mere $35. And your HELOC interest rate will be much lower than credit card interest rates.

You have not touched the HELOC, and you are astute enough to not touch the HELOC for impulsive purchases. So, why do you feel that it is like having something over your head? You owe no money for it, so it is not a liability. Instead, think of it as a security blanket. You have access to $200K of emergency cash with a low interest loan for a mere $35 per year. That's quite a bargain.

Investing my 403B

Question: I will be retiring soon. I have saved $150,000 in a 403b at work. What is the best place to put this money? Should I place it in a variable annuity now, before I retire, and where should I keep it when I retire?

-Fred

Answer: For readers who may not know, a 403b plan is a retirement plan for university, civil government, and not-for-profit employees. It has the same characteristics and benefits of the 401k plans that I have written so much about.

First, please know that I am not a certified financial planner. You should see a certified financial planner or your own financial advisor before you act on any of my advice.

One thing that is certain is that you should not have all of your retirement money in one place, whether it is a variable annuity or the stock market. Also, I do not know what other retirement assets you have besides the $150,000 in your 403b. It is quite difficult to give an answer without knowing your complete financial picture, including your age, marital status, social-security benefits, health, investing experience, risk tolerance, and the amount of income you will need during retirement. Consideration also needs to be given to any inheritance you may get from your parents and any inheritance you may want to leave your children. That is why it is best to see a certified financial planner who will ask all those questions and draw a complete financial profile.

It would help you to gain some knowledge on this subject even before you see a financial planner. One of my favorite books is "Buckets of Money" by Raymond Lucia. Lucia divides money into three buckets and invests each one based on short-term needs (next seven years), medium-term needs (eight to 14 years) and longer-term needs (more than 14 years). Additionally, Lucia published another book entitled “Ready...Set...Retire!: Financial Strategies for the Rest of Your Life” Knowing the author, this book ought to be very good.

Lucia has a network of financial advisors in every major market and has people that follow his method in Phoenix. Please contact one of them for your financial plan.

I have no affiliation with Lucia—I used to listen to his radio show, and I like his books. However, there are many other qualified certified financial planners. You should interview a few and select one based on your own comfort level.

Re-investing dividend in company stock

Question: I would like to set up a plan that automatically reinvests my dividends from my company stock in additional stock. I tried to set this up with my online account, but a message popped up indicating that this account is not eligible. I was wondering why my company does not allow us to reinvest our dividends back into company stock.

-Robert, Chandler

Answer: What you are talking about is called a Dividend Re-investment Program, also known in the industry as DRIP. Many companies have set up DRIPs so that, if someone chooses to reinvest their dividend back into the company stock, they can sign up for the DRIP. In this program, the company issues new shares to the DRIP participants instead of paying their dividends in cash.

Many companies have chosen not to set up a DRIP. The reason is often quite simple. Those companies do not want more cash by selling stock. They are paying dividends to the shareholders to get the cash out. If they were paying dividends in the form of more shares, they would be forced to keep their cash, which they do not want to do.

Why don’t companies want to keep cash? Companies usually earn only about 1% interest on cash. But the companies may earn a

15% return on our non-cash business assets. Therefore, cash is very dilutive to a company's overall return on assets (ROA), which is an important financial metric. By reducing the amount of cash, the companies can increase the overall ROA.

So, why don't we pay more to the employees if cash is such a large problem on the balance sheet? Dividends are not an expense on a company's Profit and Loss statement (P&L). The cash on the balance sheet belongs to the shareholders. If you own your company's stock, then you also own a prorated portion of its total cash.

Review any company's P&L statement. You would not find a line item for the dividend paid as an expense. That is because dividends are not an expense. They are simply a return of shareholders' capital back to them. Most of the good companies are paying dividends (e.g., Intel, Motorola, GE, IBM, Microchip, etc.). At Microchip, we also pay bonuses to our employees, which *is* a business expense.

Now, let us get back to DRIPs. Many companies do not want to set up a DRIP because it increases the cash and increases the share count. They want to do the opposite—decrease the cash by buying back their stock and decreasing the share count.

What can you as an employee do to re-invest your dividend proceeds into your company's stock? You can purchase stock in your account for the amount of the dividend. This may not be done automatically. You may have to place an order at every dividend distribution date. Just make sure that the trading window is open, and you are not in possession of any material, non-public information about the company.

Are high interest rates good or bad for bonds?

Question: I heard an expert on TV saying that rising interest rates would be bad for bonds. But I have heard other experts in the past say that bonds are good investments when interest rates are high. How can both situations be correct?

-Kimberly L., Scottsdale

Answer: I know how confusing this can be, but both situations are correct. Bonds are bad investments in a rising-interest-rate environment. But bonds are good investments when interest rates are already high. To understand this, let us first look at what bonds are and how they work.

A bond is a debt security, in which the issuer owes the holders a debt and, depending on the terms of the bond, is obliged to pay interest (the coupon), and to repay the principal at a later time, known as the maturity date. In other words, a bond is a formal contract to repay borrowed money, with interest, at fixed intervals.

Let us say you just bought $10,000 in treasury bonds issued by the U.S. Department of the Treasury, which are maturing in 10 years and have a coupon of 3%. You would get a yearly interest of $300. If the interest rates were to rise 6%, then the market value of your bond would drop precipitously. At a 6% interest rate, someone could get the same interest by just investing $5,000. Therefore, if you wanted to sell your bond, the buyer would pay you much less because they would get only half the prevailing interest. Of course, if you held your bond to maturity, then it would be worth $10,000 again, irrespective of the prevailing interest rates. So, you can see that rising interest rates are bad for the bonds that you currently hold.

Now, assume that the interest rates rise to 6% and it is now considered a high-interest-rate environment. This would be a good environment to buy bonds. In our example, if you invested $10,000 in U.S Treasury bonds, maturing in 10 years, with a coupon of 6%, you would get $600 in interest per year. If the interest rates were to drop down to 3%, the market value of your bond would rise significantly. Someone would have to invest $20,000 to get the same $600, interest at the lower 3% interest rate. That is why a high-interest-rate environment is a good time to buy bonds.

The bottom line is that high interest rates are bad for the bonds that you bought in a low-interest environment. But high interest rates are good for buying new bonds.

Of course, the bond markets are much more complicated than that. The value of your bond could drop if there were a downgrade by a rating agency because of the deteriorating performance of the bond issuer. There are also zero-coupon bonds that are purchased at deep discounts to the face value, and they pay no interest; but the bond matures at face value. A comprehensive review of bonds is beyond the scope of this column.

As I have stated many times, I am not a financial advisor. Please consult a registered financial advisor for advice before you make any investment decisions.

Which is better—bonds or stocks?

Question: Once you have researched a public company in which to invest, is it better to buy its bonds or its stock?

-Monica, Phoenix

Answer: There is no simple rule regarding whether you should invest in a public company's bonds or stock. It depends on many factors. First, let us redefine what a bond is and what a stock is.

A bond is a formal contract to repay borrowed money, with interest, at fixed intervals. A stock, on the other hand, is an equity ownership stake in a company. A stockholder owns a piece of the company that is proportionate to the ratio of his stock shares vs. the total amount of stock outstanding.

There are simply too many factors surrounding the decision of whether to buy stocks or bonds to cover them all here. But the main factor is the risk/reward ratio. In general (and I emphasize in general), bonds may offer a lower risk while stocks may offer a higher reward.

If you buy a company bond at par (face value) and hold it to maturity, then your return is equal to the coupon (the interest rate). If you sell your bond early, then your return could vary based on the market value of the bond at the time of sale. The market value of a bond goes up and down for two main reasons—one is a change in the market interest rates and the second is the company's financial position (affecting its bond rating).

If you buy a company's stock, then your return largely depends on whether that stock goes up or down in the market during the time you hold the stock. Some stocks pay a dividend, and you should account for that in the overall return that you expect from the stock.

If the company is doing very well, then the return from its stock is likely going to be much higher than its bonds. The return of a bond is pretty much limited by its coupon if held to maturity (return varies if sold early). The return on a stock has no upper limit if it is a high-flying stock and continues to rocket up.

Conversely, the downside of bonds is more limited than their stock counterparts. In the balance sheet of a company, its bonds have a more senior position than its stock (equity). Usually, the stock goes to near zero before a bondholder loses money. If the company runs into trouble, it still has to pay its bondholders. The company may also raise money by substantially diluting its stock. In that case, the stock goes down, but the bondholders still get paid. One way the bondholder can lose money is if the company reorganizes in bankruptcy; but then the stock goes to near zero, too. Recall that during the financial crisis of 2009, Citigroup's stock price sank to $1/share (its current price is a reverse split of 10 to 1), but its bonds did not lose money if held to maturity. So, it is safer to invest in a company's bonds than it is to invest in its stock.

Once again, I remind my readers that I am not a registered financial advisor. A comprehensive review of stocks and bonds is beyond the scope of this column. Please contact your own investment advisor before you make any investments.

Financial solvency in Armageddon scenario

Question: I am very concerned about the money I have invested in stocks and stock mutual funds. I am recently retired and disabled. I cannot afford to lose all the assets I have built up. If our currency plummets and the banks close their doors, so we cannot get to safe deposit boxes etc., where do you suggest we put our money (and in what form) to have the best chance of solvency, both today and in the future, should the worst occur?

-Patricia Puryear

Answer: What we should be clear about is the difference between "safety of principal" and "liquidity." You have intertwined those two distinct elements regarding investments.

Safety of principal is exactly how it reads. Is your principal safe in the investments that you are making? You have invested in stocks and stock mutual funds. Well, there is no safety of principal in those investments. Your stocks can go to zero, just as many stocks have during every major financial crisis. That does not mean that I am advising you to sell all your stocks. But you need to understand the risks associated with your stock holdings. A balanced portfolio may weather the hard times better. Stock mutual funds are more diversified and are safer than individual stocks, but they still cannot provide "safety of principal".

Liquidity means that you can quickly convert your investments to cash, to use for your needs. Some investments, such as real estate, are the most illiquid. If you want to invest in real estate and stay liquid, then publicly traded REITs may be one way to go. Investments such as money-market mutual funds and bank savings are the most liquid because you can just write a check against them.

Now, let us combine these two concepts. Money-market accounts and bank savings are the safest as well as most liquid. Real estate is the most illiquid and the myth about the safety of real estate has been broken in recent years. Large and mid-cap stocks are liquid, but do not guarantee safety of principal. Small and micro-cap stocks can be both unsafe and illiquid. Bonds, precious metals, and various derivative instruments can be both unsafe and illiquid and are beyond the scope of the average individual investor.

You have described a scenario that I would call Armageddon, where the currency plummets, the banks close their doors, and we cannot get to safety deposit boxes. Recent stress tests on banks have shown that they have been shored up, meaning they are not likely to close their doors. So, I would not move your money from the bank to under your mattress. It is safer in the bank.

The currency-plummeting scenario is much more likely, with the national debt continuing to skyrocket. However, it is more likely to be a gradual weakening of the greenback, rather than a precipitous, one-day event. But it can always happen. There are two ways to hedge against plummeting currency. One is to invest in a basket of foreign currencies, and the second is to own gold. Both are fairly liquid, but neither provides safety of principle.

Finally, a good book I would suggest is "Buckets of Money: How to Retire in Comfort and Safety," by Ray Lucia.

Once again, I remind my readers that I am not a registered financial advisor. Please contact your own investment advisor before you make any investments or follow my advice. Everything I stated above is relative. Nothing is absolutely safe, and nothing is absolutely liquid.

Why are 2nd quarter taxes due on June 15?

Question: I am a 22-year-old single man. I am a contractor working for myself. I started my business last year in 2023, and had very little income to report on my Schedule C. My business is now doing well, and I expect to make a $70,000 profit this year.

I paid my first-quarter 2024 estimated taxes on April 15, and I expected to pay the 2nd quarter's estimated taxes on July 15. However, a friend told me that the 2nd quarter estimated taxes were due on June 15. How can this be due before the quarter is over? I am worried about paying late-payment penalties.

-Justin

Answer: I am not a tax accountant. But, having done my own taxes for 40 years, I can help. Your friend is right. The first quarter taxes are due on April 15, second quarter on June 15, third quarter on September 15 and the fourth quarter on January 15. For the second quarter, you must estimate your income through May 31st and pay the taxes on June 15. Then, on September 15, you pay the estimated taxes on your income through August 31st. I believe that Congress set it up this way so that 3rd quarter taxes can be collected by September 15, which is before the end of fiscal year for the federal government.

On a $70,000 Schedule C income, for a single filer with no dependents, no other income, a standard deduction and qualified business deduction, the federal taxes are $4,697. You also need to pay $9,891 in self-employment taxes. So, your total tax bill is $13,129. You are not required to pay any more than 90% of the quarterly taxes due. So, your first quarter's estimated taxes would have been $2,954 (13,129 x 90%/4). I will assume that you paid $2,954 on April 15, 2024.

One point that is often overlooked in paying estimated taxes. You may pay estimate taxes based on the lower of your last year's taxes or 90% of your current year's taxes. With very little income last year, your 2023 tax burden was probably small. Your 2024 estimate taxes do not need to be more than your total tax liability for 2023.

Before following my advice, you should consult your own tax advisor to verify all calculations.

Return on investment is a subjective indicator

Question: I work for a manufacturing company. From time to time, we make investments in machinery and tools. Some of the equipment gives us a new capability, while some equipment improves productivity, automation, or quality. There seems to be a constant argument between our Finance department and Manufacturing about how to calculate the return on investment for the equipment. What is an acceptable return on investment? How do you sort it out?

-Gerald

Answer: This argument has raged in every company at some point. It is the CEO's job to set the guidelines for making such decisions, since return on investment is a subjective indicator.

Let us begin with the equipment that is for improvements in productivity, automation, and quality. You must first look at the current total cost of the operation, including people, depreciation, materials and supplies, utilities, and operating expenses. You do need to add the cost of quality, which is very subjective. If the new equipment is going to improve quality and lower your customer returns, how do you value that? You must come up with a method that accounts for the cost of returns, reworks, customer complaint handling, and the loss of customer goodwill (again, very subjective). So, now you have the total cost of the operation as it exists with today's equipment.

Now you must model what your costs would be with the new equipment and installation. If it takes less people to operate, saves on materials and supplies, and consumes less power, you must put all of that into your model. Include the new depreciation (the old equipment may be fully depreciated) and the interest loss. Then, include the lower cost of quality (tough to do; do the best you can based on your model and assumptions). That gives you the total cost of operation with the new equipment installed.

To calculate your savings per quarter, take the difference between the total cost of operating with today's equipment and that of operating with the new equipment. Divide the cost of the new equipment plus any installation costs by the savings, to calculate how many quarters it will take to pay back the investment that you are making. If it is paid back in one to four quarters, it is a lot easier to make the investment. If it takes multiple years to pay back, the decision becomes more difficult. But at least you can now argue based on the data whether you want to make the equipment investment.

When the equipment gives you a new capability with which you can begin a new revenue stream, then you must look at the margin created in that new business unit and the time required to break even on that. Generally, management is more comfortable with a multi-year break even for a new capability or new business unit than they are with manufacturing gear that merely improves productivity.

Chapter 15: Estate planning

I received many questions on estate planning matters. Again, I am not a certified financial planner. I chose to answer some questions because the readers wanted my opinion. The readers should consult their own financial advisor before you act on any of the advice.

Will, living trust and living will

Question: I was at a neighborhood Christmas party and a neighbor suggested that I should have a "Living Will" for disposition of my assets, just in case. Another neighbor chimed in and said that I should instead have a "Living Trust". An argument ensued, and we all decided that we would Ask Steve. So, can you please give us your views on a "Living Will" versus a "Living Trust"?

-The Three Neighbors

Answer: It is very important to do some estate planning, but getting estate planning advice from your neighbor is not a good idea; unless he or she is an estate-planning lawyer, certified financial planner, or has other credentials. I am not one of these either, but I know a lot about the subject. However, please see your own advisor before you make any decisions.

You cannot dispose of your assets through a Living Will. There is nothing in common between a Living Will and a Living Trust. Your neighbors should have been arguing between a Will and a Living Trust. A Living Will is an entirely different instrument. So, I will explain a Will, a Living Trust, and a Living Will.

A Will is a document that describes your wishes regarding how your assets should be disposed of when you die. In the Will, you can also assign a guardian for your minor children if your spouse dies before you. The drawback in disposing of assets through a Will is that a Will goes through probate. Probate is a lengthy, expensive, and very public process.

A Living Trust (also called a Revocable Living Trust) also provides for the disposition of your assets in the case of death. Its additional benefit is that it avoids probate. Therefore, a Living Trust is a better instrument for the disposition of your assets. However, if you have minor children, you still need a Will for assigning a guardian.

Finally, let us take up the Living Will. A Living Will allows you to choose your Health Care options in case you have a terminal condition. It lets you make choices about life-sustaining treatment, irreversible coma, persistent vegetative state, cardiopulmonary resuscitation, artificial administration of food, etc. You can also assign an agent and give him or her healthcare power of attorney. A Living Will would have avoided the emotional drama of the well televised Terri Schiavo case from years ago, in which a bitter moral and legal tug of war raged among her husband, parents, the courts, and even members of Congress. So, you can see that a Living Will is a totally different instrument.

There is a lot more to all these documents than the space allows here. A comprehensive estate plan should have all three instruments in it. To get more education on the subject, do a web search on "Estate Planning" (there is more information available than you will have time to read).

Estate planning is an excellent new year's resolution.

The above column on Estate Planning brought a number of follow-on questions from the readers. I chose one to answer…

Life insurance irrevocable trust

Question: Several years before we retired, we were advised to open a Life Insurance Irrevocable Trust. Our finances are no longer what we thought they would be at this point, and it has become very costly to maintain. We would like to revisit our options. Can we rescind or amend an Irrevocable Trust? Will there be tax ramifications?

-Rosemary

Answer: I encourage readers to consult with a qualified estate-planning attorney for specific estate-planning advice. However, I can point you in the right direction.

An Irrevocable Life Insurance Trust, often referred to by its acronym, ILIT, holds a life-insurance policy on the life of the person who set it up. This life insurance will not be subject to estate tax if the person setting up the ILIT does not have any involvement in the ILIT—either as a trustee or beneficiary. However, the insured will generally make ongoing contributions to the ILIT to pay premiums on the life insurance.

It appears you set up an ILIT some years ago, perhaps so there would be funds available to pay estate taxes. The estate-tax exclusion has increased significantly and is now $13.61M per person for 2024. So, you and many others who purchased life insurance for this purpose may no longer need it. Or perhaps the life insurance is just too costly, and you no longer wish to pay for it.

To answer your direct question, an ILIT is irrevocable; meaning it typically cannot be amended or rescinded. However, you do have some options. One is to simply stop paying on the policy. The trustee can then decide what to do with the policy. Most policies will lapse after a period if you do not continue paying the premiums. Perhaps the policy could be surrendered for its cash value, and then have the proceeds distributed to the beneficiaries of the ILIT. Or the trustee might be able to borrow against the policy and distribute the proceeds.

Another option to consider is selling the policy to a third-party investor. This is sometimes known as a "viatical" settlement and is becoming more commonplace. However, there can be income taxes on the sale, and the trustee of the ILIT is also responsible for this decision.

As you can tell, these are some complicated issues to consider. In addition to an estate-planning attorney, you should also look for a qualified and objective insurance expert to advise you.

I want to thank John Vryhof, an estate-planning attorney from the law firm of Snell & Wilmer, for his help on this question.

Estate planning is complicated, so consult an experienced attorney

Question: I am the owner of a boutique retail store. I am 72 years old, single, with three children, all married, and eight grandchildren. My wife passed away a year ago. I am in bad health and may not have more than 5 more years. I operate the store, and my children are not involved in it. I am concerned about what will happen after I die. The store is valued at about $18M, but it does not have the liquidity to pay the estate taxes. My overall estate is worth $21M.

-Daniel, Scottsdale

Answer: For an estate valued at $21M, including your business, home, investments, and personal property, you should seek the counsel of an experienced estate-planning attorney. Meanwhile, I can get you started.

Estate-planning laws are undergoing substantial changes. In 2024, the estate-planning exemption is $13.61M, which is the amount subtracted from your estate. The estate pays 45% taxes on the balance. For a $21M estate, the estate taxes would be about $3.33M.

In the case of a private, illiquid business, there is usually not enough money to pay for the estate taxes. Therefore, such businesses have to be sold to pay the taxes and the remainder is distributed as indicated by the Will or Trust of the deceased.

The simplest scenario would be for you to sell the business now, gift out the exemption amount and put the remainder in liquid investments, which could then be distributed among your heirs as per your instructions in the Will or Trust. In the case of your death, the business value can decline precipitously, unless someone steps in to take care of the business. Therefore, it may be best to sell it now.

If you want to stay busy operating the business, I suggest that you put the business in a "Family Partnership". You would be the general partner and should make your children limited partners. Give them a share of the business that is equal to the $13.61M exemption next year. Because of the illiquid nature of your gifts in the Family Partnership, there are substantial discounts available. For example, you may be able to gift the business's entire $18M value toward the $13.61M exemption.

Between your three children, their spouses, and eight grandchildren, you can also gift $252K per year ($18K per person) tax free. Over the next few years of your life, you can gift away a substantial portion of your estate—tax free. These gifts can be a percentage of your ownership in the business, so no cash is required.

Please do a web search on "Estate Planning" and "Family Partnership" to learn more. Please do consult an experienced estate-planning attorney.

Which insurance do I need?

Question: Our company recently brought in an insurance expert to give a seminar about various insurance products. The expert spoke about such products as whole life insurance, credit protection, and long-term care. He specifically spoke about long-term care policy being very critical to employees' long-term financial health. Is he just trying to sell us more insurance, or there is any validity to his advice?

-Kayleen, Mesa

Answer: The insurance expert that your company invited is right on the mark regarding long-term care policies. Employees, in general, can see the need for car insurance, house (or apartment) insurance, and health insurance (if their employer provides this option). Beyond that, if anyone tries to sell them any other insurance, their antenna goes up. This skepticism is somewhat justified, because so many people have been ripped off by either unnecessary or expensive insurance products. There are many insurance products out there, and they all have a time and place—providing the appropriate coverage for specific individuals in specific circumstances. But one size does not fit all. The problem is that I have seen these products pitched indiscriminately.

So, let us look at some insurance products that meet the Steve Sanghi test, beyond the standard automobile, home, and health insurance. First is a term life insurance policy. If you are the breadwinner of the house, you really should think about life insurance so that your survivors can make ends meet until they are on their feet again. If the policy through your employer is not enough, it is a good idea to supplement that coverage through a term policy. In most cases, if someone tries to sell you a whole life policy, you should instead get a term policy and invest the difference. However, whole life policies may be good for some rich folks who have maxed out on deferring their income from taxes. For others, it does not meet the Steve Sanghi test. Whole life insurance agents will not like my answer, and a protest is sure to follow.

Second, you need credit protection in these days of credit fraud and identity theft. For $16 a month, LifeLock has some of the most highly respected credit-protection insurance around. Do not confuse credit-protection insurance with credit card insurance. Credit-protection insurance helps protect you from fraud and identify theft. Credit card insurance pays off the balance on your credit card if you die. Rather than buying expensive credit card insurance, it is usually much cheaper to add to your term life insurance policy to also cover any credit card debt upon death.

Third, and to answer the specific policy you asked about, you should seriously consider long-term care insurance. There is a good chance that sometime in your life you may need long-term care—either in a medical facility or at home. No other insurance covers this expense, and the affected families sometimes exhaust their life savings. So, this insurance would be a good investment. Ask your employer to set up a group long-term care policy. It is much cheaper for you to purchase insurance under your employer's group policy than it is for you to buy it on your own.

Which estate planning documents do I need?

Question: I liked your column on "3 insurance options that make sense." It provided simple, no-nonsense advice. Our company invited an estate-planning expert to give a seminar. He covered a lot of stuff about estate planning: Wills, Trusts, Children's Trusts, Family Limited Partnerships, Charitable Remainder Trusts, etc. Can you provide similar no-nonsense advice on the minimal set of estate-planning documents one should have?

-Bobby Grant

Answer: Estate-planning laws are constantly undergoing change. Therefore, you should consult an experienced estate-planning attorney before you follow any of my advice.

In 2024, the estate-tax exemption is $13.61M for an individual. A $13.61M exemption for an individual is large enough for most of my readers to have no estate-tax liability. So, let me boil this down to the three documents that everyone should have in a basic estate plan.

Will: A Will is a document that describes your wishes regarding how your assets should be disposed of when you die. The drawback in disposing of your assets through a Will is that a Will goes through probate. Probate is a lengthy, expensive, and very public process. Therefore, you should dispose of most of your assets through a Living Trust. Any remaining miscellaneous, undocumented assets can be disposed of through a Will.

In the Will, you can also assign a guardian for your minor children, should your spouse die before you. If you do not have a Will, the state of Arizona will assign a guardian for your children. The state-appointed guardian may not be who you would have liked, based on religious, cultural, or any other values. There may be conflicts among siblings or grandparents regarding who will care for the children. That is why you should assign a guardian through a Will.

Revocable living trust: This is the best way to dispose of your assets according to your wishes, because it avoids probate. However, if you have minor children, you still need a Will for the purpose of assigning a guardian for them.

Living will and healthcare power of attorney: A Living Will allows you to predetermine your healthcare options in case you have a terminal condition. It lets you make choices about life-sustaining treatment, irreversible coma, persistent vegetative state, cardiopulmonary resuscitation, artificial administration of food, etc.

You can also assign an agent and give him or her healthcare power of attorney.

There are many other estate-planning documents, such as Children's Trusts, Generation-Skipping Trusts, Charitable Remainder Trusts, Family Limited Partnerships, Charitable Family Foundations, etc. But they are beyond the scope of a basic estate plan, in my opinion.

Power of attorney

Question: I liked your column on "3 estate-planning documents for you to consider." In that column, you wrote about the Healthcare Power of Attorney. What about the Power of Attorney for financial matters? What is the difference between a "Durable power of attorney" and a "Nondurable power of attorney," and what is the relative suitability of each?

-Barbara Simpson, Mesa

Answer: First, let us define the Power of Attorney. In layman's terms, a Power of Attorney is a legal document that allows an individual or an entity to conduct business on behalf of another person.

A Healthcare Power of Attorney grants an individual authority over making healthcare decisions on your behalf if you were to become incapacitated. In a Living Will, you can make predetermined choices about your healthcare options. Medical conditions are not predictable. If there is a decision to be made while you are incapacitated, then the person to whom you grant Healthcare Power of Attorney will make that decision.

Another kind of Power of Attorney is the General Power of Attorney, which can be durable or nondurable. It is important to know the differences and when you may need one or the other. Many people get nervous at the thought of a Power of Attorney. It can be uncomfortable to consider giving another person or agent the authority to make such important decisions. But, doing so is most often better than leaving such important decisions to chance or verbal agreements.

A durable Power of Attorney allows someone to act on your behalf until it is revoked or upon your death, whichever occurs first. For individuals facing a debilitating illness or who may be preparing to enter a nursing home, a durable Power of Attorney would be advantageous.

A durable Power of Attorney can be written so that it can be invoked at a future point in time. For someone with a debilitating or potentially debilitating illness, this type of instrument may be the best option. Usually, a physician or other recognized authority will designate the time when an individual can no longer competently manage their own legal affairs. At that time, the durable Power of Attorney will become effective, allowing the designated agent to begin managing the incapacitated person's financial obligations.

A nondurable (or limited) Power of Attorney is generally used for limited transactions. For example, if someone needs to grant authority for a single transaction, such as the sale of a house or trading stock, a nondurable Power of Attorney would be the better choice. This option is often used when you are going to be away on travel or for busy executives, or to grant Power of Attorney to your broker for the purpose of selling your stock.

Drawing Power of Attorney need not be expensive. Search on the Web for "Power of Attorney forms Arizona," and you can download free forms.

Assistance in answering this question was provided by Cristi B. McMurdie, Esq., McMurdie Law Office.

How should I take title?

Question: We are in the process of buying a house. Our realtor told us that we should take title as "Joint Tenants with Right of Survivorship". A friend told us that we should take title as

“Community Property”. What is the difference, and what are the pros and cons?

-John and Linda Turic

Answer: There are three basic ways to take the title of the house, as a married couple.

Joint tenants with rights of survivorship: Here, the married couple jointly owns the property. If one of them dies, the other owns the property outright, exercising his or her right of survivorship. This is the most common way that titles between married couples are held. But from a tax standpoint, this is not the best way—especially for an investment property.

When you buy a house, your purchase price plus any improvements becomes your tax basis in the property. If one spouse dies, then one half of the basis in the property steps to fair market value (FMV) of that half on the date of the death. For example, if your basis in the house were $200K, and one of you died and the FMV for the house on the date of the death was $300K, then the new basis for the surviving spouse would be $250K (one half of the basis of $100K steps up to FMV of that half of $150K).

If the surviving spouse sells the house, the gain of $50K is taxable income. For a residence, there is a one-time $250K exemption on gains for individuals ($500K for couples). So, for most normal-size homes, the entire gain is excluded for tax purposes. But, if it were an investment property or you had already used your residence sale exemption, then the gain of $50K would be taxable. This tax can be avoided if the title is taken as Community Property.

Community property: This is a preferable way of taking title to a property in Arizona, which is a community-property state. The main difference is that if one spouse dies, the tax basis in the property steps to FMV of both halves of the property. Thus, in the above example, the new tax basis for a surviving spouse will be $300K. And, therefore, there will be no gain on the sale of the property. This is also a preferable way to take title on your stock and your investment accounts. That way, the entire basis steps up to FMV, resulting in zero tax on the sale of assets.

Tenants in common: This is a third and rarely used form of title between married couples. This form is more often used between two friends buying a house together. Here, each party owns one half of the interest and can individually bequeath their interest to their respective heirs through a Will or Trust.

I am neither a lawyer nor a tax accountant. Please consult your own advisors before you follow my advice.

Chapter 16: Ex- employees and finding a job

Reference check on an ex-employee

Question: I manage an engineering department, and recently fired an employee. I am now receiving calls from prospective employers for a reference for this ex-employee. I am tempted to tell them about his poor performance. Should I?

-Jennifer, Tempe

Answer: As a rule of thumb, you should not tell them about his past performance. The performance of an ex-employee is personal and confidential information that cannot be disclosed without the employee's consent. You should only verify the employment dates, and the positions held by the ex-employee. You could also explain the job responsibilities without commenting on the ex-employee's performance.

Now, that was more of a legal answer. Practically, it is a small world and many employers checking the references are friends. Managers do not like their friends to hire an employee whom they know to be a poor performer. Managers are sometimes also upset with the ex-employee. It is because firing an employee can be taxing, both emotionally for the manager and economically for the company. And, given a chance to vent about the ex-employee, some managers cannot resist. So, they whisper comments about them. In a conversation, things can be implied, though never said. Most managers evaluate what to disclose on a case-by-case basis. In general, disclosing information only has a downside in if an ex-employee brings a lawsuit.

Imagine yourself on the other end, where you are trying to check the references of a candidate you are strongly considering. You would expect the other party to tell you the truth. Good questions to ask are, "Would you rehire this person?" Or "Why did the employee quit?" The answers may tell you what you want to know.

This is one area where I will tell you to do what I say and not what I do.

Religious fanatic

Question: I liked your column on March 18 regarding references for ex-employees. My company is trying to hire someone who I know from the past to be a religious fanatic. Should I tell the hiring manager? Do I have personal liability if my negative recommendation becomes known?

-Sayeed, Phoenix

Answer: It is illegal to make a hiring decision based on someone's religion. Everyone is entitled to worship in their own faith, with the full protection of the U.S. Constitution. His religion should have no bearing on his candidacy for the job.

The question is whether he brings his religion to work and creates disruptions. It would be considered a disruption if he preaches to others, gets into arguments on work time, favors and promotes others of his own faith, or creates a hostile work environment in any other way. Simply posting some pictures or teachings from this faith in his immediate workspace is not considered disruptive.

If you have knowledge from experience that he is disruptive at work, then the problem is not his religion. The problem lies in his character, because he cannot separate work from his faith and incites disruption, or in extreme cases, violence. If this is the case, you should report this to the hiring manager. Make sure that someone in human resources is involved and that your knowledge of his past behavior is documented. It would be good for the hiring manager or the human resources to check at least one more reference. They should also get a second opinion from an employment lawyer.

You did not mention anything about his performance. If he was an employee with a good performance record, then it would make the decision a lot harder. If he did not have a good performance record, then you can easily give that reference to the hiring manager.

If your company covers all the bases and then decides not to hire this individual, the company will be protected if the individual files a lawsuit. And, you would have made a significant contribution to the company by helping avoid a bad hire.

Hiring from ex- employer

Question: I left a company to join one of their competitors. I just received a letter from my old employer that reminds me of my continuing obligations to them regarding intellectual property, including names of employees, salaries, stock options, etc. I was planning to hire a couple of people from my old group. What should I do?

-Nathan, Scottsdale

Answer: When you work for an employer, you have access to information that the employer considers proprietary, such as the company's future product plans, core processes and trade secrets, proprietary architectures, upcoming patent filings, product pricing, and discounting schemes. Such intellectual property is usually well understood by departing employees.

However, companies also consider their employee lists, salaries, and stock options as proprietary information. Departing managers often consider their knowledge of their prior coworkers, their salaries, and stock options as something they just know. They often think that they can use that information to hire back part of their old group by offering raises in pay and stock options. Unfortunately, this treads on the intellectual property of their ex-employer. In some cases, the ex-employers have sued to get relief.

In general, if an employee from your old group contacts you first, applies for a posted position or comes to you through a headhunter, you are free to hire them. If you only hire one or two employees, especially from a large company, the company may just send you a letter like the one you got. If you refrain from further hiring, you are not likely to hear from your ex-employer.

In real life, each case is different. It is difficult to establish whether one of your ex-colleagues contacted you or you called them. Hiring managers also tend to feed names to the headhunters, and they then claim that the ex-colleagues came to them through the headhunter.

My real-life experience is that if your ex-colleagues are unhappy in their jobs with the ex-employer and you hire them, you usually get away with it. But if you indiscriminately call and target your former employer and recruit several old colleagues by offering them higher salaries and stock options, then you run afoul. In the end, someone who turns you down could maintain his or her loyalty to the old company by blowing the whistle on you.

What should you do? This column gives you a couple of ideas to lower your risk. But my best advice is that you should develop your own talent and not poach from your ex-employers.

Finding a job

Question: I have been searching for a job for two years. I have a master's degree in business and almost four years of HR-related experience. Please advise me.

-Lisa

Question: My job application has difficulty getting through any HR process in which the application is completed online. I have extensive background in one professional area, but if a computer does not match certain phrases in my resume, I am not qualified.

I have three college degrees and a proven track record of accomplishments, leadership, training and more, but cannot get a job in the Phoenix area.

-Barbara

Answer: I receive a very large number of questions from people searching for a job. The background of each person is different, and I cannot answer each question individually. So, I have taken a couple of representative questions to make my points on this subject.

In this globally competitive business environment, change is the only constant. In the past, you could get a job with a large company and work there your whole life. Global competition has removed that safety net. In the new economy, a lot of new jobs are being created by small companies.

There are also a lot of mergers, acquisitions, restructurings, and private-equity buyouts. They result in a lot of job displacements, further weakening the job safety net.

In the new economy, people must commit themselves to a life-long learning career. If you sit in one job doing the same work for many years and the economic winds eliminate your job, you are left with very few options. Instead, you must commit yourself to acquiring a variety of skills during your lifetime. You do not have to change companies to get this experience. (Being the last person coming into a new company that is facing layoffs is bad news.) Rather, you could expand your skill level through a few job rotations in the same company, and you could do it by taking several training classes provided by the company or in the local colleges and vocational schools.

Sometimes just a few months of training in a practical field can prepare you to find a job, such as medical technician, X-ray technician, dental assistant, security guard, and various jobs in the construction and service industries.

The problem is that most people are very narrowly committed to their field. That limits the choices so much that they cannot find a job.

I will leave you with the following quote:

"In times of change, learners inherit the earth. And the learned are beautifully equipped to work in a world that no longer exists."

- *Eric Hoffer*

Resume submitted online goes into a black hole

Question: How does one network to find job at a different company when most of the human resources departments just refer you to the company web site? I am finding that they do not want to give out the hiring managers' name or email address so that I can try to talk more in depth about a job opportunity. I have submitted my resume to many web sites, and they just go into a database.

-Donald

Answer: You are correct that most companies would not give out the names of hiring managers. The reason for this is that a lot of people try to collect such names and then use them for purposes not intended. Some examples include selling the contact information to telemarketers and spammers, giving it to headhunters to recruit away from the company and giving it to competitors.

However, I do not think that your resume just goes into a database. Except for entry-level positions, there are generally more job opportunities than the number of truly qualified candidates. Usually, a company will try to match your resume from the web site to an open position and act if there is a match. Unfortunately, companies are busy, and most do not respond if there is no match. This is what creates the perception that the resume just goes into a database.

The challenge really is as you described—how does one network to find a job at a different company? I wrote a column on networking in this space. Here is a summary:

There are several networking organizations that you should join. My favorite one is the "Association for Corporate Growth" (www.acg.org/arizona). Their primary product is a monthly gathering where a prominent local business executive presents the story of his or her company. The audience consists of business executives, entrepreneurs, and service providers. There is an hour of networking followed by dinner and the presentation.

You will find that if your resume goes into a company through someone you know or met at a networking event, then it is likely to get looked at more closely. And you are more likely to get a response.

New college graduate cannot find a job

Question: I graduated from college with a major in history one year ago. Since then, I have not been able to find a respectable job. I have been waiting tables in a restaurant for five months. Can you make some suggestions?

-Nick, Mesa

Answer: I hear about new layoffs often. It is never easy to get a good starting job coming out of college—unless you graduated in an applied field such as engineering, law, or medicine. Companies that are hiring are looking for experienced candidates with critical skills that can improve their operation.

But how do you get experience without first getting a job? That is the proverbial "chicken or egg" question. I believe that you need application-specific skills. A bachelor's degree in liberal arts is not enough.

First, there is nothing dishonorable about being a waiter. Many successful businessmen and women have waited on tables early in their careers. It teaches you the discipline of getting to work, absorbing training, serving your customers, and earning a paycheck; all of which helps you learn responsibility. There is nothing dishonorable about that.

To land a higher-paying job, you should get some applied skills. If you have the ambition, stamina, and patience for three to four years of additional schooling, you could investigate law, medical, or dental school. In two years or less, you could earn a master's in business administration, with a major in finance, marketing, or a host of other specialties. If you seek a quicker path, then vocational training may suffice. Examples include computer-repair technician, X-Ray technician, dental associate, corporate-security training, culinary school, etc.

While in training for an applied skill, you should develop contacts within your target industry. Your school's job-placement office can be a very good help here.

By the time you finish earning a degree in any of these applied areas, you should be able to land a decent job that will start you on the path toward a successful career. Meanwhile, you must find a way to support yourself, which may include continuing to wait tables.

Options for work

Question: I am a teacher, and at the age of fifty-five, I am ready for a change. I followed my passion and taught young children for years. This is a high-energy job, and now is the time to back away from this 60-65 hour a week job and spend time with my family and aging parents. I still want and need to work - just not so vigorously. What are some options for further work?

-Claire

Answer: First, I want to thank you for being a teacher and educating our nation's children. Our teachers do not get enough thanks. It seems that you are ready to retire and have some more leisure and family time. At the same time, you still need to work but not as vigorously. Here are some options:

- Move up from teaching young children to teaching adults, either at a community college or a vocational school. These teaching assignments can be part time. This way, you will be working and will also have leisure and family time.

- There are many families who educate children at home. Some do so because of religious beliefs and others to keep children away from bad influences in public schools. In most cases, a stay-at-home parent is educating the children. However, they often need part-time help or for a given subject such as Math, Science, English or American History.

- You could enlist yourself with a temporary agency. When a company needs temporary help, they usually call these temporary agencies. These are usually short-term assignments with sufficient flexibility.

- Many charitable organizations—the United Way, Food Bank, YMCA, and hundreds of other agencies have part-time paid positions that will work for your situation.

- Tutoring is another option. This could include preparing high school students for the SAT, ACT, or AIMS tests, or helping a student in certain subject after school. Tutoring opportunities are more abundant on college campuses if you can make the leap in your skills to tutoring college students.

Chapter 17: Proper email and phone etiquette in the office

Executives: Dial the number yourself

Question: I have a business associate who bugs me every time I get a phone call from him. He always asks his administrative assistant to initiate the call. Only when I am on the phone and waiting for him, does he come on the line. Is it proper business etiquette for him to make me wait, as he is the one who wants to talk to me? I do not mind his assistant answering the phone when I initiate a call, as I want to talk to him in that case.

-Keith, Scottsdale

Answer: I have a business associate who does the same thing. This "etiquette" is not uncommon in business. But your question is whether this practice is proper etiquette, not whether it is commonplace. My answer is that this is not a polite practice.

The person who is engaging in this practice is making a subtle statement that he is somehow more important than you, or that his time is more valuable than yours. Is it OK to do this occasionally, if you have an unusually busy day, or you are running to the airport, or you are calling one of your subordinates or you asked your secretary to locate the contact number and initiate the call? Yes, ... *occasionally*. Even then, I would start the conversation with apologizing for keeping the other person waiting.

However, doing this all or most of the time clearly sends a negative message. Executives are all very busy. Your business associate is assuming that you can wait 30 seconds for him, while he cannot be bothered to dial your number himself. I tend to believe that executives who continuously engage in this practice just have a showmanship attitude. The negative feeling it engenders among their peers is not big enough to elicit a strong response. So, they keep doing it because they think they are getting away with it.

What can you do about it? My feeling is that the irritation is not big enough to warrant a strong conversation, which may have unintended consequences. Depending on your relationship with the person, you might casually mention it. You could also work with human resources to issue a set of phone-etiquette guidelines. But that may seem excessive; and your business associate may be from outside of your company, as is in my case. I always have much bigger issues to deal with, so, this one will never get on the priority list.

Your best bet may be to cut out this article and find a way to place it on your business associate's chair. He will get the message.

iPods at the office

Question: I am writing to seek your opinion on whether my office environment is professional. I work in an office that has engineering, customer service, and sales sitting very close together. It seems that just about everyone is now working with an iPod of some sort in their ear. I come from an old school of thinking and cannot understand how the executives or human resources department find this acceptable. I do not want to complain and disrupt the staff or look like the bad guy. Can you give me your professional opinion on this subject of wearing iPods around the office all day?

-Anonymous

Answer: My first reaction was like yours—unprofessional! After some investigation, I was surprised to find out how prevalent this is at Microchip, too—and I do consider Microchip a very professional environment. So, I asked around to see why this was so common. The first reason that came up is that the cubical environment is noisy, and people find it difficult to focus. Customer-service areas can be especially noisy, with constant phone calls. Engineers and technical writers, for example, tend to be more computer-task focused. Mixing these two modes in the same area does create a problem.

I also found the headset becoming more prevalent for work-related tasks. Teams and other computer-to-computer phone programs save money and improve productivity. Conference calls (and therefore headsets) are a byproduct of globalization, telecommuting, and distributed teams. Online training, which usually requires a headset, can be a highly effective tool.

But it is very annoying to drop by someone's desk to ask a work-related question and feel like you are interrupting them because they have their headphones on, and you have to physically tap them on the shoulder to get their attention; especially if they seem at all put-outs that you have "interrupted" them. I also find it very unprofessional for people to wear headphones as they walk around the office, creating a safety issue as well as a barrier to interaction.

It seems new workplace social rules are needed to help make this work, both for the interrupter and the interrupted. The interrupted must be sensitive to the issue and always drop the headphones quickly, to make the visitor feel like their issue is clearly a higher priority. I notice that some people put little mirrors on their walls so that, even if their back is turned and their headphones are on, they can see someone has arrived. Similarly, a little note on the desk with "Conference Call" would be easy to point to and the interrupter should be very understanding.

However, like all workplace social rules, someone in HR or management must take the initiative to raise the issue, ensure everybody knows the rules, and that people follow them in both spirit and practice.

Practice proper email etiquette; do not use all caps

Question: My boss, who is the department manager, writes his emails to me in all capital letters. It is very annoying and hard to read. What is the message behind writing in all capital letters and what can I do about it?

-Charlie, Scottsdale

Answer: Writing an entire email in caps is the equivalent of yelling. If someone writes a word, sentence, or paragraph in all caps, this can be viewed as adding emphasis. However, writing the entire email in caps is very rude and hard to read. Therefore, it can hardly be seen as adding emphasis. And, if you are annoyed while reading through all caps, then it is hard to focus on the content of the email. So, I would see this as being yelled at.

What can you do about it? First, you need to evaluate whether he is writing in all caps to just you or everyone in the department. You should look at an email written to someone else to which you were copied. Also, discretely try to find out whether the emails he writes to others, where no one is copied, are also in all caps.

If your boss is writing to everyone in all caps, then he is just a person who is annoyed with the world. Yelling is his way of keeping his sanity, and it has become a bad habit. If I have a bad habit, then any employee from the lowest level to a vice president can tell me. And I WILL try to modify my behavior. Based on the culture in your company, your job may be harder.

You might try printing, "PLEASE DO NOT WRITE IN ALL CAPITAL LETTERS", in big and bold letters on an untraceable communal printer. Then, slip the paper under his door. He will get the message. Will he change his behavior? I do not know. But I think that he might tone it down for a while.

If you find that he is writing in all caps to you alone, then it sends a different message. He is probably not pleased with your performance. And, instead of facing you and telling you so, he gets his frustration out by yelling in writing.

So, ask for a meeting with your boss. Ask him how you are doing in your job. Ask about his expectations of you and then compare them to your expectations of yourself. Where you find gaps, commit to your boss that you will improve.

THEN GET ON WITH IT AND START IMPROVING.

People writing emails in ALL CAPS sound off

I received a record number of email responses from my column of June 22, 2008 "WRITING IN ALL CAPS IS VERY UNSETTLING."

It started with a simple comment posted on my AZCentral blog that read, "Find something meaningful to complain about." But then the feedback poured in in a way that seemed like I had shot into a hornet's nest.

Most emails were from senior citizens complaining about vision issues and not being able to read the screen. The second most common complaint came from people who did not know how to type, so ignoring the shift key made it easier. Here are some examples:

"I am 83 years old. I grew up without computers. However, when most papers stopped printing stock tables, I had to buy a computer. I have been typing letters probably since before you were born and want to tell you why I use all caps. As we age, our vision diminishes and caps are easier to read," *Dory.*

"I am glad you directed your 'All Capital Letters' to the working office, because we senior citizens and people with vision problems are delighted to be able to use all caps to communicate with our friends," *Katherine.*

"People who type in all caps are not necessarily angry; there are a lot of people who are somewhat inept when it comes to typing. It is just easier for them to type in all caps," *Barbara.*

"The all-caps format helps with my vision issues. I am seventy-two. If you cannot or would not deal with it, contact a MD to address your mental issues," *Larry.*

"Your article reminded me of when my 60-year-old mother first discovered email. She would send emails to everyone in all caps. We told her that it was the equivalent of yelling at someone. But she could not read the little letters. I had to adjust her computer setting to display in larger font size and disabled the caps lock key, before her emails came in lower case," *Tracy.*

"Both our daughter and son, two journalist graduates, state that I mean to be shouting when writing in all caps. That is the farthest thing from my mind. My reason for all caps is that I do not have to use the shift key, and therefore can type much faster," *Lorraine.*

"My sister and I exchange emails. The recipient replies by inserting comments in between lines of the original message in all caps. This makes it easier for the other to pick out the responses. Having said that, I must admit that if I respond to a message from someone other than my sister by using all caps, I start with,"' I am not shouting, just differentiating,'" *Leo.*

This was a small sampling of the emails I received. Clearly the question I received, and my response, was regarding the office environment. I did not mean to extrapolate it to social emailing between consenting senior citizens, or when the eyesight challenge of the sender is well known. I also did not realize the large number of computer users who either do not know how to type, or are grammar challenged. I thank the readers for educating all of us on these exceptions.

I contacted a couple of literary as well as journalistic organizations. They agreed with my opinion that all caps amount to yelling. They—and now I—note that there are significant exceptions to this opinion.

But how does Charlie, the original questioner, feel about all of this? I sent my response to Charlie a month before it was queued for publication. Charlie's boss did not write to everyone in all caps, just to Charlie. Charlie met with his boss and discovered that the boss was indeed unhappy. I am happy to report that Charlie is making good progress in repairing the relationship with his boss, whose emails are now in lower case.

Chapter 18: Political views and impact of elections

I received several questions on political views and the impact of elections. I do not share my political views at work and would not share them here. I answered many of the questions from the viewpoint of a businessman.

How to pay down the national debt

Question: As a nation, the United States is spending more than it earns in tax revenue, which creates a deficit. We have been running a deficit for so long that now we have a total of thirty-six trillion dollars in debt. Clearly, we have a spending problem. Assume for a moment that the United States were a corporation. As a businessman, how would you proceed to tackle this huge debt overhang?

-Sundar, Phoenix

Answer: You have handed me a political hot potato. The nation's voters and its politicians are not ready for the necessary pain therapy. Therefore, a businessman like me who is willing to tell the truth could never get elected.

If you break down the budget into entitlement spending and discretionary spending, and then you take the entire discretionary spending to zero, you will still not balance the budget. But discretionary spending is all that the politicians keep talking about. If anyone tries to address the entitlement spending, they are immediately shut down by both sides.

Next, let us look at tax increases. There is an old saying, "If you want more of something, tax it less; and if you want less of something, tax it more." So, if we want the nation to have more wealth, taxing it more is simply going to produce less. Currently, 51% of the people pay no federal taxes and therefore have no skin in the game. They are the tax consumers, and they have no problem in taxing the taxpayers, which keeps making the government bigger. If you keep robbing

Peter to pay Paul, you can get Paul's vote. If much of the country becomes the "Pauls," the problem becomes irresolvable. The Pauls would keep electing the same people, who would keep robbing the Peters and supporting the Pauls.

The nation's debt and continuing deficit has become so large that we cannot tax it away, and we cannot pay it by just tinkering with discretionary spending. The only way to balance the budget is to cut spending deeply, including all kinds of entitlement spending. This is something that the nation, including both voters and politicians, has no stomach for.

As a CEO, I have veto rights on the spending of Microchip Technology, and it has been profitable for more than 100 consecutive quarters. But, with no national consensus and no term limits for politicians, their primary goal is to get re-elected. And promising to take the country through a difficult session of pain therapy is no way to get re-elected.

So, what is likely to be the end game for our budget crisis? I see three possibilities. The first is to inflate the debt away through hyper-inflation. The second is to devalue the debt away by devaluing the dollar. And third is to continue till a significant event forces our hand. Any significant event (e.g., a hedge-fund blow up, a major bank failure, an unmanaged default of sovereign debt) could trigger a cataclysmic event. When we finally resort to deep austerity measures, we are sure to see the kind of violent street protests that took place in Greece. One way or the other, the price for our runaway spending and the huge national debt must be paid.

Readers respond to national debt debate

In my last column, "Nation not ready for measures that will cut deficit" I tossed a political hot potato to my readers. You responded in record numbers—too many to publish. Below is a sampling of your emails, both positive and negative, followed by my comments…

R. Glenn Williamson: "Very well written! As a Canadian who recently became an American citizen, it pains me to see the inaction of recognizing this problem. As one of Peters paying for the Paul's, it is becoming silly."

Rusty Davis: "Bravo. I wish there were a few more of us that felt we should live within our means. The longer we wait, the less chance we have of it happening without real trouble for the country. My parents lived through the depression and taught me to work hard, live within my means, pay cash for everything, or not buy it, and to save a portion of every check. It is too bad that more people did not have parents like yours or mine. Thank you for your courage to speak today."

Jerry Watterworth: "I found your article completely misleading. You, like the rest of the Republican Party, seem to only focus on spending cuts as the path to fixing our budget problems. What is it about this one-sided approach that seems so compelling? You completely dismiss the revenue side of the equation. You also use the false statement that "51% of the people pay no taxes." If anybody eats, they pay taxes when they buy food. If anybody rents a room, they pay taxes on the price of the room. Therefore, everybody pays taxes of some sort."

Dwayne Witten: "You stated some of the issues in a way that is understandable even to those who do not have a PhD in economics and finance. Unfortunately, the Pauls will reject your arguments because, after all, they are the Pauls. So, in effect, you end up 'preaching to the choir.' It is very sad that politicians do not have the guts and appetite to face the eventual reality."

Ben Click: "Thanks for the straight -talk column. It is frustrating to see politicians shy away from the hard decisions just to get re-elected. The answer to our debt/deficit problem is not complicated, but it is painful in the short term for some. I have sent your article to friends around the U.S."

Keith: "I really appreciated your article. I thought you explained the situation of our country's debt situation very well. As a business owner and investor, I want to face reality, and your article illustrated it well, in my opinion."

James Rush: "Do we now add your name to the list of people obviously parroting Sean Hannity of Fox? Your statement, 'Currently, 51% of the people pay no taxes and therefore have no skin in the game' is not true. And yet you use it as a springboard to demonize a very large portion of low-wage-earning Americans as 'tax consumers', and then profess that 'they have no problem in taxing the taxpayers'."

Julian Schmidtke: "I was pleased that your answer to the deficit is right on. It is obvious that our politicians are the main reason we continue to add to this extremely large deficit. Protecting their votes and turf is also part of the problem. I feel we need term limits in America. Most representatives spend very little time on the job, as they are campaigning continually to keep their jobs."

Ron Badowski, former Mayor, Town of Wickenburg: "I enjoyed reading your thoughts on our nation's disastrous financial situation. You could not have been more 'on point'. I fear we are very close to, if not past the point of financial recovery. We are no longer a country of self-reliance, personal values, and helping one's family and neighbors. It appears many parents do not wish to teach those values and responsibilities to their children. The majority now believe the government is responsible for our needs. This country needs business and community leaders like you to continue bringing your message to our government representatives, our schools, and to the public."

David Lawrence: "From my perspective, you gave some real clarity to the subject and some realistic observations regarding the spineless politicians kicking the can down the road. It is a simple solution, but there is definitely a lack of will."

Joe Bacskay: "Your column was the most common-sense, simple explanation of what is wrong with our elected officials and many of our voters. I will be making copies and giving them out or mailing them out to many people that I know."

Vick Koll: "First, I must say, very interesting and truthful article. Very unbiased and understandable economics. Politicians will continue to rob Peter to pay Paul (subsidies, welfare, unemployment, food stamps, section 10 housing, political salaries, and benefits). But what happens when Peter disappears?"

Jim Histand: "Thanks for the excellent and timely article. You expressed the facts of human nature and their implications for this subject so succinctly and simply."

General Craig Ferguson: "I will bet 'you have got mail' after Sunday's deficit column. I used to hear Peter and Paul illustrations from my father when I was growing up in the fifties and sixties. He was a self-employed businessman and was always worried about taxes and economic recessions. I think the difference is today's crass, immoral, and totally corrupt congress."

My comments: Some readers objected to the statement that 51% of the people pay no taxes. They cited taxes on food, fuel, etc. The debate in this country is not about raising taxes on food or fuel. The debate is about federal income taxes. And 51% of the people in this country pay no federal income taxes.

One reader objected to my statement that those paying no federal income taxes have no skin in the game. He believes that all the tax consumers have skin in the game, because their subsidies and government handouts are important to them. Well, with that definition of "skin in the game", I agree they do have skin in the game. They have *other* people's skin in the game.

"The problem with socialism is that eventually you run out of other people's money." - *Margaret Thatcher*

Liberal and conservative spokespeople will spin one side of the equation or the other. "The top 1% of earners pay 40% of the taxes," say Republicans. "The rich do not pay enough as a percentage of their income," say the Democrats. You cannot get democrats to talk about the dollar amount paid by the rich in taxes, out of the total, while 51% of people pay no federal taxes. And you cannot get Republicans to talk about any increase in the tax rates. That is why I predicted the endgame that I did in my column.

U.S. national debt compared to that of Japan

Question: Thank you for your two great columns about U.S. national debt. I am a Japanese citizen living in U.S. on assignment. As I understand it, Japan's national debt is even higher than that of U.S. Yet Japan is very slow to change if changing at all. The Japanese government continues to have large budget deficits. Doesn't Japan face even worse scenarios than you predicted for the U.S., and can it affect global economy?

-Yuki, Phoenix

Answer: Japan has the second highest government debt in the world while U.S. Government debt is the largest. What is even more important is to look at the government debt as a % of total GDP. U.S. debt has surpassed 100% of its GDP while Japan's debt is 200% of its total GDP. So, one could predict even more dire consequences for Japan. However, I beg to differ. Here is why.

My analysis is based on five fundamental differences in Japan versus the U.S.

1. Japan's military spending is negligible at 2% of their budget. U.S. military spending is 13% of our budget. I am not passing judgment on our military expenditure and commitments around the globe. That is a national policy debate. I am simply stating the facts in comparison to Japan in answering your question.

2. Japan has no immigration problem. Japan is a homogeneous society essentially closed to outsiders. Japan is not a hyphenated country – there are no designations as Mexican-Japanese, Indian-Japanese, African-Japanese, or Chinese-Japanese. Japan does not publish its public ballot in multiple languages. Japan does not have the burden of millions of illegal immigrants on its schools, health care system, justice system, and education system. Japan protects and defends its borders. All the boat people of the 1970s landed in the U.S. even though Japan was much closer. Again, I am not passing judgment on U.S. policy, just stating facts.

3. Japan's government debt is owned by its citizens. In comparison, U.S. government debt is owned by the foreigners. If Japan taxes its citizens to pay for debt, it goes back to its citizens. So, it is a self-contained loop. In U.S. we need Chinese and others to fund our budget deficit. And the interest payments go out of the country.

4. Japan's society's ability to prevail through hardship is incredible. Just compare the behavior of Japanese citizens after earthquake and tsunami with the behavior of Americans after the hurricane in New Orleans. Japanese suffered through cold, hunger, lack of clean water and food in the affected areas, but they persevered with no looting and no civil disobedience. The Japanese citizens turned off heaters in their homes to preserve power for their industry. Such behavior will be considered unprecedented and very unlikely in the U.S.

5. Japanese largely purchase Japanese products. In a recent trip to Japan, I visited an appliance store. It only displayed Japanese brands for refrigerators, washers, dryers, and

cooking appliances. When I asked for Whirlpool, I was escorted to the back of the warehouse where there was a Whirlpool refrigerator in not too good of a condition. There is no such "buy American" sentiment in U.S. So, we continuously send money to the foreigners.

While there are significant issues in Japan with their government debt, the liability is not national since it is owned internally. U.S. government debt in contrast is a national liability. Japan's economy has been stuck in neutral for 35 years. Nikkei peaked in 1989 at 38,915. It recently exceeded that number and is now at 39,594. So, Japan has already gone through a muddle through economy with frequent recessions which is one of the outcomes I predicted for the U.S.

Japan has two possible options. The first is to go through an extreme contraction of government spending which its citizens are more likely to bear than the citizens of any other country. The second option will be to print the money and devalue the Japanese yen. That seem to be already happening. One U.S. dollar was equal to 78 yen in 2012. Today it has halved in value and is now one U.S. dollar is worth 156 yen. The devaluation makes Japanese exports more competitive, something the Japanese love.

Dealing with oil crisis

Question: With oil over $80 per barrel and gas prices over $4.00 per gallon, I see plenty of opinions about our energy strategy from the radio, TV and print media. I would like you to look at this from a businessman's viewpoint. What is it that our nation should do?

-Ron, Phoenix

Answer: Oh boy, you have handed me a political hot potato. It is a very difficult subject when you look at it from the standpoint of Presidential politics, effects on the environment, national security and economic effects of public policy. I am politically independent in my views. Therefore, I am going to look at it from a businessman's viewpoint and sort through other effects.

Let us assume that our nation is a business (and it is) and the job of the President and Congress is to run our nation's business as a corporation. This corporation has a huge demand for one of its products (Oil). The demand for oil in U.S. alone is twenty-one million barrels per day. Out of this demand, our nation only produces about thirteen million barrels per day ourselves. The rest of the demand is served by other corporations and our competitors (Saudi Arabia, Iran, Venezuela, Russia, Mexico, and others).

So, from a businessman's viewpoint, it seems that we have a never-ending demand for the oil. If we initiate efforts on all fronts – drilling offshore, Arctic national wildlife refuge (ANWR), Green River basin, and build new nuclear plants, new coal plants with newest technology, wind energy, solar energy, Electric cars and others; we will still be importing oil from other countries. For a brief period during Donald Trump's presidency, U.S. did become energy independent when we drilled a record amount of oil ourselves.

So, I do not understand why we will not pursue all these avenues to reduce demand as well as produce more to satisfy that demand. Most of the large oil exporters are not our friends and our national security is compromised by putting our future in their hands.

There are obvious environmental implications that we need to be mindful about. Chinese will be drilling ninety miles off the coast of Florida. Why is it good for Chinese to drill, but not for us to drill off our own coasts?

We should also build renewable energy plants – wind and solar. We should build new nuclear plants. France relies 75% on nuclear energy, US 15%.

We should reduce consumption by switching to Electric cars, hybrids, and more fuel-efficient gasoline cars. But here is a fact from a movie "A Crude Awakening." If you were to magically hybridize all cars on the road, we would still be using the same amount of gas seven years from now. It is because with the growing economy and growing population, demand is increasing.

At the end, no matter what opinion a given Presidential candidate has, the situation will become so grave in the next few years that we will land up following most of what I am suggesting above. What is not palatable at $80 a barrel oil, becomes acceptable at $140 per barrel. And if there are some still holding out, they will fold at $150, $160 or $170 per barrel.

So, a businessperson will marshal all his resources to meet the demand he sees, and in the process, help the budget deficit, create US jobs, protect national security, reduce demand through conservation, produce renewable energy and hope to someday become energy independent. But with 40% of oil being imported, energy independence is some distance away.

CEOs running for president

Question: Have you considered running for President? I have seen the progress of Microchip over the years, and I have been reading your columns for quite some time now. I was wondering if you could clean up the mess in Washington.

-Melanie, Phoenix

Answer: Thanks, but I do not consider myself even remotely qualified to be the President of the United States. But I read your question more broadly. I think what you are really asking is why doesn't any large public-company CEO run for the office of President?

It is true that large public-company CEOs have a lot of executive experience, and they make a lot of very difficult decisions, on which the health of the business and the prosperity of their shareholders, customers and employees depend. These CEOs also have a lot of experience in communicating with the government, community, and media. So, could those skills translate to the Presidency?

How a President gets the work of the nation done is quite different than how a CEO gets the job of a corporation done. Most things that a President wants to do have to be passed through Congress. Congress represents one of the most partisan groups of people. Roughly one half of the people are pulling the country in one direction and the other half in a different direction.

I cannot imagine a CEO getting work done with half of his or her managers working against the corporate agenda. In the case of a CEO, he or she can fire and replace the managers. But the President has no such power.

A public-company CEO enjoys veto power over any decision. A CEO may empower the subordinates in making certain decisions, but he or she holds the ultimate line-item veto. Many of our nation's governors also have the line-item veto, but not the President.

Most public-company CEOs are very well known in their field, but they are not very well known nationally. The Washington machine is often very critical of outsiders. They are likely to be criticized for a lack of experience in foreign policy and national defense, even though many have negotiated large multinational deals in the private and public sectors. Are they ready to be commanders-in-chief? Some of the same questions have been raised about past presidential candidates.

Despite the many differences cited, some CEOs manage a budget that is much larger than some of the actual candidates have ever managed. They could become good Presidents and have the judgment to lead our nation. But most CEOs that I know would dread the process of running for office and the intrusion into personal and family life that it creates.

As for me, I am not even eligible because a candidate for the President of the United States must be a citizen by birth, not by naturalization. Besides, I have never had any desire to run for any political office.

Should we make new business investments right now?

Question: I am the VP of operations for a distributor of retail goods to small and medium-size businesses across the Southwest. Our company is considering major new investments in capacity expansion, automation, and logistics. However, our management team is having a raging debate about the economy's prospects and the outcome of the November elections. How should we decide regarding new investments in such uncertain times? We have the forecasts, news analysis and the like, but we are also looking for some opinions from business leaders. What would you do?

-John C., Scottsdale

Answer: That is a very good question, and the timing could not be more appropriate. However, it is difficult to answer without touching on the politics of the November elections. I usually avoid such topics, but to provide you with complete business advice, I will include the political considerations in my answer.

I believe the economy faces very significant challenges next year, irrespective of the outcome of the November elections. If a Democrat is elected President, they would see that as a referendum on President Biden's policies of big government, higher taxes, open borders, expansion of the entitlement society, and big deficits. Consequently, the gross domestic product (GDP) of our nation would not be likely to do much better than it is doing today. The growth rate of the economy is likely to be lower. Continuation of current policies would also put the country into a long-term fiscal mess, which could lead us to stagnation and debt problems, a few years down the line.

On the other hand, if Donald Trump were elected President, he would close the borders, deport some of the illegal immigrants, make us energy independent, cut the size of our federal government, and make tax cuts permanent. He will also try to cut spending and reform entitlements, but will largely not get passed through Congress, even though such austerity measures may be the correct bitter pill that our country needs to swallow for long-term fiscal health. The effects of stimulative tax policies would take longer, while spending cuts would curtail GDP growth immediately. So, the economy could start to recover significantly in the later years of his presidency, but short-term contraction would be unavoidable.

I do not have enough knowledge about your business, in terms of how long it takes to implement new initiatives, lead times for capital investments, etc. But, if your capacity additions need to be productive next year, you may be too early in making such investments. In addition, Europe is in a recession and China's economy is in trouble. In this global environment, businesses need to be very careful about making investments—especially if they will be borrowing money. I have never seen a company go out of business because they missed some expansion opportunity. I have seen plenty of companies get in big trouble because they made risky investments, and the business was not there to fill the capacity.

The best course for a business to take would be to hold off until next year. Specifically, it would be best to wait for the results of the election and see what Congress does about the fiscal mess. Do not get a false sense of security from the Fed's expected rate cut. These cuts will take time to have some effect.

Both political parties will most likely disagree with my analysis of the economy, and their protest responses are sure to follow.

Businessman's viewpoint on QE

Question: So much of the discussion regarding Quantitative Easing (QE) focuses on macroeconomic policies with theoretical and difficult-to-measure, long-term impacts. However, there are immediate, real-life impacts on businesses and employment at microeconomic levels. Some of the ramifications are negative and worth sharing.

I am the plant manager of a large manufacturing facility selling to the beverage industry. Our products go right to the American consumer, and our sales are directly dependent on the consumer's disposable income.

Did QE increase our sales, allowing us to increase our production and add people? The answer was no, and in fact the opposite happened.

QE fueled price increases in commodities, fuel, and metals, and devalued the dollar. The lower dollar immediately raised the costs of components from overseas. When costs went up for components, cuts needed to be made in other areas to compensate. This forced us to cut labor costs by reducing overtime and head count. With the American consumer increasingly strapped, our business saw decreasing sales and increasing costs. A terrible recipe for employment!

I believe it is time for other businesses to speak up.

-Shawn McQuitty, Tolleson, AZ

Answer: I basically agree with your views. The best analogy I can come up with for QE is giving a drug dose to an addict who is in pain. Rather than going through a difficult rehab process and working through the withdrawal syndrome (which is, long-term, good for the addict) it is much easier to just shoot more drugs to ease the pain.

Here, the drug addict is the American economy. The long-term solution is to cut the runaway growth of budget deficits, shrink the size of federal government, reform entitlement programs, reform the tax code, and put the country on a long-term path to fiscal health. But, with a divided Congress and the President not being able to pull the two sides together, they are not even talking about any long-term solution.

With near-zero interest rates that remained so for a long time, what could the Fed do? It chose to inject the economy with another dose of drugs, in the form of QE3. The financial markets liked the relief from this drug, and the stock market shot up. But gold and commodity prices also moved up, fuel prices increased, and the value of the dollar went down. All these price increases worked in the economy to raise the price of everything, hence bringing inflationary pressures. With high unemployment, low job creation and a general lack of disposable income, the inflationary increases strapped the American consumer even more. A new cycle of pain began which will require a new dose of drugs to feel temporary relief.

On November 5th, Americans go to polls to elect the next President and Congress. I cannot advise you on how to vote. Will Kamala Harris be able to bring the next Congress together and put the country on a path toward fiscal health and away from runaway deficits? Or will Donald Trump bring the new Congress together to cut the budget deficit, reform entitlements and the tax code, and pull the country away from runaway deficits and toward fiscal health?

Chapter 19: Work life balance

Balance work with family

Question: I am the VP of sales for a global public company. I do international and domestic business travel all the time, visiting customers, distributors, and our own sales offices. I have a family, including a wife and three children. How do you balance your work with home life?

-Robert, Scottsdale

Answer: This question could have come from any of my executives, or from me. How do I balance my work with my home life? Honestly, I do not. So, you should not necessarily do what I do.

The fact is that, in the global business environment today, business travel is constant. I spent 83 days away from home last year and have done this for the last 20 years. I am deeply indebted to my wife and my two children who always saw me packing my bags.

My wife did not work outside of our home. (I called her a domestic engineer.) She was deeply committed to the children. She made up for all the times I did not make it to my daughter's soccer games or dance performances; and when I missed my son's lacrosse games and the award ceremony at his school for his national merit scholarship recognition. (My daughter still rubs this in every time she gets a chance.)

Most successful executives do not balance their lives well. That does not mean that you cannot, and you should always continue to try. In life, you make choices. If you accept being the VP of sales for a global business, it comes with tremendous responsibility. It requires personal sacrifice and commitment to the job. Yes, it comes with a good compensation package with which you can afford a few luxuries. But, trust me, any of my executives would gladly give up a few luxuries if it meant less travel away from home.

You have several choices. You can certainly take a less demanding job with less travel. The other option is to take your wife with you on a trip occasionally. But that is harder to do with kids in school. Another idea is to make up for it when you are at home or on vacation with the family. I even take my laptop on family vacations, and check emails every day to stay connected. Is this necessary? I find that it is. This may not have been the answer that you wanted to hear. But you asked Steve, which will always get you an honest and practical answer—not some theoretically concocted, idealistic, or politically correct answer!

Executives are like soldiers who are not in harm's way. When duty calls, they go. I feel deeply indebted to our actual soldiers, who make the sacrifice for our freedom. And I feel deeply indebted to my executives who make the sacrifice for the success of our customers, shareholders, and employees.

Build culture of trust, not big brother watching

Question: I am the CEO of a small business employing fifty people. We have strict limitations regarding company e-mail addresses being used for personal e-mail, and we do monitor all employee e-mails (to and from our company address). However, some employees always find ways to circumvent these policies using other means, including personal e-mail accounts, internet chatting, and texting using a smart phone. I suspect that they are involved in online communications not related to company business because of their reduced productivity levels. How should I solve this problem without implementing stricter policies (or monitoring) that may also punish our sincere employees? Do I have certain wrong employees on the bus, or is this a current trend that I must live with?

-Bill, Phoenix

Answer: I am sorry, but I am not at all in sync with the culture that you are describing at your company. If you build a culture that says, "big brother is watching", that is the level of trust you will get back from your employees.

I wrote a lot about this in my book "Driving Excellence", published by Wiley. If your company has a mission, strategic objectives, well-defined individual roles, short-term and long-term objectives, and a set of key results to be achieved, there is no need to watch your employees' use of email to send a personal greeting or take care of personal business from work.

If your company is anything like Microchip, employees work long hours—including some evenings and weekends. And they do not get paid overtime for any of this. I would rather have employees take care of their personal business during lunches or breaks using work computers instead of bringing their own PCs to work and risking infections on our network or leaving early to do their personal email at home. Employees (me included) who own smart phones work all hours of the day (and night), reading and answering the emails and texts of other employees. I do not see the point in employees carrying a second phone to take care of personal email.

So, I am not in tune with the whole idea of employee monitoring. I would rather build a performance culture that is goal oriented. Employees can relax and take care of a personal emergency or stay in touch with a spouse or child during the day without the employer coming down on them. We also set high goals and expect our employees to work hard and persevere in achieving these goals.

I cannot finish this answer without saying that a company's compensation system should be designed to ensure that all employees benefit from the extraordinary results they achieve. Once the employees understand that they have skin in the game, they act as owners and the need for intrusive monitoring disappears.

Chapter 20: Outsourcing and changes in business

Change is certainty in global economy

Question: My company is headquartered in Phoenix and does business globally. It is making too many changes in its product lines and global subcontractors and is transferring some jobs to Asia facilities. It is making me and other employees nervous and anxious. Why are so many changes necessary?

-Kate

Answer: In global businesses today, change is the only constant. Given the brutally competitive global environment, your company is likely trying to survive and thrive for the benefit of its customers and employees (including you). Companies are competing with Asian competitors, where production employees make $4 an hour and the regular work week is six days. In that environment, it is essential to make changes to re-align the company's cost structure, its product lines and subcontractor base. And sometimes it is necessary to transfer some lower-skilled jobs to Asia to remain competitive.

At Microchip, we remember a quote by *Eric Hoffer*, "In times of change, learners inherit the earth. And the learned are beautifully equipped to work in a world that no longer exists." If you study it carefully, it has a profound meaning.

The stress that you feel is simply being human. The best resource is the book "Who moved my cheese" by Spencer Johnson. It describes two scenarios in the middle of a chaotic change. One group refuses to adapt, blames the management, and is left in a desperate situation. The other group takes responsibility, embraces change, adapts, and comes out for the better. It teaches you an amazing way to deal with change in your work and in your life. The second book I would recommend is "The World is Flat" by Thomas Friedman.

A company can also use "change" to its competitive advantage by adapting faster than its competitors in the areas of competitive pricing, lower cost structure, and higher quality. In the past, I created an annual theme at Microchip that said, "We must accelerate the rate of change. Change is our ally. Driving and managing change is our winning strategy."

Rebuttal on "change is certainty in global economy"

Question: In your column on outsourcing, you suggest that it is OK for a company to outsource its jobs to Asian factories for low-cost manufacturing. What about the risk to our businesses and American way of life if the relationship between the U.S. and Asian countries were to go bad?

-John, Mesa

Question: Thanks for your excellent column on outsourcing. Due to the intertwined parts of manufacturing, it is no longer possible to distinguish products based on where they are made. With such deep economic ties, the chance of a world-war style conflict is zero.

- Rick, Glendale

Answer: I thank both the readers for their opposing views. This is a very complex issue. Outsourcing to low-cost countries has been going on for over 50 years. First, it was to Japan in the 60s and 70s, it then moved to Taiwan, Korea, Singapore, and Hong Kong in the 80s and 90s. In the last 20 years, outsourcing has been moving to China. With rising political tensions with China, the outsourcing is now moving to India, Vietnam and Mexico. The U.S. is the most innovative and creative nation in the world. We have always invented new industries and new products; and have rapidly redeployed our workforce. At 4.1%, the U.S. has the lowest unemployment rate in the western world. Compare that to France's 7.4% unemployment rate, Germany's 6%, Italy's 8.1%, and U.K.'s at 4.4%.

John mentions, very broadly, that our relationship with Asian countries could go bad. Asia consists of many countries, each having independent government, laws, currency, trade policies, and business practices. A company should carefully consider all these factors before using Asian manufacturing and should keep some diversification.

Rick is correct in saying that production is so intertwined that you no longer know where a product is made. Toyota is now the third largest car manufacturer in the U.S. and employs a lot of Americans. Similarly, GM is the largest car manufacturer in China and employs a lot of Chinese.

I would not be totally complacent about wars, though. After all, bombs are not made to shoot pigeons on holidays. The British economist Sir Norman Angell argued in his book "The Great Illusion", published in 1910, that deep economic ties between superpowers made large conflicts irrelevant. That book was still in stores when some European armies invaded their neighbors in 1914.

How to prioritize changes?

Question: I liked your column on "Change is certainty in global economy". I see many opportunities at our company for making changes. Some of the changes are under my control. Others need to be initiated above me. I want to oppose some of the changes that are taking place. How do I sort these things out? How do I prioritize these changes? And how do I decide what to oppose?

-Grace, Scottsdale

Answer: Your question is very generic in nature. I do not know what kind of business you are in and what kind of changes you are dealing with. So, I cannot provide any specific advice. But I will provide some general advice that will apply in many situations.

There are two opposing management theories. One says, "If it is not broken, leave it alone." And the second says, "If it is not broken, break it and put it back together to see if there is a better way." Both have merits. You must look at a variety of business indicators. If you have knowledge of your business, then set up goals for certain indicators to improve. Do not change them all and leave a few that are working fine alone—that fits the first theory.

Then take some that need to be improved. Even when they are not broken, assume that they are broken and try to put the process flow or the recipe back together. The point is that many times our eyes and mind gloss over things and we do not see the process beyond how it is configured today. Putting it back together from the start gives the mind a fresh look as you are not limited by how it was done before. And many times, this can improve the process—that fits the second theory.

Change is often hard on everyone. Employees have a natural, built-in resistance to change. They often do not understand the importance or need for change. They fear the ramifications of change. It makes them feel insecure. In my book "Driving Excellence", I dedicated the entirety of chapter 11 to "The Human Change Process".

I usually start every New Year with the serenity prayer:

God, grant me the serenity to accept the things I cannot change; courage to change the things I can; and wisdom to know the difference. Amen.

Chapter 21: Global financial crisis and housing crisis

I received numerous questions on the global financial crisis and housing crisis during 2007/2008. Some of the answers are still relevant today.

Who is to blame for the financial crisis?

Question: I was wondering if you have any thoughts on who is to blame for the global financial crisis of 2008/2009? I do not need a political answer. I need a business answer.

-Barbara, Phoenix

Answer: Thank you for being quite blunt with me. As an independent, the only answer you will get from me is a business answer. I believe that there is plenty of blame to go around for the current financial crisis. So, let us round up all the suspects.

1. The U.S. Congress: It is not a Republican or a Democrat problem. The entire Congress is to blame. Congress enacted the Glass-Steagall Act in 1933, which prohibited banks and investment banks from combining. This combination had supposedly contributed to the crash of 1929. Congress repealed this law in 1999, setting up the scenario for the current crisis. Apparently, after 70 years we had forgotten the lessons of 1929.

2. The Mortgage Companies and Banks: Congress pushed for a dramatic increase in home ownership. And the mortgage companies readily complied. They made homeowners out of a record number of renters. The basic assumption was that home prices only go up. So, the mortgage companies and banks gave mortgage loans to non-creditworthy borrowers, often without verifying income and ability to pay. They tempted potential homeowners with teaser interest rates and people bought bigger homes with larger mortgages than they could afford. The moment

the interest rates went up, the homeowners could not pay. Default rates and foreclosures went up. The glut of unsold homes drove down prices, which further deepened the crisis.

Then, banks started writing off bad loans. The stock market tumbled. Many banks and investment banks failed. The cycle had reached Wall Street.

3. Fannie Mae and Freddie Mac: These were two government-sponsored mortgage companies that should have been outlawed many years ago. They were able to borrow money at a lower cost than their competitor banks. So, they borrowed record amounts of money and bought up mortgage portfolios. They then packaged those portfolios and sold them as securities. (They had plenty of help from investment banks.) When the underlying mortgages defaulted, the house of cards came down. The Treasury Secretary eventually took control of these mortgage giants, but not before colossal damage had been done.

4. The Securities and Exchange Commission (SEC): The SEC is a regulatory body that did not do its job. When it came to the global financial crisis, Congress, the SEC and the Financial Accounting Standards Board (FASB) should all be ashamed of themselves. They have socked U.S. public companies with $50B+ of financial and legal costs for Sarbanes-Oxley compliance, internal controls, and stock-option expensing, which did nothing to prevent this crisis.

   I do not know who was responsible for revoking the short-sale rule in July of 2007. Under that rule, short sales were allowed only on an uptick. Revoking it allowed an uncontrolled downward spiral on any weakness in a stock.

5. The Federal Reserve Board: The Fed did not do its job either. They created excessive liquidity, which led to the housing bubble. They had the authority to regulate, preventing the formation of

derivatives for underlying mortgage securities, sub-prime mortgages and "Alt A" mortgages in which borrowers secured mortgage loans without any verification of income.

6. Homeowners: Homeowners cannot be left off this list. No one put a gun to their heads to buy a house that was larger than they needed and larger than they could afford. They knew the risks of interest rates adjusting higher. Yet, they took the teaser interest-rate loans that were set to adjust after a period. They also bought second and third homes as vacation homes or investments, thinking that home prices would go up forever. When you make bad decisions, you lose money. That is the fundamental law of economics.

7. The Bush Administration: I name the Bush Administration because, ultimately, the buck stopped there. President Bush must take some responsibility for the crisis. With his bully pulpit, he ultimately takes responsibility for driving the SEC, the Fed, Fannie/Freddie, the Treasury Department, and I say very reluctantly, the U.S. Congress.

The next obvious question is, "What do we do now?" Is the $700B bail-out plan enough? But that is a subject for a different column.

Follow up on blame for financial crisis

The column on October 19, 2008, about "placing blame in financial crisis" brought a record number of emails and web responses. Several readers noted some additional suspects that I did not name in my column. After a thorough review, I add the following suspects to the list of those responsible for the global financial crisis.

Excessive leverage: There is one major factor that is the largest contributor to this mess—excessive leverage. The major investment banks (Goldman, Merrill, Bear Stearns, Lehman Brothers and

Morgan Stanley) deployed increased leverage and record debt-to-equity ratios. Unfortunately, leverage works both ways. When the underlying assets appreciate, the excessive leverage creates record profits. But, when the assets depreciate, they wipe out the equity. This is what happened here, and three of the above banks—Merrill, Bear Stearns, and Lehman Brothers—did not survive.

–Rich Burrit

Realtors and appraisers: They encouraged people to buy homes who had no business doing so. In the state of Arizona, there was an influx of new realtors as well as mortgage companies that are no longer in business. They made their commissions and are no longer around. Realtors and appraisers work together, don't they?

–Maryellen Kitchen

Rating agencies: The true cause of the housing crisis was because sub-prime loans were mixed in with prime loans and sold as AAA-rated securities. Wall Street bankers bought them at a premium price. They used them as collateral to borrow even more money. As some of the sub-prime loans went into default, it was clear that the rating companies had falsely rated the securities. Then, those holding the mortgage securities as collateral called them due, and those buying the securities stopped doing so. I think the biggest blame goes to the rating companies.

–Robert Morse

Bill Clinton: I think one must be fair in assigning blame. The one part of your Sunday column I thought remiss was not noting that President Clinton enthusiastically signed off on the repeal of Glass-Steagall Act in 1999. If one is going to point a finger at Mr. Bush, then one must note Clinton's hand in today's imbroglio. I wonder if Mr. Clinton acknowledges his mistake.

Rating agencies, Bill Clinton, and Alan Greenspan: Your article "Placing Blame..." was excellent. It should have been on the front page of the paper. I would, however, like to point out that you missed one major area of blame, which is the ratings companies (Moody's, et. al.). These companies acted in a complicit manner by keeping artificially high ratings for the Goldmans, Lehmans and AIGs of the world. This ratings fraud led many average investors to believe that everything was okay.

Also, I noticed that you rightly called out the Bush administration. In all fairness, and in your effort to remain apolitical, if you are going to name Bush, then it would have also been appropriate for you to name Alan Greenspan and Bill Clinton. The easy-money policy began during Clinton's administration, and Clinton was the President who signed the repeal in 1999. I agree that the "buck stops here" with the current administration. However, the seeds for this crisis were planted before Bush was in office, so the buck also stopped with Clinton.

–Dwayne Witten

Steve's take: These readers correctly pointed out the culpability of "Excessive Leverage by Investment Banks", "Rating Agencies", "Realtors and Appraisers", and "Bill Clinton and Alan Greenspan." I was particularly remiss for leaving Alan Greenspan off my previous list. As the chairman of Federal Reserve Board for 18 years, he presided over the formation of the biggest financial collapse since the Great Depression; and he has largely gotten a pass (including from me in my first write up). I stand corrected, and Alan Greenspan has much to answer for.

Do not bail out housing speculators; incentivize home buyers

This question was asked during the housing crisis of 2007/2008. The answer is relevant even today.

Question: There are many ideas floating around for solving the housing crisis. This is more of a business question than a financial one, because it is affecting the economy, businesses, the stock market, etc. Can you share your opinion about how to solve this crisis?

-Mark, Phoenix

Answer: First, let me say that I am glad it is not my responsibility to solve this crisis. At the very same time, I feel that the ones responsible for solving it are not going to do so, either. Good solutions have a very hard time emerging in an election year. Politics dominates everything. Every idea is weighed by how many voters it would please. Therefore, I am skeptical about most of the ideas that are floating around right now.

One idea is that we should freeze interest rates for homeowners. Haven't we learned from history that price controls do not work? Besides, it penalizes homeowners who made a conservative decision of getting a fixed-rate mortgage at a higher rate. And it rewards speculators who took on teaser interest rates to buy bigger houses than they could afford.

Additionally, if you freeze rates for five years for existing homeowners, it could drive rates for new mortgages sky high, because banks will have to make up the shortfall. That, in turn, will hurt the very housing market that you are trying to prop up.

There are other solutions being proposed, such as spending $300 billion to create a federal agency to buy delinquent home mortgages and bail out homeowners. That is also a moral hazard, and it incubates a culture that the government will bail you out if many people were to make the same mistake and bet on the wrong side.

It is a lot easier to criticize other people's ideas than it is to come up with your own viable ideas. I do not have a solution, either. So, I am going to share with you a good idea that I read in the *Financial Times* during my recent visit to Europe. However, the following is a paraphrase, with some of the words and twist being my own.

We should use the $300B housing-crisis budget that is being proposed to create a tax credit for homeowners. The tax credit would make houses more affordable and would move the line between when it is more cost effective to buy versus renting. Therefore, it would create additional demand for houses, which in turn would help to prop up house prices. This would also enable current homeowners to sell their houses and avoid a downward financial spiral. Additionally, new mortgages should require reasonable down payments and verified credit worthiness. This tax credit could phase out above a certain income, to avoid any "helping the rich" arguments. And, the entire tax credit could phase out over time, as the crisis is slowly resolved.

I like this idea because it provides stimulus to housing demand among those who are best positioned to put upward pressure on house prices. This demand, in turn, would provide an exit route to those currently unable to sell their houses.

Dealing with volatile home values

Question: My wife and I have a house in Escrow that is undergoing loan approval. The contract price on the house is $290K. We are putting down 5% and getting a loan for $275K. The lender has already received an appraisal for the home that meets the loan criteria. However, a home in the same neighborhood with the same floor plan just closed escrow at a price of $270K. Thus, we will owe more to our house than its value. Can we get out of our contract without losing our $5K earnest-money deposit?

-John and Melinda, Phoenix

Answer: We are in one of the most volatile real-estate markets in decades. Even in a normal market, the price of two similar houses can vary by 7%—which is the difference in your case. The price of the other home does not tell you everything. The other house may have a smaller yard, fewer upgrades, a lesser view, or it may be in a less desired location.

During the current mortgage crisis, house prices can vary more than normal. In your case, the seller of the comparable home may be in foreclosure or behind in payments or could be motivated for a different reason to sell at a lower price. They may have a more able buyer who paid in cash for a quick close. For all we know, the other buyer could have paid part of the price in barter by allowing the seller the use of his condominium in Hawaii or by throwing in a boat. My point is that you do not know all the conditions under which the other house was sold.

You made a deal with your seller in good faith. The seller took his home off the market while you underwent loan approval. The appraisal verified the value of the property to satisfy the loan requirement. So, if you back out of the deal now, your seller would be financially damaged and entitled to keep all or part of your $5K earnest-money deposit.

The only way you can get out of the deal is if there are still some closing conditions that have not been met. For example, your contract calls for your approval of the home inspection as a condition. You could object to certain findings in the inspection. And if the seller does not agree to correct some expensive finding, then you are entitled to break the contract. However, you may already be past such closing conditions.

At this point in time, I see only one feasible option. You should call your lender and tell him the price of the house in the neighborhood. Then tell the lender that you will not make the payments on a house loan that is upside down from the start. Ask the lender to reject your loan application. The lender will likely get spooked and reject the loan. This will, in turn, get you out of your real-estate contract without losing your deposit. And your seller will hate me.

More on negotiating real-estate deals

I have received many emails regarding my above column, "Use care—Housing is Volatile", from both home buyers and realtors. I appreciate all feedback—positive or negative. The feedback from buyers was largely positive, as they were looking for some protection in their contracts, should their prospective homes' value drop precipitously. The feedback from realtors was universally negative. They labeled my advice as, "not acting in good faith", "unethical", and they saw it as cheating the realtors out of commission (both the buyer's and the seller's realtor). Some have written that both realtors can sue the buyer for the loss of their commission. So, let me add some color to my response.

I talked to the buyers, whose names were disguised on the paper upon their request. They had no realtor involved. The seller did not have a realtor involved, either. It was a "For Sale by Owner" scenario. They did not use a standard real-estate contract. They drew up a contract, and they did not have all the clauses that a standard real-estate contract would. Why did they do it this way? They did it to save money. The seller did not want a realtor so they could save on commission. The buyers saw the sign while driving by the property and negotiated the sale themselves. They were under the impression that this yielded a better deal from the seller. That is why they were so disturbed when another house, which was sold through realtors, sold for 7% less than the house they were purchasing.

So, as far as the contract is concerned, there would be no breach of contract if the buyers followed my advice. In retrospect, I realize that readers of the column would not have been aware of all these details, but I could not put all that into the paper because of space constraints. The buyers were essentially resigned to the idea that they would lose their security deposit if they walked away from the contract. If they had gone to a lawyer, they would likely have asked, "What can I do to get out of this contract?" Instead, that is what they asked me.

I am not a lawyer, but the contract was very skimpy, with a price and a few escrow instructions. While it did stipulate that the deal was subject to loan approval. It did not even say that buyers were required to do their best, in good faith, to obtain a loan. So, I felt that the seller tried to sell the house without a realtor, a lawyer, or even the knowledge to write an adequate contract. Any lawyer would have given the buyers the same advice regarding how to get out of that contract.

Some of the realtors writing to me asked, "Who are you to be providing real-estate advice?" They are probably correct. I do not have a real-estate license. However, after buying and selling more than thirty investment properties over the last 23 years, I know more than many real-estate agents with just a year or less of experience;

and have often corrected them on many mistakes. But I accept the criticism that I should not be dishing out such advice in writing.

My column is a business-advice column. Occasionally, I end up selecting a question that deviates from business advice. Such deviations have been in finance (401k, managing money), estate planning and this time, in real estate. I have seen some financial advisors jump on my financial-advice columns as invading their territory, and now I am hearing the same thing from realtors.

One of my questions is, why am I getting so many questions on personal finance and real estate? I have found the answer to be that readers are not satisfied with the advice they are getting from some financial advisors and some realtors. I have personally spoken with many of my readers. They see the advice they get from licensed practitioners as serving their own commission interests, and not the interests of their clients. So, readers are turning to independent advice/opinions. Most of my columns that are not directly related to business advice have stated that readers should seek further advice from licensed practitioners before taking any action. I realize that I did not give such a warning in the column under question. However, I did tell the buyers directly that they should seek professional advice.

This story does have a happy ending. The buyers, upon receiving my advice, decided to spend a few hundred dollars on getting a new independent appraisal. The appraisal was consistent with what they were paying. Additionally, the appraiser discovered that the lower-priced house in the neighborhood was sold as a fixer-upper and needed a lot of work inside. It was a distress sale by a divorcing couple. After receiving this new information from the appraiser, the buyers decided to go ahead with the purchase. They obtained loan approval and have since closed escrow.

The buyers and sellers are both happy. So, this saga ended well. But the plight of hundreds of homeowners continues in this volatile real-estate market.

What created the housing crash?

Question: I have heard various answers as to what created the housing crash. Some are blaming homeowners, others are blaming banks, the Government, the economy, etc. What do you believe led to the housing crash?

-Jonathan, Phoenix

Answer: It is a very good question that does not have a simple answer. Historians will probably argue about this for a long time, and many books will be written on the subject. I have a very simple way of explaining what caused the housing crash.

It all started with two issues—an incorrect public policy and an incorrect assumption about home values.

There was a public policy that homeownership was good for everyone. Under that policy, the higher the percentage of homeowners in the country, the better it was. Homeownership as a public policy became a symbol of success, as if the renters were second-class citizens. Really? When someone buys a home with a 100% mortgage, is he or she really an owner? The bank is the owner, and that person is simply a renter who, instead of paying rent, is now paying a mortgage payment.

The second false assumption was that home values could only go up. There is no asset in this world that only goes up, including stocks, bonds, gold, oil, commodities, foreign currency, etc. Real-estate prices have crashed before, in prior U.S. recessions. They also crashed in Japan, resulting in two decades of no economic growth. So, why everyone assumed that home values would only go up is beyond me.

With these two bad assumptions, the rest of the course was set. Banks were willing to lend 100% of the home's value, because they assumed that housing prices would only go up. So, if the borrower lost his job, he could sell the house at a higher price. Government institutions implemented the public policy that homeownership was good. They started pushing lenders to loan money to non-creditworthy buyers to show higher home-ownership percentages. Then lenders, in trying to outbid their competition, started making riskier and riskier loans. Eventually, they had many sub-prime mortgages, and even ALT-A mortgages in which the homeowner does not even document their income, expenses, and ability to pay.

How could we not have known that this would end badly? The interest rates went up, some adjustable-rate mortgage rates adjusted up, homeowners could not pay and went into foreclosure, the home values came down, and the negative spiral set in.

Now, I am not saying that homeownership is bad. But homeownership should be promoted with reasonable down payments and credit standards. This will build public policy on a strong foundation, and not on a house of cards.

As always, I welcome readers' responses—both for and against my analysis. I will publish a follow-up column if there are enough good responses.

Diversify income to weather financial storms

Question: My husband and I are real-estate agents. Because of the mortgage crisis, we have not sold any houses lately. Our friends who are also real estate agents are in a similar situation. What can you suggest that we do to ride out this worst market in residential real estate in decades?

-Kathy and Tom, Phoenix

Answer: I wrote an earlier column in these pages, "Success demands lifelong education," which applies to your situation. But let us tackle this subject more specifically for your case.

In the new economy, people must commit themselves to a life-long learning career. If you sit in one job doing the same work for many years and the economic winds eliminate your job, you are left with very few options. Instead, you must commit yourself to acquiring a variety of skills during your lifetime.

In your case, there are a few related fields in real estate that are not suffering as much from the debt crisis. For example, can you migrate to selling commercial real estate, which is not as affected?

There are a lot of homeowners who are delinquent in their mortgage payments, and the banks do not want the properties back. Banks have already foreclosed on too many houses. They would rather work with homeowners, but many do not have the skills and they just stop paying. Can you represent delinquent homeowners in negotiating with the bank to lower their interest rates, accept short sales, or write off some principal in exchange for the homeowner staying in the home and making payments?

Can you put together a program where you pool money from investors to buy homes in foreclosure sales at a fraction of the fair market value? Can you then fix up the homes, rent them, and manage those investments for the pool?

With many baby boomers heading into their retirement years, reverse mortgages are becoming more popular. Can you market a program where you can help senior citizens acquire reverse mortgages? This would provide them with a steady paycheck from the bank every month, instead of having to rely solely on social security or their children.

Being in the real-estate profession, you must see many other job functions, such as property appraisers, property inspectors, escrow officers, foreclosure-sale specialists, and maintenance coordinators. However, I know that it is a lot easier for me to suggest all of this than it is for one to act on this advice.

It would have been better for you to diversify your income stream into some of these areas when times were good. But most people do not think of diversification when times are good. What should you do now? You or your husband should get a job to bring in a steady paycheck. The other spouse should venture into one or two of these alternate areas in real estate, along with continuing to sell residential real estate. Good luck.

Why don't the banks lower the interest rates to prevent foreclosures?

Question: With the financial turmoil largely being blamed on mortgage-backed securities, why don't the banks simply lower the interest rate across the board to reduce the number of foreclosures? For those who are totally tapped out, this probably would do nothing. But for those who are in marginal situations, this could make the difference between foreclosure and keeping their homes. Since foreclosures are bad for everyone except bottom-feeding investors, it would seem to be at least a short-term solution. With the knowledge gained from this type of action, the actual value of mortgage portfolios should be much better known. Companies would be better off having a known asset of lower value, rather than an unknown asset or liability.

-Foley

Answer: Your suggestion does have merit. I am not a banker, but I do not think banks could do this unilaterally without the cost of funds coming down or a government-backed program. Some rules needed to be put in place for implementing the government's rescue plan. Without such rules, there is no way of knowing who needs help. It is reported that many worthy homeowners with jobs, but with no equity in their homes, are going delinquent. That is so that they can negotiate with their banks to lower their mortgages.

I have chastised banks and mortgage companies for their culpability in lowering the lending standards for home mortgages, which has contributed to this mess. But now if banks were to unilaterally lower interest rates, they would be even deeper in the red. This is because they would lose money on many performing loans, too.

Therefore, the interest rates need to be brought down in an orderly fashion, with the Federal Reserve Board setting short-term interest rates. The Fed has taken interest rates down to historical lows of zero to 0.25%. With that, the longer-term rates to which mortgages are tied are starting to move down.

Adjustable mortgages have a time lag. Many of them adjust every six months, tied to some cost-of-funds index. As interest rates come down, many homeowners in marginal situations will start to be rescued. At the same time, lower rates will make homes more affordable for new buyers. The first-time home buyers' credit will also help to generate demand. This starts to create a bottom in the housing crisis, and a housing recovery could begin.

This scenario, in turn, would start to stabilize mortgage portfolio values, which would then begin to stabilize banks' balance sheets.

The downward spiral from housing got us into this mess, and even a hint of an upward spiral could start to get us out of it.

Can the bank seize my account to satisfy a delinquent mortgage?

Question: I can no longer afford to keep my home. The mortgage is under water, so I cannot sell it. I will have to let it go back to the bank. Meanwhile, I am trying to save some money to pay for an apartment after the foreclosure. I have heard that the bank holding my mortgage can seize the money from my account, even though it is not in the same bank. Now I cannot sleep at night. Do I need to put the money under my mattress to prevent that from happening?

-Liz M., Phoenix

Answer: Before I answer your question, please know that I am not a lawyer. Please consult your own lawyer, accountant, or tax advisor before you act on any of my advice. You can also check out the Web site www.homerecovery.org. They have good information and a number to call for free help with your options.

Arizona is a "non-recourse state". If you put the mortgage on the home when you bought it, then that mortgage is considered a "non-recourse" loan. This means that the lender has no other recourse, other than recouping its money from the house itself. The lender can foreclose on the home. But if that does not fully recover the lender's losses, then it cannot go after any of your other assets. In that case, there is no need for you to put your money under your mattress.

However, if it was a "refinance mortgage", where you received a loan more than the value of your previous mortgage, then the mortgage becomes a "recourse" loan. In that case, the lender can go after your other assets if the foreclosure does not completely recoup its losses.

There are other loans that can be recourse loans or non-recourse loans. Many car loans, for example, are non-recourse loans. If the repossession of your car does not satisfy the loan on the car, the lender cannot go after your other assets. Some other types of loans can be recourse loans. In those cases, the lender cannot just seize your account—even if the account is in the same bank. The lender must sue you and get a judgment. Only then can it attach that judgment to your bank account, hence recouping its losses. No such avenue is available to the lender for a mortgage loan that was a "purchase mortgage".

Before you decide that you will let your house go to the bank, you should talk to the counselors at the web site I recommended. There are several other options available to you, such as a "short sale", "deed-in-lieu of foreclosure" and "loan-modification programs". Please review those options before you let your house go into foreclosure.

The rules on "recourse versus non-recourse" loans vary by state. In this time of significant turmoil with the mortgage markets, many states have been modifying their rules. The rules also get complicated if there is a second mortgage involved, regarding whether it was at the time of purchase or was added later. That is why I strongly recommend that you seek expert legal advice before you take any action.

Chapter 22: Higher education and applied skills

Take a job or get master's degree

Question: I am graduating from ASU with a bachelor's degree in engineering. I have a good-paying job offer from a local company. However, my dad wants me to continue for a master's degree. He thinks it will be good for my career, long term. I would value your opinion.

-Keith, Mesa

Answer: Your father is not wrong in saying that this will be good for your career, long term. However, a good job offer is hard to decline. You may be tired of studying and want a break from the college routine—and by getting into the job market, you will have more money.

There is a way to accomplish both. It is usually a good idea to get some practical job experience between a bachelor's and master's degree. Many companies will pay for your expenses (tuition and books), if you seek higher education in your field. So, you could accept the job offer and then pursue a Master's, part-time, after a year or two.

The problem, often, is that it is easy to get busy in life, get married, have children, and never get around to obtaining a higher degree. So, if your dad pays for your Master's, you may want to do it now. Otherwise, you can do it later when you can get your company to pay for it. The graduating classes of today will have to compete with Chinese and Indians for their entire lives—two nationalities with a very high commitment to higher education. Look at any graduate-school engineering class, over 80% are Asians. Therefore, for your long-term career success, an MS or MBA will be very beneficial.

I am aware that there are many successful businesspeople who would disagree with me, as they only have a bachelor's degree. They are entitled to their opinions. But you did not ask them—you asked Steve.

How to help STEM education in Arizona

Question: I know that you are a supporter of the FIRST Robotics competition, which is helping to improve Science, Technology, Engineering and Math (STEM) education in Arizona. How can an individual and corporations participate and help to increase the reach of this competition?

-Doug Diehl, Phoenix

Answer: FIRST, in this context, stands for "For Inspiration and Recognition of Science and Technology". It is a nationwide non-profit 501(c) (3) organization that was started about thirty years ago in New Hampshire by Segway inventor Dean Kamen. The goal of FIRST is to inspire high-school students, teachers, parents, and community in the appreciation of science and technology.

The way we achieve that goal is to team up students with engineers and mentors from professional corporations in solving an engineering problem in a very intense and competitive way. That engineering problem happens to be the building of a robot that competes with other robots in a sports-like competition.

We brought the Arizona FIRST Regional Robotics competition to Phoenix in 2003. Last year, we had fifty-two high-school teams with 1,075 students participating in this exciting competition.

The students work in teams to design, manufacture, build, and program a robot from a very general kit of parts over a six-week period. In the process, the students are learning about the principles of STEM. At the same time, they are also learning about fundraising, brainstorming, teamwork, conflict resolution, multi-tasking, communication skills, web site development and working under schedule pressure. These are all real-life skills that the students need in their lives and careers.

Per a study that was conducted by Brandeis University and funded by the Ford Foundation, 88% of FIRST students attend college and 55% major in science or engineering. FIRST alumni are ten times as likely to have a co-op or internship job during their college freshman year.

The Arizona Regional competition requires $200K a year, which comes as sponsorships from various corporations and individuals. In addition, each team raises ~$10K for the cost of the kit of parts and other expenses. Here is how individuals and corporations can help:

- Arizona allows each couple a $400 tax credit ($200 for singles) for donations to an after-school activity. This can help a school raise $10K for its entry into the Robotics competition. You get dollar-for-dollar credit from your Arizona taxes, costing you nothing.

- If you are donating to United Way, you may ask them to redirect a portion of your contributions to AZFirst. This will help us raise the $200K needed to run the competition.

- As a corporation, you can help drive the $400 tax credit initiative and the United Way donation initiative in your company. You can also become a sponsor of the competition with significant recognition opportunities.

- There are also numerous volunteering opportunities as referees, judges, mentors, planning-committee members, and various duties at the competition.

The reason AZ companies should care about the FIRST program is that it is an investment in the education of our young people as future employees.

For further information on all these opportunities, please contact Annalisa.Regalado@Microchip.com.

Getting youth excited about science and technology

Question: The United States is seeing a continuous decline in the interest in science and technology among high-school teens. How can we get young people more involved in science and technology? What is your take on science and engineering competitions?

-Marcos, Phoenix

Answer: You have really touched on one of my passions. You are correct that there is a precipitous decline in the interest in math, science, and technology among high-school students. Talk to today's high-school students. Their role models are sports figures, singers, or Hollywood stars.

Today's society takes all the inventions of the past for granted. Cars run, planes fly, personal computers work, smart phones are great, water is drinkable, and information is at your fingertips on the internet. These are all inventions of the last century, which were improved by a successive generation of engineers. And, no, Al Gore did not invent the internet—engineers did.

But it is evident that engineering is in crisis today. Enrollment for undergraduate and graduate engineering majors is dropping precipitously. As a direct result, the country stands to lose its technological superiority in the next decade or two.

Enter FIRST, an organization that has been trying to stem this tide. FIRST stands for: For Inspiration and Recognition of Science and Technology. The dream of this organization is that one day the work of scientists and engineers will be as revered as the sports figures and Hollywood stars are today. That is a very tall order.

The mission of FIRST is to inspire students, and their teachers, schools, parents, and communities to appreciate science and technology. They accomplish this by training students, in partnership with mentors and engineers from professional corporations, to solve an engineering problem in an intense, fun, and competitive way. And, that engineering problem just happens to be building a robot. With FIRST, the high-school students are learning the concepts of science, electrical engineering, mechanical engineering, programming- and computer-aided design.

At the same time, FIRST students are learning about fund raising, team building; brainstorming; conflict resolution; web site development; multitasking; speaking to tournament judges; and how to document their work. In other words, these high school students are learning real life skills. So, the end goal of this competition is not about building a winning robot; the end goal is to build productive citizens.

Many universities and corporations have pitched in, with more than $60 million in scholarships reserved for students participating in the FIRST robotics competition.

The Arizona Robotics championship is held in October every year at Arizona State University. You can find more information about FIRST at www.firstinspires.org. For the Arizona regional competition, you can go to www.azfirst.org.

Hands-on experience versus a degree

Question: I want to build a good foundation for the rest of my life. Being from another country, trying to fit into the American lifestyle has been easy except for one thing. I have always been a hands-on person. But employers here are more focused on education and having a college degree, rather than hands-on experience. What do you think is more important in my young life—getting a degree or doing what I am comfortable with and building experience in the field?

-Alex, Chandler

Answer: First of all, you are likely to thrive in your career if you choose a path that you love and enjoy. If you are comfortable with building hands-on experience, as you described, then there is nothing wrong with choosing that path. But, if you are not willing to make sacrifices to gain more education, then there will be consequences and limitations in your career.

From your question (which was abridged for this column) I know that you work for a technology company. Technology companies hire a large number of new colleges graduates every year. Some of them have bachelor's degrees, some have master's, and some may even have PhDs. These graduates are hired in various engineering positions in research, manufacturing, marketing, IT, etc.

Technology companies also hire many non-degreed people. But they are mainly hired in manufacturing operations (production), as maintenance technicians, electricians, plumbers, shipping/receiving clerks, etc.

Can a person with years of hands-on experience but without a degree rise to executive positions within a company? The answer is yes, but it is rare. It takes a unique individual to achieve that kind of success. I do not have the exact data, but I believe that 95%+ of the executive positions at technology companies are held by degreed individuals.

So, you have a choice to make. If you stop at high-school graduation and then work your way up with hands-on experience, you may do what is comfortable to you, but you may also limit your ultimate career success.

There is a way to accomplish both. Many companies will pay for your expenses (tuition and books) if you seek a degree in your field. So, you could be gaining hands-on experience and pursuing a degree.

The problem, often, is that it is easy to get busy in life, get married, have children, and never get around to obtaining a degree. The graduating classes of today will have to compete with the Chinese and Indians for their entire lives—two nationalities with a very high commitment to degreed education. Non-degreed individuals will have a harder and harder time competing with this tremendous foreign competition.

I understand that this is a controversial topic. Not everyone thinks and believes the same in this respect. There are successful businesspeople who would disagree with me because they have made it without a college degree. They are entitled to their opinions.

Which foreign language to learn

Question: I am an undergraduate engineering student at ASU. Which foreign language would you suggest for studying and why?

-Gil, Mesa

Answer: First, I would say that learning a foreign language is a wonderful thing. I always admire people who can speak multiple languages. Deciding which foreign language to study is a complicated subject. There are a lot of personal and family-background related biases that play a role in the selection of a foreign language. I will assume that your question relates to which foreign language would be best for you in your career as an engineer.

Your obvious choices are French, German, Italian, Japanese, Chinese, Portuguese (Brazil), Spanish, or Hindi (India). So, let us take them one by one.

On average, the French do not speak English well. Even if they do speak English, they do not like it. So, if you speak French, they will like you more. Most multinational companies do business in France. So, French is a good choice.

Germans speak English very well. So, unless you have a social or family-background related bias, I would skip German.

Italian will help you conduct business in Italy, but not as much as French will help you in France. Besides, France is a larger market than Italy.

Japanese is very difficult to learn unless you learned it as a child. Japanese will help you a lot when conducting business in Japan, but it would not be my first choice for a Kanji-character-based Asian language. My first choice would be Chinese.

China is the fastest growing large economy in the world. It is almost certain that an engineer working for a multinational company within the next 30 years will either do business with China or compete with China. So, Chinese is my runaway #1 choice.

Portuguese is useful only in Portugal and Brazil. Both are relatively small markets. Spanish is most useful socially in Arizona and other areas of the U.S., but Spanish-speaking countries are also relatively small markets.

All Indians speak English reasonably well, due to the country's historical British influence. Different parts of India have different local dialects, so Indians speak English among themselves. And English is the language of business in India. Therefore, I would not invest in learning Hindi.

Bottom line: If you need to select one language to learn, I will pick Chinese. I may receive letters from various nationalities objecting to my answer. Others are entitled to their opinion. You asked Steve, and my answer is time tested with extensive international business travel over the last 40 years.

For your great question, I say Xie Xie (thank you in Chinese).

Which skills are useful?

Question: I am an engineering student. Other than the Chinese language that you recommended in your column, what other skills would be useful in my engineering career; skills that I am not likely to learn as a part of my engineering curriculum?

-Isaac

Answer: There are many skills that will be helpful in your career. But you will have to make an extra effort to seek out and practice these skills.

Get an internship during the summer in an engineering corporation. Intern work demonstrates a student's real-world accomplishments, beyond just bookwork. It also gives you a feel for the work environment and the traits needed to become successful.

Teamwork: The workplace is made up of teams. Most schoolwork requires individual talent and knowledge. I would not want to replace schoolwork, but you also need to learn teamwork. (The closest an engineering student comes to teamwork is working with his lab partner.) Teamwork entails understanding the goals of the team and prioritizing them above the goals of the individual. Find opportunities to learn about teamwork.

Engineering project management and time management: You need to be familiar with subjects like schedule development, Project (or Program) Evaluation and Review Technique (PERT) charting, workforce needs and planning. You also need to learn about organizing your work, multi-tasking, and time-management skills. In corporations, you are rarely working on only one project. Multi-tasking can very quickly get out of hand if proper time and project-management skills are not utilized.

Written and verbal communication skills: Most students never have to address a group of people or write—beyond dry, technical jargon to describe their technical work to other technical types. Many times, I find engineers in the workplace are unable to express themselves in a meeting. So, developing and practicing good written and verbal skills will help you in your career.

Presentation skills: After a new college graduate joins our company, it does not take very long before they need to stand up in front of a group of people and make a presentation. In learning presentation skills, you need to overcome stage fright and develop a presentation style. You only get one chance to make a first impression, and that impression better be a good one.

People skills: In the workplace, I constantly see people that get along and ones that do not. It is an oversimplification, but the famous Dilbert cartoon series does reflect how the public views most techie types. It depicts that most engineers cannot make themselves understood well, especially to non-tech types. Many are often offended by this stereotyped image, but there is some merit in the implied criticism. Engineers are often difficult to manage, and they manage themselves poorly. I believe that acquiring and developing people skills can begin in school.

All of this is probably too much to swallow. But anything you can practice here will give you a leg up over the average engineering graduate. Good luck in your education and call us when you graduate.

Chapter 23: Consumer related questions

Restocking charge

Question: I bought a PC from a retail store as a Christmas gift for my son. After my son opened it, he did not like it. He wanted one with a totally different brand and operating system. So, I tried to return it to the retail store. The store charged me a 15% restocking fee for returning the product. I was very upset. Is this fee fair? Should the government not pass a law against this restocking fee?

-Vicky, Scottsdale

Answer: It is not uncommon for a merchant to charge a restocking fee for a returned product, especially an expensive one like a PC. Think of it this way. The store inventoried the product, displayed a demo on their floor, the salesperson probably helped you with your selection and checked you out. Then, depending on the inventory situation, the product was unavailable to be sold to anyone else. You kept the product for many days, and then presented it as a gift to your son. He opened it, hooked it up, used it and then did not like it. Then you took it back. The plastic wraps were cut open, it was not factory packed anymore. And, for all we know, it may be damaged.

If you were the second buyer of that PC and took it home and then found that you got a PC that had been returned by someone, would you be happy? I know that most people would not be happy. They bought a brand-new PC and expected a brand-new one that is factory wrapped.

So, you see the problem. When you took your PC back, did you destroy some value for the retailer? After his initial investment in stocking, displaying, and selling it to you, if he takes the product back, he has to spend more money to re-pack it to look like the original or he has to discount it. Either way, he has some cost involved and he is entitled to pass that cost to you in the form of a restocking charge.

Your retailer should have told you about the restocking charge at the time of sale. And there is often no restocking charge if you did not open the package and returned it within a short period (usually 14 days).

As a consumer, I hate these charges, too. But, as a businessman, I think they are fair. I believe that the government should not legislate the restocking charge. The free-market economy should drive it. If another retailer does not charge for restocking, then your retailer will start to lose a lot of business. This competitive factor should drive the market and the restocking charge.

Baggage transfer

Question: I took a Southwest Airlines flight from Phoenix to Los Angeles connecting to a United Airlines flight to Tokyo, to visit my son for Christmas. At the check-in counter, the agent would not check my luggage to Tokyo. She would only check it to LAX which was the Southwest portion of the flight. In LAX, I had to go to baggage claim, wait for my baggage and then recheck it. With all the holiday traffic, I missed my flight and had to go through a lot of frustration to get home with my luggage. Is it reasonable for Southwest Airlines to not transfer my baggage to another carrier?

-Natsumi, Phoenix

Answer: Southwest Airlines is a business, and a business is allowed to define their product and then sell and provide that product consistently. Southwest is a low-cost, point-to-point carrier. They do not transfer luggage to other carriers, provide assigned seating, or serve food on the flights (other than pretzels). This is how they define their product, and then they deliver that product consistently at low cost and better than any other carrier.

Most frequent fliers are aware of such Southwest practices and only choose Southwest when they are flying point-to-point within Southwest's network. If they have to make a connection to another carrier, they allow sufficient time to receive their baggage and recheck it. If this was your first time making a connection with another carrier from Southwest, then your frustration is understandable.

So, your question is whether these Southwest practices are reasonable? Southwest prides itself in its service and does not want to be responsible for lost luggage by other carriers who have worse records. (I do not imply that United has a worse record.) And most fliers feel that for what Southwest saves them, the lack of certain privileges is reasonable. You must make your own decision as to what is reasonable for you. As a business, Southwest Airlines has the right to define its product. As a consumer, you have a choice of carriers and the right to choose the appropriate product for a price.

I invite Southwest Airlines to answer the question in a different way if they like. Subject to editorial review, I would be happy to publish their comments.

I am very sorry for the hassle that you went through. My responses in this column tend to represent objective business advice. The person asking the question may not always get what they want to hear. In this case, I have a hard time pinning the blame on Southwest Airlines.

Discounting product versus mail in rebate

Question: Our company makes aftermarket automotive products that are sold through auto-parts retailers. We have an excellent new product that is better than the competition's. I believe that it should be discounted for market introduction to create awareness. But management insists on offering a mail-in rebate. Mail-in rebates are annoying to the customer. What is your opinion?

-Paul, Scottsdale

Answer: One thing that you and your management agree on is that your product is superior to the competition, and it should be promoted at market introduction. However, you are arguing about the best method for promotion. Should you offer a discount or a mail-in rebate?

Offering a straight discount has the benefit of a better price for the customer on the retail shelf, compared to the product from your competition. However, this type of discount does not promote your product as having superior quality. It only seems better in terms of price. And it can cheapen your brand.

A mail-in rebate, on the other hand, establishes the price of the product at a higher value, perhaps equal to or even higher than the competition. This gives the impression to consumers that your product is superior. Often, this will cause them to read the details of your packaging and ask questions of the retail clerk, as they tend to become interested in finding out why the product is better. If the customer can then buy your product with a mail-in rebate, they believe that they are buying a superior product at a sale price.

A good portion of the customers buying with a mail-in rebate will never send in the rebate request. In those cases, your company gets a higher margin. If the customer does send the mail-in rebate request, your company gets the benefit of obtaining their contact details. These can be used to market future products or upgrades.

So, even though mail-in rebates can sometimes be annoying, customers usually perceive the price of the product to be equal to the price after the rebate. Marketing is more of an art than a science, so the results of marketing campaigns are not always predictable.

A possible hybrid approach would be to offer an "instant rebate" that is subtracted from the price at the register. Such rebates are usually offered for a very limited time. This establishes a higher price for the brand and acts as a discount to the customer. It also puts control in your company's hands as to how to proceed after the expiration date. Based on the results, you can renew the rebate or take the price higher. It also avoids the costs of administering a mail-in rebate program. A trade-off with this plan is that, while you achieve the lower-price promotion, you do not get the contact details of the customer. So, this approach could be a compromise for your company to consider.

Marketing is the art of achieving higher sales and profits than the science of cost and competitive pricing would indicate. Good luck with the marketing of your new product.

Do not sweat the small stuff

Question: I was shopping at a retail store, and the buzzer went off when I tried to walk out with my purchased merchandise. I was very embarrassed for seemingly being accused of stealing. What can I do?

-Kenneth, Phoenix

Answer: This has probably happened to everyone at some time. Let me tell you my story. I was shopping at Walgreens. After checkout, when I started to walk out, the buzzer went off. I was angry for the same reason that you were—seemingly being accused of stealing. So, I went back to the cashier, threw my bag on the counter, and told the cashier, "Check my bag to see why the buzzer went off like I was stealing something." The woman politely said, "Sir, it must be your electric personality that set the buzzer off. You are all clear to go out." My anger changed into embarrassment. I felt small. But I was also very impressed with the customer-service skills of this woman, and I continue to shop at this Walgreens.

I am not sure how the episode concluded in your case. The doors of these stores have coils on both sides that create a field. When an identification tag enters this field, it sets the buzzer off. The cashier is supposed to remove or disable the tag, but sometimes the cashier forgets. Other times, the ID tag reader can misread.

If you have not stolen anything, you have nothing to worry about. This minor embarrassment is no more than what you feel at the airports, when you are getting wanded down with your arms spread. Neither the technology nor the operators are perfect, and sometimes a mistake will happen.

I do not have a very good suggestion for you regarding what to do. If your question implies getting some compensation from the store for your embarrassment, that is a tough row to hoe. I am not a lawyer, but a lawyer may not take your case on contingency. Spending your own money to pursue this would be throwing good money after bad. If your episode ended well like mine did, you should forget it. If you were not treated well, you should not patronize that store again.

In general, I feel that there are much bigger problems in this world. Let us tackle some of those, and not sweat the small stuff.

Customer service at airline counters

Question: I am a trainer at Sky Harbor Airport for a major airline, and one part of my job responsibilities is to train our ticket counter and gate agents in customer service. Today, we do not rank very well among the ten major airlines that report customer-service complaints to the Department of Transportation. In Phoenix, we want to improve and provide the best customer service in our industry. What are the best resources and books to read on customer service?

-Chuck, Phoenix

Answer: In my opinion, diving straight into many of the great books available may not be the right starting point. If the employees are not performing, there may be several reasons for their lack of improvement. It may be that they are denying the existence of the problem. So, the first step often entails helping the employees gain awareness that a problem or issue exists. You have the data from the department of transportation to show that your airline does not rank well.

The second reason is often that the employees blame any and all factors for the problem. They blame the circumstances, other employees, the entire system, or even the customers. It is often good to make some disarming statements such as, "I agree that some factors, such as late arrivals and departures, are to blame. And customers can be a pain." Then, coach employees to take some level of ownership of the issue.

In the next stage, employees often give the appearance of taking ownership of the issue. However, they may just be saying what management wants to hear. They have not taken ownership of the issue, nor do they have a desire to change. They are just playing the game. When the pressure to improve subsides, they revert to their old ways and there is no lasting change.

In the final stage, employees embrace the desired improvements. They set about adapting, acting, and growing. They say, "I own this issue, and I am going to improve." At this stage, the manager and the trainer have two responsibilities. First, they must help the employees gain insight into how the improvement will benefit their performance, increase their value, and enhance their careers. Second, they should assist employees in establishing a development plan that outlines the changes to be made (how, why, and when). I documented this Human Change Process in chapter 11 of my book "Driving Excellence".

One of the best resources in today's business world is Ken Blanchard (author of "One Minute Manager" and "Situational Leadership" www.kenblanchard.com). His three best books about customer service are "Raving Fans", "Whale Done", and "Johnny the Bagger". There are also webinars and other services available on his web site. Three other great books are "FISH" by Stephen Lundin, "Customer Astonishment" by Darby Checketts, and "The Customer Shouts Back" by Ross Shafer. All are great reading materials that will make you stop and think.

Chapter 24: International business issues

Where to set up shop in Asia?

Question: I am the vice president of manufacturing for our company. We own an electronics assembly plant in Singapore that is no longer cost effective because of high labor costs in Singapore. We are evaluating other lower-cost sites in Asia. Everyone says that we should go to China. Can you share your experience in various low-cost Asian countries?

-David, Phoenix

Answer: First, make a list of what is important to your company in site selection for a manufacturing plant, and then prioritize that list. Some of the common attributes companies are looking for include:

1. Lower cost of labor—for both hourly production workers as well as salaried employees.
2. Availability of trained personnel in your line of work.
3. Infrastructure for manufacturing support of your products—availability of equipment, repair services, raw materials, chemicals, water supply, industrial gases, and electricity.
4. Proximity to an international airport with facilities for customs clearance.
5. Business-friendly local and national government.
6. Foreign export zones and the availability of tax incentive (often called tax holidays).
7. Lower rate of business tax.
8. Non-union labor environment.
9. Stability of local currency against the U.S. dollar.
10. Local rate of wage and general inflation.
11. Availability of houses and schools for U.S. expatriate management and their families.
12. An English-speaking workforce is usually scarce, but a huge plus.

Then, you should visit the target countries and meet with other businesses in local industrial parks to understand their benefits and challenges. You should also meet with government officials to understand the tax incentives. Here are some of my recommendations:

1. China: The local currency, the Yuan, is appreciating making it less competitive. Managerial talent is scarce, driving salaries up amongst competitors. Merit raises are about 15% per year—at this rate, China would be uncompetitive in a few years. And, from a diplomatic as well as economic viewpoint, China is on a collision course with the U.S. I would avoid China as a place to build a manufacturing plant. If you go to China, use the subcontracting route rather than owning a plant.
2. India: India is good for software, but not for a hardware manufacturing plant. Labor is very unionized, infrastructure is poor, government policies are not steady, and bureaucratic hurdles at customs make India unattractive.
3. Malaysia, Taiwan, Hong Kong, and Korea: They are all developed countries with higher cost structures, like Singapore.
4. Thailand: Thailand meets every single need I mentioned above, except the labor class is not English speaking. Microchip has a large manufacturing plant in Thailand, and it would be a good choice for you.
5. Philippines: The Philippines meets every single need, and the labor class is English speaking. The Philippines is another great choice.
6. Vietnam: Vietnam offers the lowest labor cost and excellent tax holidays. But you sacrifice a bit with immature industry and developing infrastructure.

So, there you have my analysis. Some countries' consulates may disagree but need not protest. My recommendations are Thailand, The Philippines or Vietnam. I would love to know your final selection and your reasons. Good luck.

Asia business etiquette: Top 10 tips

Question: In my new job, I will be traveling to Asia quite often. I was intrigued by your recent column regarding where to set up shop in Asia. I am a bit apprehensive about the business culture and etiquette in Asia. Can you share a few pointers?

-Frank, Mesa

Answer: The business cultures and etiquette in Asia vary. I will cover ten areas where I see that Americans often stumble. There are plenty of books on the subject if you would like to learn more.

1. The people of most Asian countries, especially Japan, Korea, and China, are very proud of their cultural heritage. So, do not put anyone down or brag about the American culture. The average Chinese person you meet does not feel that he is not free. They are proud of what their country has accomplished.

2. Exchange business cards with both hands. After receiving one, pause to study it a bit. Then, safely put it in your pocket or display it on the table during the meeting. Do not play with the card or mutilate it. In Asia, a business card is an extension of a person and bending it is a form of disrespect.

3. Do not use slang while speaking in Asia. Asians would not understand it. Speak slowly and clearly. Do not make jokes, as Asians do not understand most of the American jokes.

4. Do not tell other businesspeople that their English is good. This may be considered disrespectful, as an educated businessperson is supposed to speak English well.

5. "Yes" does not mean the same thing in every country. If you ask someone to do something in Japan and they say yes, it simply means that they heard you. It does not mean that they agree with you or will do anything for you. In Asia, ask the people to repeat exactly what they are going to do. Then, follow up with a letter or email that restates what was agreed upon.
6. Every restaurant in Japan, Korea, Taiwan, and China will bring you a wet towel to wipe your hands. Use it. In some Asian countries, people will eat anything that once moved. Many of the items that we would lose our appetites over are

delicacies in Asia. Unless you are an adventurous eater, politely decline these items to avoid having to spit out anything you find unpalatable.

7. It is OK to not use chopsticks—just ask for a fork. But, if you try chopsticks, do not lick your chopsticks, and do not stand them in your food. Just place them horizontally on your plate. When taking food from the table, first offer some to your neighbor. Fill his cup of tea before you fill yours.

8. In many Asian countries, it is considered offensive to blow your nose in public, and especially during dinner. This is an absolute no-no in Japan. I wish Americans would not blow their noses at the dining table in the U.S., either. If you need to blow your nose, excuse yourself to the bathroom.

9. Asians take their street shoes off before they enter a private home, religious places, and certain dining establishments. Americans hate to take their shoes off (airports included). Be prepared to take your shoes off in Asia. No smelly socks or holes in your socks, please.

10. The risk of offending someone goes up exponentially when visiting a private home because spouses are often not used to Americans. So, bring a gift for the host/hostess, take your shoes off at the door and do not talk too much. The risk also goes up when you go to bars. Most Asians, especially Japanese and Koreans, will drink you under the table. So, do not make a fool of yourself.

Rating India's progress in electronics

Question: I am asking you this question because I know that you are originally from India. How would you rate the progress India has made in the field of electronics? And what should India do to further use electronics to develop its economy?

-Sunil, Mesa

Answer: I first want to say that, as an American, I am much more concerned about the well-being of the U.S. economy.

When I came to the USA in 1976, the American electronics industry was experiencing rapid growth. The large companies of today, such as Microsoft, Intel, Dell, Apple, Cisco, and Google, were either small companies or not yet formed.

During this era, there were four Asian tigers: Hong Kong, Korea, Taiwan, and Singapore. They were all considered third-world countries. But the economies of these countries were going through rapid growth. In the subsequent 25 years, each of these countries took advantage of the first wave of the electronics and semiconductor manufacturing outsourcing trend. They all, first, focused on building semiconductor assembly/test plants and later fabs. In addition, Taiwan built a PC infrastructure, Korea built a cellular-phone infrastructure, Singapore built a disk-drive storage infrastructure, and Hong Kong built a variety of subcontracting plants while positioning itself as the gateway to China. Today, these four countries are neither poor nor third world countries.

During most of this era, I watched India miss a series of opportunities on the international scene to establish itself as an outsourcing hub, and to rapidly grow its economy. It missed the semiconductor assembly/test plants, the fabs, the computer manufacturing, and then the cell-phone manufacturing. There were two main reasons. First, India went through a series of government and policy changes that sought to protect local companies and viewed foreign investments with suspicion. It was not until the 1990s, when India shifted from its historical socialist bent to a free-market environment, that the economy started to rapidly grow. The second reason was that all the earlier industries were hardware industries. India, with its traditional bureaucracy, has a difficult time providing the infrastructure and logistics support required to manufacture hardware efficiently. For example, it used to take days to clear an incoming or outgoing international shipment.

Then, the software and IT industry came. And this time, the chips were stacked in India's favor. Software has no bureaucratic shipment hurdles because you can ship it over the internet. Helped by significant policy changes from the Government, the special focus of a few state Governments, and aided by world-class educational institutes (IITs); the traditional, hard-working Indian engineers rapidly seized the opportunity and turned India into the software and IT outsourcing capital of the world. Large outsourcing companies like Infosys and Wipro are common names in the USA. Old Indian conglomerates like Tata and Larson & Toubro also formed divisions to grab IT work outsourced from western nations. The industry grew further when American corporations began opening technology centers in India. Today, most American corporations, such as Microsoft, Intel, Dell, Cisco, TI, and Microchip Technology have a significant presence in India.

One challenge westerner has with India is high employee turnover. Indian engineers, especially in high-tech centers like Bengaluru, change jobs rapidly. This slows down the formation of experienced, high-performing teams, and is an impediment blocking the continued and increased commitment of American corporations to India. Many are now building competitive technology centers in places like Romania, Hungary, and the Philippines.

While the IT industry is providing excellent opportunities to educated engineers, there is still more that needs to be done to employ the very large uneducated class. This is where the hardware manufacturing industry comes in. India must find a way to attract the next wave of semiconductor fabs, assembly/test plants, computer, cellphone, and other consumer-electronics manufacturing plants. China is clearly the runaway leader, here. India has a lot to do to even get started. Setting up a few export zones with good infrastructure and logistics support, lowering import duties, and reducing bureaucratic hurdles and bribery would be good starting points.

I would close with two comments that I made to my two children about their grades. I say to India- a very nice job, and there is room for improvement.

Negotiating international contracts with a weak dollar

Question: I am the purchasing manager of my company, and I am sourcing one of my components from Japan. My supplier recently informed me that they will renew the contract in Japanese Yen only. With exchange rates moving around, this makes my bill of matcrials cost uncertain. What is my recourse?

-Christina, Scottsdale

Answer: With significant turmoil in the financial markets during 2008/2009, the weakening of the U.S. economy and substantial cuts in the interest rates, the U.S. dollar had plummeted against most major currencies—including the Japanese Yen. This squeezed the profits out of Japanese manufacturers because the weakening dollar lowers the price of their products, while their costs are fixed in Yen. In the prior year, with your contract in dollars, your supplier had absorbed significant price reductions due to the weakening dollar.

By moving to Yen, your supplier is attempting to tip the scale in their favor. It is because with cost and price both in Yen, their profits will be more predictable and yours would not. What can you do about it?

It all comes down to how widely the product is available and who has the leverage. If a similar product is available from other manufacturers, then perhaps you should switch suppliers or at least bring another one in for the negotiations. In the end, maybe you should split the business between two suppliers and demand prices in U.S. dollars.

If your product is single sourced from a Japanese supplier who will only do business in Yen, then you have a more difficult situation. Here are a few ideas…

First, you should investigate currency hedging. When you sign the contract in Yen, you can hedge a fixed number of Yen to a fixed price in U.S. dollars. There is a small cost to hedging, but your product cost will be fixed and predictable.

The second thing would be a natural hedge if your company also sells their products in Japan. By pricing some of your products for

Japan in Yen, you can create a natural hedge. Sales and purchasing are often separate and independent departments. So, this plan requires cooperation and the involvement of a common "Economic Buyer" with "Total Cost of Ownership".

The third possibility is to suggest to your supplier that the price be set in dollars (or Yen), but, if the currencies move in either direction by more than a certain amount (say 5%), the two sides would split the difference. This is probably the fairest scenario.

If none of these things happen and the price is fixed in Yen, it is probably not the end of the world. The U.S. dollar versus Yen fluctuates. U.S. dollar has recently strengthened and may continue to do so further. So, if your cost is fixed in Yen, and the dollar strengthens, your cost may drop in dollars and yield a windfall.

And your Japanese supplier, after taking losses during the dollar's weakness, will be hurting again if the dollar strengthens.

Chapter 25: Legal questions

I received a good number of legal questions from my readers. I am not a lawyer. But I have forty years of business experience with plenty of legal challenges, court cases, patent cases, and business disputes. I asked my corporate attorney why I was getting legal questions. Her answer was that the readers believe that I had access to some free legal advice which they do not. My attorney was correct. So, I answered many of the questions with help from attorneys in my network. I still advise my readers to get advice from your own attorney on a specific matter before they decide to act.

Copying artwork from internet

Question: Can you provide guidance about copyright laws, regarding which images can be saved or printed from the internet? I wanted to print a picture of a necklace from the internet, but a friend told me that it would be a copyright violation. I was going to use it for inspiration and to study the person's technique, not to make a duplicate. The necklace was on a web site where the designer sells them, but I did not see anything about copyright. What about saving or printing pictures from blogs or web sites?

-Rita Kopinger

Answer: Circular 92 from the U.S. Copyright Office provides general information on copyright and Circular 40 covers visual arts like jewelry design. You may do a web search for "copyright laws" and "fair use," and you will get enough material to make your head spin. These materials will take you some time to review, so let me offer some simplified guidelines in the meantime.

Copyright protects original works of authorship fixed in a tangible medium. Original works of authorship include literary, dramatic, musical, and artistic works, such as images, jewelry designs, novels, movies, songs, computer software, and architecture. A work is protected when it is created and fixed in a tangible form that is perceptible either directly or with the aid of a machine or device. Works made after March 1, 1989, need not be marked with "©" to be protected.

There are two copyrights here—the necklace design and the picture. Copying a necklace from a picture violates the copyright holder's rights. However, it is not a violation to look at or get inspiration from the photo. It is likely allowed as a fair use or implied license to download, save or print a copy of the photo for your own viewing, unless the web site terms specifically prohibit this. The same is true for copying, saving, or printing pictures from other blogs or web sites. But as soon as you start to copy any part of the design, including the curves or shapes of the necklace, you start to tread on the copyright. There is no firm rule about how much a work must differ from the original to avoid infringing the copyright. This depends on the facts of each situation.

I am not a lawyer. If you are going to make a lot of jewelry for sale, you should consult a lawyer. But there are laws and then there is the everyday application of those laws. In general, if you make one necklace inspired by a design from the internet, it is likely not cost effective for anybody to sue you. But if you deploy that technique in volume in your business, you are exposing yourself to a copyright-infringement claim.

Software piracy

Question: A customer in France reverse engineered our proprietary software and is threatening to publish it and/or hold us hostage with the threat of doing so. He is offering to become our new software developer and sell his version of our software after adding functionality. He proposed that he sell the software and provide support, or that we sell the software and pay him royalty. Reverse engineering our software violates our click-through software licensing agreement.

If he publishes the re-engineered software, then we would experience substantial damage. If our competitors discovered how we capture, analyze, and report data from our Doppler-radar based applications, then they could either discredit our methods or copy them.

What rights do we have in France and what actions can we take (i.e., restraining order, arrest, etc.)?

-Ken Starr

Answer: Software piracy is a huge problem, globally. I do not have official estimates, but I believe that over 10% of the software sold globally is pirated. There are many approaches to this problem. None are simple or cheap.

I will assume that: your company owns the copyright to your software; it was created or first published in the U.S. recently; the click-through license is enforceable, prohibits reverse engineering, and does not allow creation of derivative works; and that the customer's work is a derivative.

If you have not registered your copyright in the U.S. and France, and have not marked your product, you should. It will make future enforcement and award of damages easier. Next, consider sending a cease-and-desist letter, but be aware that this may result in a declaratory judgment being filed against you.

Under U.S. copyright law, if someone publishes an unauthorized derivative of your work then you could sue in U.S. District Court and include your breach of contract claim. This means a large upfront investment; but, if you win, you could be awarded attorney's fees and actual or statutory damages.

Under the Berne Convention and the WIPO Copyright Treaty, France commits to protect U.S. copyrights from infringement in France and has specific courts for copyright matters. An interim injunction to cease infringement may be requested (France and U.S.), but you must do this quickly after learning of the infringement, or injunctive relief will be denied. France allows infringement seizures, including gathering accounting data to show damages. Customs assistance is available, but not useful for downloaded software. Copyright infringement is a criminal offense in France, with stiff fines and jail time possible.

www.wipo.int is a good place to start your research. Also review the case 126 F3d 365 Computer Associates International Inc. v. Altai Inc. The case is old but shows what a mess multi-jurisdictional software copyright dispute is.

Thanks to Microchip's in-house general counsel, Ms. Kim Van Herk, for her help and research on this topic.

Legal doctrine of clean hands

Question: I allowed my 18-year-old son to take my car for a night out with his friends. My son drinks beer but assured me that he would have a designated driver. Unfortunately, the designated driver, who was my son's 19-year-old friend, also ended up having a couple of drinks. He drove back anyway since he had the least to drink. While backing out, he hit a pole. Can I sue him for the damage to my car? This was my second car, and I had let the insurance lapse.

-Jake, Phoenix

Answer: First of all, I want to remind you that I am not a lawyer; you really should see a lawyer to get advice on this. That said, from what I know about your situation, I do not believe that you will be able to prevail in your lawsuit.

You were not there. So, you really do not know what happened. You only know the version that your son likely told you. You must know by now that teenagers are habitual liars when it comes to drinking and their friends.

Even if your account is 100% accurate, your case fails what I know to be "the legal doctrine of clean hands". It is a rule of law that a person coming to court with a lawsuit must not have done anything wrong regarding the subject matter of the claim. No one in this case—you, your son, or your son's friend—has clean hands. You knowingly allowed your underage son (the legal drinking age is 21) to go drinking with his friends in a car that was illegal to drive because of lapsed insurance. You also trusted him to use good judgment after having several drinks. Apparently, he did not make a good judgment call and handed the keys to a friend who drank too, albeit less than others (which I am not so sure about). Then your son's friend, also an underage drinker, proceeded to drive and caused an accident.

You are fortunate that you are only dealing with damage to your car. If there had been a more serious accident with people hurt, you could have had significant liability. Clearly the driver has the responsibility because he got behind the wheel after drinking illegally. But your son is responsible for knowingly handing over the keys to an illegally drunk friend and then getting in the car with him. And you are responsible for allowing your underage son to go drinking with his friends in your car with no insurance coverage.

All three of you share responsibility for this, and I believe that your case clearly fails the doctrine of clean hands. If a reader or a lawyer writes to me with a different opinion, I would be happy to publish a rebuttal.

New license plate law has valid purpose

Question: Can you give your opinion on the new license-plate law in which everyone needs to remove the dealer frame from their autos, so that the word "Arizona" is visible? Do you not think that our state government should make better use of its time, rather than passing this stupid law that preys on senior citizens and others who do not know about the law or are otherwise unable to reinstall their license plates?

-A concerned senior citizen, Scottsdale

Answer: As most of you may know by now, Arizona implemented a new law at the start of the year requiring that the word "Arizona" on all license plates must be unobstructed—by dealer frames or otherwise.

When I first heard about this law, I had the same reaction as our concerned senior citizen. Our state, county and local governments should have better things to do in this very difficult economy than to pass, implement, and enforce this ridiculous law. But then I learned the reason for it, and it made sense.

This law is driven by the increasing use of photo radar on our streets and highways. Photo radar is a very cost-effective way for the authorities to collect speeding fines and slow down the traffic, with either stationery or mobile cameras detecting speeding drivers. Mobile cameras can be relocated very easily, to keep drivers guessing. The authorities can then send tickets to their homes and make them pay up. If an individual must be served at their home, the extra cost is passed to that person.

Photo radar is ineffective for out-of-state drivers because the state authorities cannot trace their license plates and issue tickets. When a dealer frame hides the word "Arizona," this makes it difficult for the authorities to differentiate an out-of-state plate from an Arizona plate. Therefore, many Arizona drivers could evade paying tickets for their traffic violations. So, the new law is effective in helping the authorities enforce speeding laws.

There is an entirely different controversy about photo radar. Is it legal? Is it accurate? Having experienced photo radar more than once myself, I can assure you that I have tested the system and found that it is legal. Is it accurate? You will never be able to prove otherwise. Therefore, your best defense is to avoid cutting it too close.

I have a lead foot and a fast car. So, I do not like photo radar or the new license-plate law. It may be repealed someday, but for now it is the law.

Please drive safely.

Getting homeowners to pay association dues

Question: I have a home in Scottsdale, which is part of a homeowner association consisting of ten homes. We have a new owner for one of the homes, and he just would not pay his homeowner dues on time. We are a small association and choose one of the owners to be president. Ordinarily, there is very little work because the only common property is a community gate, two roads, and some trees and bushes. But this new homeowner is very demanding, and it takes many reminders to get him to pay his dues. Can you suggest some remedy?

-Keith, Scottsdale

Answer: I have been there. I used to live in a community of only six homes, and I was the president of our homeowner association. Two of our homeowners were delinquent for several years, and both eventually went bankrupt. One of them sold his house after two years of non-payment of association dues. The other had been delinquent for four years. This property was eventually transferred to the bank and the old dues were finally paid off.

In a large homeowner association, there is a management company that runs the business by the book. If a homeowner is delinquent, it can send a notice, levy late charges, file liens, and start foreclosures. A small percentage of homeowners are always delinquent in any association, irrespective of the economy. A large association's balance sheet usually supports this delinquency and the burden on any single homeowner is insignificant.

However, when you have a small association and one or two homeowners are delinquent, it is a considerable burden for the others. And, because small associations do not have a management staff, delinquencies create a substantial workload for the president. The legal costs can be quite steep and must be funded by a small number of homeowners.

In my experience, delinquent homeowners are usually very demanding. They may nitpick issues around the neighborhood to justify non-payment. And the more you try to appease them, the more belligerent they get.

My advice is to send all homeowners a fresh copy of the association's bylaws and Covenants, Conditions and Restrictions (CC&Rs). Then, start to manage by the rules. Give the appropriate notice to any delinquent homeowners. If needed, escalate the matter by filing a lien, and finally, start foreclosure proceedings. Legal pressure is the only thing that I have found to bring results.

Even though the remaining homeowners have to chip in for the costs, all costs are eventually recovered. This is because, in Arizona, a homeowner-association lien is superior to mortgage and other liens. In particular, the title to the property cannot be transferred without satisfying the association lien. If the homeowner is not in bankruptcy, the association can then foreclose to recover the dues. So, retain a good law firm and pursue the association's legal rights—without any undue emotions attached.

HOA liens clarified

I have received many email enquiries regarding my column of January 14, 2009, which erroneously stated that, in Arizona, a homeowner-association lien is superior to mortgage and other liens.

A.R.S. 33-1807(B) states that the association's lien is superior to all other liens and encumbrances, except:

1. Liens and encumbrances recorded before the recordation of the declaration.
2. A recorded first mortgage on the unit.
3. Liens for real estate taxes and other governmental assessments or charges against the unit.

My statement that the association's lien is superior to mortgages was partially correct; the lien is superior to 2nd and 3rd mortgages, but not the first mortgage. I apologize for the error and the confusion I may have caused among many homeowner associations where property values are below today's first-mortgage values.

If a homeowner is not in bankruptcy, the association can foreclose to recover the dues. However, it only works if the property has equity after the superior liens. The laws are relatively complex. So, retain a good law firm to pursue the association's legal rights.

This clarification was provided, pro-bono, by Ms. Kathryn Battock, an attorney with the law firm of Ekmark and Ekmark. They have helped me collect several times for my homeowner association.

Who should I sue for child's injuries?

Question: My daughter was assaulted by a girl who is known to be a bully in her high school. She was injured badly on her back, arms, and face. I have medical expenses and time off from work to take care of my daughter. Are my expenses and time off from work recoverable from the bully. Should I sue the bully, who is seventeen, or her parents?

-Denise, Phoenix

Answer: You should watch a few episodes of Judge Judy for ideas. I remember her dealing with these kinds of cases, though the laws vary from state to state.

In Arizona, it would be best to sue both the minor and her parents. Parents or guardians with custody and control of a minor (under 18) are responsible for the damages (up to $10,000 for each tort) caused by the malicious misconduct or willful acts of the minor (A.R.S § 12-661). Parents may also be liable for failure to supervise the child. If you do not sue the parents, in most instances minors have no assets and the judgment is uncollectable until they are adults.

Arizona schools also have a duty to protect children from foreseeable harm. If the event happened while the school had an obligation to supervise the children, it may bear some responsibility.

Another question is who should sue. Minors cannot sue another person on their own. A minor must sue through the help of a "guardian ad litem" (Arizona Rule of Civil Procedure 17 (g-i)). A guardian ad litem is a special guardian appointed by the court to represent the minor. Often, the minor's parents can bring the suit.

Your daughter may be able to recover for her pain and suffering, medical expenses, and possibly punitive damages. Your time off work may also be compensable if it was caused by the event.

Battery is a crime. If the girl is convicted, then restitution for damages may also be ordered. Damages in a criminal case would only be for actual expenses and your lost wages, but not pain and suffering or punitive damages.

I must caution my readers that I am not a lawyer. My advice is general advice and should be treated as a starting point. Readers should seek their own attorney's advice, as the specifics of each case vary.

My thanks to Kim Van Herk, Microchip's in-house general counsel, for her help in answering this question.

Ex-CEO should move on after 16 years

Question: About 16 years ago, I was forced out of my position as the CEO of a technology company. Since that time, the new CEO has laid claim to all the strategies I initiated. As the head of this now-successful public company, he recently participated in a defamatory article that praised him and denigrated me. Should I sue for libel and defamation? Or should I tell the real story?

-Name Withheld

Answer: In a world of rapid change, 16 years is too long for you to now lay claim to the strategies of that company. You were its CEO 16 years ago and you said that you were forced out, though you did not give the reason.

You say that the new CEO has laid claim to your strategies. That would be like John Scully or Gil Emilio denying that Steve Jobs was the architect of Apple's success. A new CEO always faces the challenge of figuring out what to keep and what to shed. So, there will always be some continuity of strategies. You also said that this is now a successful public company. If you trusted in your plans and the new CEO executing them, then you could have kept most of your stock ownership and would have benefited handsomely.

If you believed that your termination was unjustified, then you should have sued back then for wrongful termination. At this point, the statute of limitations has long since passed. And the target of your suit would have a great defense under the "doctrine of latches". I am also skeptical of your claims regarding libel and defamation. It is unlikely that a successful CEO would denigrate you. Have you considered that the writer may have brought up old dirty laundry, against the CEO's wishes? Life is too short, and I would suggest that you move on.

Most terminated executives seek other executive positions. They want to get back in the saddle and prove their worth to themselves as well as others. That is what Steve Jobs did at Apple and Jamie Dimon did at JP Morgan Chase; and there are numerous other examples of terminated executives becoming very successful elsewhere. Sixteen years is enough time for you to have racked up two to three successful stints as the CEO of major corporations. For all I know, you may have already achieved that kind of success. If that is the case, then my congratulations and you should be pleased.

If you have not run another company and are still lamenting the loss of your job from 16 years ago, then you should look forward and take on another challenge to run a new company; not sue the old one.

Chapter 26: Miscellaneous topics

Using the segway in my business

Question: I know that you are a Segway Personal Transporter user. Do you just use it for joy riding, or do you also use it in your business? I am evaluating using the Segway in my business, which provides building security to several large clients. My security guards are at the command station, as well as walking or driving around the perimeter and the inside of buildings. How should I evaluate whether the use of Segways will be cost effective?

-Denny, Phoenix

Answer: I own two Segways, personally. We use them for recreational riding in parks, as well as at fairs, parades, and high school robotics competitions.

Microchip also uses Segways in our business. Our manufacturing plant in Oregon is the size of three football fields, and most of that is an ultra-clean-room semiconductor manufacturing environment. A production operator walks an average of five miles a day, moving products from station to station. We deploy several Segways with specially designed product carriers to transport the product from one part of the manufacturing plant to another.

We also deploy the Segway in our marketing and sales operations. We use it at trade shows, exhibitions, conferences, customer appreciation functions, "bring your children to work day" for giving rides to children, etc. Two years ago, we donated a Segway at an engineering conference for a tear down, so engineers could study how it was made—including the use of Microchip's semiconductors.

Now, how can you use the Segway in your security business? The Segway is ideally suited for security businesses in which you cover a large campus. It moves the security guards faster, enabling them to cover more ground in less time. And it enables you to forgo the use of gasoline-powered vehicles, helping the environment as well as saving on operational and maintenance costs.

The security guard on a Segway is also clearly noticeable as an effective deterrent. Riders stand an additional eight inches off the ground; allowing them to be better seen and giving the rider better sight lines, including over cars in a parking lot or boxes in a warehouse. It allows the officers to be more visible and respond more quickly to crimes and emergencies.

Go to www.Segway.com. This site has a lot of information, including a productivity calculator that allows you to analyze the dollars and cents for your planned usage.

Postal worker sounds off

Question: I am a mail carrier with the U.S. Postal Service. The carriers are harassed daily to "pick up the pace" (e.g., "Why did it take you six minutes too long in the office, yesterday morning?" "Um...I had to take a poop.")

While we are being watched and prodded to "save the company", our six top dogs in Washington, D.C. have given themselves huge bonuses during a year that the Postal Service lost $2.8 billion. The salary and bonuses of the Postmaster General and his five vice presidents totaled $2.7 million last year. Yep, and they sit there at their desks worrying how they can get the mail carriers to save the sinking ship by doing more work for eight hours of pay What do you think of that?

-Lynn

Answer: The problem of paying executive bonuses while the company is losing money is not exclusive to the U.S. Postal Service. This problem seems to be prevalent throughout corporate America. Just look at the automotive companies, major banks, airlines, AIG, Fannie Mae, Freddie Mac, and the large number of Wall Street firms that have received TARP money.

What was TARP? It was the Troubled Asset Relief Program. It should have been renamed "Taxpayers Again Raped by Politicians", but I will save that subject for another column.

I do not condone the executives of any of these companies earning large bonuses. Given that, your complaint is very genuine.

My concern is whether there is an overall plan for the Postal Service to avoid losing money. Over the last decade or two, very successful shipping companies have emerged, such as Federal Express and UPS. They have taken a lot of business away from the Postal Service, and their customer satisfaction is much higher than that of the Postal Service.

Federal Express and UPS can choose the area they want to serve. They can choose to not serve remote areas with low density of people where it would not be cost effective for them. The U.S. Postal Service does not have that choice. They have to serve every area based on federal mandate.

So, that is a real issue. There seems to be a lack of long-term business development. I am not an expert on your industry, but in every industry, there are players that win market share and those that lose market share. If an organization finds itself in the latter category, the management must work in close cooperation with the employees to design a business formula and culture that can transform the company from a money-losing enterprise into a winning one.

I know that this can be done because I have been there. I wrote about Microchip Technology's turnaround story in a book titled "Driving Excellence: How the Aggregate System turned Microchip Technology from a losing company to a market leader", which was published by Wiley in April 2006. And my second book "Up and to the right- my personal and business journey building the Microchip Technology juggernaut" published in 2023 shows dramatic rise of Microchip starting from humble beginnings.

I have not seen the math done on your business, so I cannot determine whether picking up the pace and cutting out another minute at the office gets you there. My general belief is that employees work in the system, while the management works on the system. When things are not working, it is usually not the employees' problem; rather, it is a system problem that must be owned by the management.

Sanghi deciphers his own compensation

Question: At a little company I worked for years ago, the other workers resented the owner/CEO because they felt they were inadequately paid, and he kept too much of the profits to pay his salary. As I see it, if he had put more of his profits into their salaries, they would have become more productive and felt more valued and would have ultimately helped the business overall and the local community to be more prosperous.

Would the entire US economy not be better off if CEOs like you voluntarily turned back a significant part of their salaries to the lower echelon workers? June 29, 2008, *AZ Republic* said your salary was $13.5 Million; surely you would not be incredibly dissatisfied with $7.25 million, instead?

-Name withheld by request

Answer: The purpose of a CEO for a publicly held company is to deliver value to the company's shareholders. Executives can be compensated based on a flat salary or company performance, or a combination of both.

Let us break down my $13.5 million salary, which covers the April 2006 to March 2007 period. (You can download our filings at the Security and Exchange Commission website www.sec.gov.)

Annual Base Salary	= $515,010
401K/Life Insurance	= $5,005
Performance Bonus	= $1,195,743
Stock option exercises	= $11,762,117
Grand Total	= **$13,477,875**

You can see that my compensation mainly consisted of two elements—the performance bonus and stock-option exercises.

Performance Bonus: The performance bonus depends on quarterly and yearly performance. The targets are set by an independent compensation committee of the board of directors.

The bonus resulted from a year of particularly good performance by Microchip. We achieved record sales of $1.04 billion, up 12% from the prior year. Our earnings per share also reached a new record, up 16.5% from the prior year. Microchip also secured the number one position in our key market space.

There have also been times when my bonus was zero. My investors like large bonuses because they usually reflect strong performance, which then typically increases the stock price. My employees like them too, as they all participate in a bonus plan at various levels, depending on their responsibility. When the company prospers, everyone shares in the rewards.

Stock Option Exercises: Each year, all Microchip employees receive certain stock options, which gives them the right to buy Microchip stock at a price on the grant day for up to 10 years in the future. The options vest over four years before they can be exercised, and they expire after 10 years.

In 1996 and 1997, the board of directors granted me certain stock options to acquire Microchip stock between $6 and $8 (the stock price at that time, split adjusted). I held onto these options for almost 10 years. If I had not exercised them, they would have become worthless at their expiration date.

During this 10-year period, Microchip's stock went from ~$7.00 to ~$40, up 471%. Microchip's market capitalization rose from about $1.2 billion to about $8 billion. About $6.8 billion of economic value was created for shareholders. Microchip's revenue went from $286 million to $1.04 billion. Total employees grew from 1,200 to 4,700, creating new jobs that supported the economy and our community. Additional tax revenues were generated as well. In fact, Microchip outperformed all the companies featured in the popular book "Good to Great" by Jim Collins.

Now, what would have happened if Microchip's stock remained flat during this same period? In that case, my stock options would have expired worthless. My performance bonus would have been zero. Then, my compensation for the year would have been $548,482. Investors would have made $6.8 billion less, and there would have been 3,500 fewer jobs.

Determining what is fair in executive compensation can be quite subjective. But, in my case, I would have you ask Microchip shareholders whether they think it is fair.

The subject of executive compensation draws a curious amount of interest. People rightfully get disgusted by the headlines caused by bad apples like Enron and WorldCom. Just because there are a few bad apples does not mean that everyone acts that way and is unreasonably paid without appropriate results.

What about the compensation of sports stars, actors, and singers? A high-school graduate who is the right height and excels at dribbling a ball can earn $20 million a year, and everyone stands up and cheers. How is he adding more economic value to the community than what I have described above?

Stock options versus restricted stock units

Question: Our company has given stock options to employees for many years. The company is now talking about giving Restricted Stock Units (RSUs) to employees instead of options. Would you please comment on this subject?

-Andy, Tempe

Answer: Starting with the fiscal year after June 30, 2005, companies are required to expense stock options on their income statements. This is having a profound effect on businesses.

In the 1980s, there was a cry from investors that the boards of directors at public companies needed to tie the interests of employees to the interests of shareholders. Stock options did that very well, because if the stock went up, then both the investors and the employee's made money. It sounded fair. In fact, the 1990s was a very successful period for investors and employees alike.

But then the stock market crashed in 2001, and stock options got a bad name. Yes, there was corporate malfeasance at Enron and WorldCom. However, overall, stock options were a great tool. With stock-option expensing in place, the cost of giving RSUs to employees has become reasonably like the cost of expensing options (depending on the volatility index of the stock). Therefore, an increasing number of boards of directors has shifted toward RSUs. The employees like them too, because RSUs are guaranteed to make money. The exercise price for RSUs is zero and the employee makes money whether the stock goes up or not.

The ironic thing is that investors also like RSUs. Stock options got such a bad name that nearly 99% of the investors and analysts prefer RSUs. This is the biggest "upside down" scenario that I have ever seen in employee and executive compensation. How RSUs tie the interests of employees to the interests of shareholders is beyond me. With RSUs, employees make money irrespective of shareholders making money. But shareholders and employees both love RSUs, so companies are converting their programs to RSUs, and everyone is happy.

In a few years, there will be a period when employees make money and investors do not. The wheel would then have gone full circle. Executives and boards will be criticized for giving RSUs and uncoupling the interest of employees to the interest of shareholders. A new class of MBAs would have graduated and will be managing America's money. And they will take their turn in criticizing executive compensation levels and perceived greed.

So, call me cynical, but I believe that stock options were a better tool to tie the interests of employees to those of shareholders. Stock-option expensing changed all that. This is one case where the accounting tail has wagged the dog big time, and to the serious detriment of the long-term interests of shareholders.

A question can be asked why Microchip does not give stock options to employees instead of RSUs. The answer is because of competitive reasons. If all our competitors gave RSUs, and we gave stock options, we would lose valuable talent.

Put options instead of stock options

Question: Our company has given stock options to its employees for many years. With stock options, I only make money when the stock of the company goes up. If the stock goes down, my stock options are worthless. For the last several years, the stock of our company has done nothing except go down. A "Put Option" would allow me to sell the stock to the company at a fixed price in the future. In this case, I would make money only if the stock of the company went down. Why don't companies adopt "Put Options" instead of stock options in this environment?

-Jonathan, Scottsdale

Answer: I must hand it to you to be creative. However, I believe that your creativity is misdirected. I assume that your question is serious, and you are not kidding with me or your company.

Stock options are meant to align the interests of employees with those of the shareholders. A stock option gives the employee a right to buy his or her company's stock in the future at the grant price, which is usually the stock price on the day of the grant. This right to buy in the future usually extends up to 10 years, but it may be granted for a shorter period.

Through stock options, the company is enlisting your creativity, efforts, and emotions toward improving its business results. This, in turn, improves the stock price of the company, which benefits the company's shareholders as well as its employees.

When you request a "Put Option" from your company, you are asking the company to grant you the right to sell its stock to the company at a fixed price in the future. This means that you benefit only when the stock of the company goes down. How does it benefit the company or its shareholders to align your interests in a way that drives its stock price down?

I understand that the stocks of many companies have not performed well in recent years. In many cases, employees have done a good job, and the company has good earnings and cash flow, but the stock has not performed because the price-to-earnings ratios have compressed due to an uncertain economy. Still, the company, through its stock options, wants you to stay committed over the long term. The company wants you to make money from stock options only when its shareholders make money. And that only happens when its stock goes up.

Now, I do not think that you should work for a company where you cannot invest your time, creativity, and passion to improve its business results. While you can buy Put Options on your company from the open market, you really should not buy Put Options on a company where you are currently employed.

If you and many of your fellow employees were to begin buying Put Options on your company from the open market, then this would be a clear sign that your company is in serious trouble. If that happens, I want to know the name of your company so I can buy its "Puts", too.

Dad starved for appreciation from the kids

Question: My question crosses the boundaries of family and business. I am a dad of two teenagers. I am very busy at work trying to earn a decent living for my family. All I get from my children are complaints about the time I am not there to be with them at school activities. I try to do my best, but I never meet their expectations. My wife is not very helpful and adds her own complaints. At times, I feel demoralized and unappreciated by my children. How can I get some appreciation?

-George, the dad

Answer: Dads are among the most unsung heroes in this world. They often do not have someone who smiles at them at the end of a hard workday, looks them in the eyes and says, "Thank you, Dad". There is usually no one there to appreciate the dads because their work is taken for granted.

Often, a dad's satisfaction can come only from knowing that there is a tide out there—a tide the size of a tsunami, coming from a bottomless pool. This tide is the family's finances, which, if left unfulfilled, will rob most families of their happiness. It is a need that can deprive families of their ability to live in their own homes, drive nice cars, go to good schools and colleges, and even prevent a child from asking mom and dad if they may have $25 to go out for dinner and movie with their friends.

In many families, all everyone else does is talk and criticize; but it is the dads (and many moms) that get up in the morning, get dressed and go to work. Rain or shine, scorching hot or freezing cold, they go to work, day after day for nearly 40 years. And they do it without any thanks or so much as a pat on the back. But they do it because they are the wage earners and know that if a family cannot be fed, housed, clothed, educated, and entertained, they do not have a chance to be happy.

So, what is my advice? Love your children unconditionally and give them everything unselfishly that you can afford to give, without destroying their motivation to succeed in life. Do not expect anything back—especially from your teenagers. A hormonal switch goes on when they are fourteen and does not turn off until they are over twenty-five. Then, they will come around and you will get some appreciation. Meanwhile, get a pet.

My elders told me one more thing. Spoil the grandkids and you will get all the appreciation for which you are longing.

-Steve, the dad

Rebuttal on dad starved for appreciation from kids

My column on December 9, 2007 "Unselfish fathers keep family afloat" brought a number of responses from the readers.

"Your comments about fathers that work hard to provide for their families were outstanding. It was right on target,"

-Steve R.

"I was disappointed and do not feel you really addressed George's issues properly. Husbands and wives need to appreciate each other, and he clearly says his wife complains and is not helpful. You may feel it is not politically correct to tell this man's wife to shape up. But that is where you should have started. She should be grateful that she has a husband who feels a responsibility to her, and their children and she should teach gratitude to her children.

Your advice should have been more sympathetic to his situation and called his wife to task. My father seldom was able to make school plays etc., but my mother fully appreciated his role as breadwinner and knew it was a challenging and crucial role for our family. My mother led the way, and my brother and I followed her example of appreciating our father. Life is full of trade-offs and this wife, and these children, need to face reality. They should support him and thank him rather than complain. He can only do so much, and he deserves better from them....and you."

- *Nancy*

Another comment from a mother was less than favorable and essentially dumped on George for being a materialistic father and not carving out time for children's school activities. But she withheld permission to print her full comments.

Answer: It is quite understandable that a column about fathers working hard to provide for the family and often missing school activities will draw a varied response from the readers because of individual experiences. I thank all my readers for their comments.

All the responses were positive on George, the dad's, situation except one who withheld permission. One of the unique responses from Nancy is printed above. She supports George and thinks that I should have been harder on the mother. So, I will choose to answer this one.

My answers tend to be practical, to the best of my ability. You can nudge the wife to role model appreciation, but you cannot force the wife to appreciate and teach that appreciation to the children. Most fathers try and it works sometimes, but not always. By making it a problem of the mother, you will simply get the mother upset. There is an old saying "If Mama is not happy, no one is happy".

I take plenty of strong stands in the business world. But at home, the logic often does not work. You must make a choice between "being right or being happy". Many fathers who always choose to be right are the divorced ones or in the doghouse. My advice to George was to choose to be happy. George agreed.

How do you choose charities to donate to?

Question: As a small business owner, I believe in being a supportive member of the community. As such I do not discourage donation solicitations from community groups. Lately, we have been swamped with requests. With so many requests we are no longer able to give to everyone who asks. I am aware that Microchip gives a great deal of fiscal support to the community, especially the FIRST robotics program. Is there a formalistic method for determining how much fiscal support a company should/can contribute to community organizations? Additionally, do you have specific qualifications, as a business, that you look for before choosing who to contribute to?

-Ken, Glendale, Arizona

Answer: First, let me commend you for being a supportive member of the community. A company depends on the community for its resources, and it must help to nurture those resources as well as improve the quality of life.

I went through the same dilemma many years ago at Microchip. The needs of the community are endless, and you must make choices regarding what you believe in and where you want to focus your efforts. We believe in helping seven broad categories: (1) Hunger and homelessness, (2) Senior needs, (3) Children's support programs, (4) Battered wives and broken homes, (5) Healthcare, (6) Education and (7) Entrepreneurship.

We support the first five categories through a large annual corporate donation and company-wide fundraising for the Valley of the Sun United Way (www.vsuw.org). The United Way supports over 150 community organizations across five themes.

The last two categories—Education and Entrepreneurship—we choose to passionately support ourselves. FIRST Robotics (www.firstinspires.org) fits under Education, and Microchip's role in the Association for corporate growth (www.ACG.org/Arizona), and this very column, fit under helping entrepreneurs.

You can also create a small yearly budget and form an internal committee, through which you can donate to miscellaneous charities. We assign a senior Microchip employee to be personally involved in each, to prevent our money from being wasted.

What is a good annual charity budget? How big is your heart?

Dividends not a cost on company's P&L statement

Question: My company keeps telling employees that they must control costs and operating expenses. At the same time, the company keeps increasing the dividend paid to its shareholders, while the company stock is stagnating. Are dividends not an expense to the company?

-Clint, Chandler

Answer: Dividends are not an expense on a company's Profit and Loss statement (P&L). The cash on the balance sheet belongs to the shareholders. If you own your company's stock, then you also own the prorated portion of its total cash. Company officers are allowed to use this cash for making capital purchases and other business investments. Those purchases must be expensed through the P&L as either a business expense or depreciation for capital purchases.

Review your company's P&L statement, you will not find a line item for the dividend paid as an expense. This is because dividends are not an expense. They are simply a return of shareholders' capital back to them. Most of the good companies are paying dividends (e.g. IBM, Cisco, Microsoft, Texas Instruments, Microchip, etc.).

You said that your company's stock price does not seem to go up with dividends. Imagine putting money in the bank and getting no interest. You would quickly take that money out. Similarly, if a shareholder is invested in your company's stock and it does not go up and you do not pay a dividend, then no one will want to own that stock and it will quickly fall. Therefore, in a market economy, the return to shareholders is important.

Lastly, it is important to understand who the shareholders are. Shareholders are not some fat cats somewhere who just get a bunch of dividends. Most shareholders in many companies are ordinary people and employees like you (often investing through 401(k) plans). Most Companies' 401(k) plans are invested in mutual funds. The dividend your company pays goes to these mutual funds, which usually own stock in investing companies. The mutual funds then redistribute the dividends to individual 401(k) accounts, like your own. Therefore, a large number of dividends goes back to the employees of corporate America, who have their money invested in 401(k) plans through various mutual-fund companies.

Your CEO should be commended for controlling expenses while increasing dividends. Such governance would have partially avoided the corporate malfeasance of the late 1990s.

Chapter 27: About executives and managers

The Six powers of a manager

Question: My boss continuously manages his subordinates through carrots and sticks. He routinely threatens employees' jobs and dangles perks to motivate. Otherwise, he is incompetent in providing the needed resources, guidance, or expertise in leading us to success. What do you have to say?

-Sabina R., Phoenix

Answer: There are essentially six main powers vested in a boss. An appropriate mix of these powers and using the correct power for a given situation is a managerial skill learned and perfected through experience and practice. Your boss needs help and training in using these powers more effectively. Here are the six powers:

1. <u>Legitimate power:</u> This is the power granted to bosses by their position. They can approve resources, expenses, and projects, and assign priorities. Proper use of this power requires knowledge of the business, the company's technology capabilities, the competitive environment, and the staff's capabilities. Incompetent managers will misappropriate this power and decide by their bias, closeness to employees, etc.

2. <u>Connection power:</u> Managers often have more connections to the important people in the company or the industry. They can help their employees by making appropriate use of this power. The bosses who continuously drop a lot of high-level names are misusing this power by trying to influence others with their connections.

3. <u>Expert power:</u> This is the power enjoyed by a boss who is an expert in their field. Managers in technology fields often enjoy this power. Subordinates want to work for these people because of their tremendous expertise.

4. <u>Referent power:</u> This a power enjoyed by a boss who is very likeable. People want to work for this boss because he or she is very nice to work for. Likeability is often a good power, but any

power taken to an extreme can be bad. If the boss is becoming likeable because he or she does not deal with poor performers and lets everyone slide while the projects are failing may be a nice boss, but a poor performer himself or herself.

5. Power of reward: A boss has the power to reward the employees with bonuses, raises, promotions, perks, or praise. Excessive use of this power is considered negative and seems to be the case with your boss.

6. Power of punishment: A boss has the power to punish, demote, withhold merit raises or fire an employee. Judicious use of such power with non-performers is a necessity, but managing by using such threats, as in your boss's case, is a misuse of the power.

The best managers use a combination of all six powers in moderation. Excessive use of any one power is not good. And, removing any of the powers from a manager's toolbox would compromise his or her management ability. I have been learning and practicing the appropriate use of these powers all through my business career.

Your boss can learn and can get better. But motivating or requiring him to get help is a difficult task. Discretely slip this column under his door.

One more caution—do not try these powers at home with your spouse or kids. It does not work.

Executive perks

Question: Our company's executive team seems to enjoy huge perks. Beyond their salaries and bonuses, they have company cars, private golf-club memberships, and access to company planes for personal and family use. Are these perks legal, ethical, right?

-Matthew, Queen Creek

Answer: First, let me tell you that neither I nor any member of my management team at Microchip has a company car, company paid golf-club membership, access to company planes for personal business, or any other perks.

It is not uncommon for company executives to have such perks. Is it legal? Yes! The company's board of directors can give executives a larger salary or they may pay a portion of compensation in the form of perks. To be totally legal, the executives must report the cash value of those perks on their tax returns, and the company should report this value in SEC filings.

Is it ethical? The answer is also yes! All forms of compensation to an executive need to be approved by the independent compensation committee of the board. If all compensation and benefits are properly approved and disclosed, then perks do not violate any ethical obligations.

So, is it right? There, my answer is no. Such perks to executives create an "us versus them" atmosphere between employees and management. It is better for the board to give the executives a competitive salary and let them pay for their own perks.

The best way to create a strong company culture is through "servant leadership" and "employee empowerment." In my two books "Driving Excellence" and "Up and to the right". I show the organizational chart of Microchip. The chart is drawn upside down, with the CEO at the bottom. The role of the CEO is not to accumulate, wield, and show off power and wealth. Rather, the CEO should distribute power throughout the organization and then teach, guide, and motivate others in its use.

Retired Southwest Airlines CEO Herb Kelleher did his business traveling on their commercial airliners instead of taking a private plane. Additionally, he took the place of one of the scheduled flight attendants. This way, he got a first-hand feel for his company's product and service.

Such "servant leaders" are not motivated by personal power, wealth, and perks. They, instead, channel their energies toward the betterment of the company, employees, customers, and shareholders.

So, excessive executive perks are legal and ethical, but they often do not set the right tone, and therefore are not right.

Assigned parking spaces

Question: Our company has assigned parking spaces for executives, which are located right next to the entry door. The rest of us must park farther away and walk in the heat or rain. Is it fair and ethical?

-Christy, Mesa

Answer: In the column above, I wrote about executive perks in response to a reader's question about whether such perks were legal, ethical, or right. Executive perks, if properly disclosed, are perfectly legal and ethical. But they do not set the right tone and are therefore not right.

Assigned parking spaces for executives are a kind of perk. There is nothing illegal or unethical about them. But do they set the right tone? I think not.

Parking spot choices tend to be very personal and not always driven by the proximity to the front door. Some employees will choose covered parking, even if it is farther away. Others will park at the end of an aisle to minimize the chances of getting door dings. There are even those who will park their sports cars all alone, far away, covered with car covers, so everyone can get curious about them.

Still, if the company assigns parking spots to the executives, it will be seen as a perk and, in general, will be resented by the employees.

One way to resolve this is to create a certain number of choice parking spots and then sell them in a silent auction on a yearly basis, with the proceeds going to a broad-based charity such as the United Way. Everyone has a chance to win, so it is fair. Executives do have higher disposable incomes, so they can bid higher. However, the charitable cause is worthwhile, so everyone can live with it. It is important to donate to a broad-based charity, to avoid a discussion about everyone's pet causes.

You can supplement this idea with a spot for "Employees of the Month" and create a couple of spots based on a random raffle. This gives everyone skin in the game and a chance to win a choice parking spot. And that makes it fair.

For many years, I won a parking spot in a similar auction at Microchip. One year, I parked my Mercedes next to the beat-up pickup truck of a great employee who won a spot next to me. I think that is totally fair.

Rules versus values-based cultures

Question: I work for an electronics technology and manufacturing company. Our company just has too many rules, procedures, and specifications for its size. In my opinion, too many rules are handcuffing employees and stifling creativity. Can you opine on simplifying a rules-based culture?

-Cindy, Mesa, Arizona

Answer: I wrote an entire chapter on rules- versus values-based cultures in my book "Driving Excellence" published by Wiley in April 2006.

Corporate cultures can be differentiated into two basic varieties: rules-based and values-based. What distinguishes a rules-based from a values-based culture is the degree of emphasis placed on attempting to control or steer human thoughts and behavior.

Rules-based cultures emphasize establishing an extensive set of rules that govern behavior. In values-based cultures, the goal is to instill in the enterprise a common set of values that guide individuals' behaviors.

Rules and values-based cultures each have their virtues and shortcomings. Healthy and thriving cultures rely on an optimal blend of both types of cultures. Exceedingly rules-based cultures tend to drive conformity, status quo, and bureaucracy. Values-based cultures tend to encourage more freedom and empowerment. This leads to greater inspiration, enthusiasm, resourcefulness, commitment, creativity, and innovation.

Some rules are necessary to bring structure and order to societies, companies, and families. The enterprise and the individuals desire some sense of structure, uniformity, and consistency. For instance, we expect other drivers to stop at a red light. We want highly detailed policies and procedures for employees who are operating nuclear power plants. Soldiers might not "take the hill" if they were not indoctrinated into a strict rules-based culture that does not allow them to opt out of a mission.

Policies, procedures, and specifications represent company rules. However, the company's rate of improvement is impeded when employees perceive the rules as excessive. If employees need to overcome a non-value-added policy or procedure at every turn, they will conclude that it requires too much energy to make any improvements. In such an environment, it is difficult to truly empower employees. However, the rules-based mindset assumes that additional rules fix problems.

In values-based company cultures, the enterprise is designed around what it truly values: customers, quality, profitability, technology, employees, continuous improvement, innovation, communication, teamwork, employee empowerment, etc. The values are clearly stated, defined in detail, and communicated to employees. Values serve as a beacon in the night. They are where discussions begin and how wayward discussions are brought back on track. The company values guide employees' strategies, decisions, and actions.

The transition from an overly rules-based to a values-based culture is difficult but achievable. Managers and employees will be skeptical that management and the culture will change. Some employees will embrace the change, others will watch from the sidelines, and a few will resist. The leaders must convey their sincerity and commitment to the new culture. The *Aggregate System* described in my book "Driving Excellence" is a how-to tool to systematically instill a value-based culture, in a way that demonstrates the change is real and ensures its permanence.

Best performers not always best managers

Question: My company just promoted one of my colleagues to the department-manager role. He was a very technically competent person and a very good performer. However, he really lacks the people skills and the traits necessary to manage people. What can be done?

-Eric S., Phoenix

Answer: Firms frequently promote employees into manager positions because they are the strongest performers or the most technical members of the group. This approach is fine if the individual is competent and has the necessary managerial skills required or has the commitment to go through managerial training and master these skills. However, this is often not the case. The unfortunate subordinates are then saddled with a manager who possesses marginal management skills. We have all directly or indirectly witnessed this scenario, just as you are now.

The sporting world learned this lesson long ago. Rarely are former superstars hired as managers or coaches. They typically gained stardom by focusing inward. They are gifted with amazing skills and driven to outwork and outplay the other guy. As coaches, they cannot understand why their players do not work harder; why they do not play up to the former superstar's expectations.

With their inward focus, superstars commonly fail to learn the little things, those things that many less-gifted athletes learned. Examples include how to listen, the mechanics of the game, effectively interacting and influencing people, cheering on the other guy, as well as patience and humility.

Companies should avoid the temptation to automatically promote the highest performer or most technically proficient individual. Look for people who have a natural aptitude for managing others, have worked to acquire managerial skills, and take pleasure in helping others succeed. In fact, companies should instill within their corporate cultures the training and promotion of individuals who exhibit those traits.

Now, what can you do in your case? First, you may be jumping the gun a bit. If the manager was just promoted, give it some time. See if the company puts in the necessary investment to provide this individual with some managerial training. If that does not happen and the manager does not improve through on-the-job trials, then you and your colleagues obviously have a problem. There are the usual avenues for addressing this challenge—going to human resources, complaining to your boss's boss, etc. However, they all have perils and a limited success rate, depending on the culture of your company. Seeking a transfer within your company may be the best bet.

Characteristics of successful managers

Question: I am a systems engineer for an electronics company. Later in my career, I would like to grow up to become a manager. What are the characteristics that I need to acquire or develop to become a successful manager?

-Neil B., Phoenix

Answer: First, I would like to say that there is no cookie-cutter formula that makes a universally successful manager. Over the years, I have seen a lot of very different managers succeed in business. The desired characteristics of a manager are also highly dependent on the culture of the company and the style that flows from the CEO on down. A very aggressive style can be seen as confident and desirable in one company, while another may consider the same person a rude, arrogant non-team player. So, it is important that a successful manager develops flexibility above all other characteristics.

In my book "Driving Excellence" I compiled the following comprehensive list of desired managerial characteristics. You should match this list to your company's culture, selecting the characteristics that are a good match, and then work to develop and acquire them. You should also find a successful manager in your company who will mentor you, as you train yourself for a future managerial career.

The 25 Desired Characteristics of Managers:

1. Consistently achieves the desired operational performance goals and demands quality.
2. Displays professionalism and role model the culture.
3. Has technical competence in their field.
4. Drives continuous improvement.
5. Is bright and has good common sense.
6. Seeks to satisfy customers (internal and external).
7. Demonstrates excellent people skills.
8. Practices a dynamic leadership style (i.e., situational leadership).
9. Empowers employees to foster their involvement.
10. Has solid performance-management skill.
11. Has good judgment and decision-making abilities.
12. Demonstrates initiative, is a creative problem solver, and utilizes analytical methods.
13. Is a strong communicator with good selling, persuasiveness, and negotiating skills.
14. Hard worker who demonstrates initiative, perseverance, and follow-through.
15. Is flexible, adaptable, and works well under stress.
16. Fosters continuous learning by developing employees.
17. Is a good organizer and planner.
18. Listens actively and considers others' input and feedback.
19. Recognizes good work, takes interest in the individual, and does not play politics.
20. Is a team player, builds good team chemistry, and is a consensus builder.
21. Respects, praises, and supports other groups rather than seeking control over them.
22. Operates with limited ego; acts ethically and honestly.
23. Is a good motivator who effectively deals with poor performers.
24. Is frugal (i.e., profit & loss and cost sensitivity).
25. Is concerned with maintaining a safe workplace.

I published my first Ask Steve column in the business pages of the Arizona Republic in 2006. With weekly columns for several years and later a monthly column, I offered my services to share the practical business know-how I had gained over many years I led

Microchip to the top of an extremely competitive industry. But all good things must come to an end. Because of many other very pressing priorities in my business and personal life, this was my last column. For about seven years, it was my pleasure to answer readers' questions. It is my sincere hope that I have shared a fresh perspective on business, personal, career, political and financial topics, which has benefited all the Republic's readers. And through the publication of these columns in this book, I hope that it will continue to benefit the readers of this book for years to come.

Original column reprints

ASK STEVE

Understanding layoff criteria

Microchip Technology Inc. Chief Executive Officer Steve Sanghi offers practical help for your real-life business challenges.

Question: I worked for five years for an engineering company that was suffering financially because of the weak economy. I was recently laid off. What angers me is that certain employees who were recently hired from other companies are still there. I can't get any answers from my company. Can you help?

— *Scott, Phoenix*

STEVE SANGHI
ASK STEVE

Answer: First, I'm very sorry that you have become the victim of a layoff because of the weakening economy. It's understandable for a laid-off employee to be confused and angry at his company. The most frequently asked question is, "Why me?"

Sometimes, it is the first layoff for a company. In that case, the criteria for selection was recently developed and probably not yet communicated to the employees. But, in most cases, the laid-off employee either did not agree with the criteria or did not agree with how he or she was evaluated against that criteria.

Most employees would like the No. 1 criterion to be length of service. In a brutally competitive global environment, that method does not work.

The first criterion is often "critical skills." If the company is going to have fewer employees, it is important to keep the ones with most critical skills. If your company was not doing well and still hired employees, I'm sure that this was done to acquire skills that were critical for its success.

The second criterion is often job performance. Imagine that there are two employees with similar critical skills. The first one applies his skills and gets good results. He gets along with everyone, helps the others to succeed, is well engaged and is seen as an excellent employee. The second one has a chip on his shoulder, does not get along with others, is not engaged and is seen as a disruptive influence. If you were the manager, it is clear whom you would choose.

The third criterion is length of service, which should be used only as a tie breaker.

The next issue is how to apply the above criteria fairly. Prior performance appraisals may give guidance. However, critical skills and job performance are not absolute measures. My experience has been that when a laid-off employee disagrees with the application of first two criteria on him, then in most cases, he had also disagreed with prior performance appraisals. In those cases, there were signs for the employee to improve. But, the improvement areas weren't internalized, and therefore never improved upon.

There is one other scenario. Anti-discrimination laws require that a company not impact the distribution of minorities, females and employees over 40 after a layoff. During the application of these laws, a more qualified employee can sometimes get laid off.

Is that fair? I think not! But that is the subject for another column.

Ask Steve by writing to steve.sanghi@microchip.com.

Mixed-race kids enjoy a special perspective

Question: I'm 16 years old and my father was filling out the 2010 Census form, which created a discussion in our house: What is my race? My father is half Cuban and half American. My mother is half Filipino and half Mexican. So, who am I?

— Natalie, *Phoenix*

Answer: I've chosen to take an essay that my daughter Christie wrote in 2003, which I publish with her permission.

"During my years of growing up, every time I filled out an application, I encountered a section called ethnic background; and every time I wondered, who am I? Not fitting any of the choices given, I always checked "Other." I am Christie Sanghi, born in Sacramento, Calif.

STEVE SANGHI
ASK STEVE

"My mom is from Nicaragua; she came to the U.S. in the middle of a civil war in Nicaragua in 1979. Her first language is Spanish. She speaks English well, but I find myself correcting her English to this day. My dad is from India.

"My mom was born and raised as a Christian, whereas my dad was raised as a Hindu and converted to Christianity before he married my mom. My mom does not speak Hindi, and my dad does not speak Spanish. Therefore, they speak English – my first language. I grew up in this household influenced by these two cultures, learning to live with the differences, celebrating the similarities, learning the values from both, and yet forming my own identity.

"I have learned to embrace the values, lessons and traditions that each of my parents has taught me. From my mom, I have learned conservative values, high morals and a sense of self-worth. From my dad, I have learned the value of hard work, honesty, career success and the drive to make this world a better place to live.

"I have been to Nicaragua with my mom and to India with my parents, and I have known the extended families on both sides. Both sides have some admirable qualities and have worked hard to make their cultures a major part of my life. I respect them completely ... "As I leave home after 18 years, I leave with a sense of confidence that I have the values, courage, honesty and commitment to deal with the challenges I face ahead. I am from a Spanish heritage with the values I have learned from my mother, and an East Indian heritage with the values I have learned from my father. I am American from what I have learned from my parents and friends, and 18 years in the U.S. So, who am I? I still check the same box — "Other."

— **Christie Sanghi Wieger**

Steve Sanghi is the CEO of Microchip Technology. Please "Ask Steve" by writing to steve.sanghi@microchip.com.

ASK STEVE

Merger may expand worker's opportunities

Microchip Technology Inc. Chief Executive Officer Steve Sanghi offers practical help for your real-life business challenges.

Question: I'm a middle-level manager in a company that recently got acquired by its larger competitor. My former boss and many of my former colleagues left the company soon after the merger. We were very resource-constrained in the smaller company. As you recently wrote, the merger may give us the opportunity to provide the complete solution. Because of my skills, my job seems safe. But my old boss wants to rehire me at his new company. I'm afraid that we will face the same constrained environment that we just came out of. Please help me evaluate whether I should stay or leave.

Steve Sanghi

— Phil, Scottsdale

Answer: When a company is acquired by another company, the combined company sees some duplication of resources. And the bigger company has paid a premium to acquire the smaller company. So, some rationalization of resources, and hence the elimination of redundancies, is very likely. However, if you are one with critical skills and you feel that your job is safe, then you are in a very good position.

The biggest problem I see in a merger is that the employees of the acquired company continue to march in the direction they were marching before. Maybe the acquiring company has better technology in certain areas. And, in those areas, the development pipeline for the acquired company will be terminated or modified.

The employees of the acquired companies may wear the new company's badge on their shirt pocket. But they really need to be wearing the badge in their heart. They always need to think of the right answer for the new company (and not for their old company). If you are able to use your skills in advancing the agenda of the new company and wear its badge in your heart, then you will be very successful and you should stay there. You should also evaluate the culture of your new company and your opportunities there. Do they promote from within? How have the people from prior acquisitions done with this company?

Beware of the offer from your old boss. Is your old boss giving you a more senior position than you had before, and thus providing an opportunity to grow? If you work for the same boss for a very long time, I believe that you amass less skills overall. Your strengths remain your strengths and your weaknesses remain your weaknesses.

Working for different bosses gives you a broader perspective, and you can professionally grow to take on more challenging tasks. I have always managed and led my employees to build their loyalty for the company, and not for me. Therefore, my advice is that you should throw your loyalty in with your new company and not with your old boss.

Ask Steve by writing to steve.sanghi@microchip.com.

About the Author

Steve Sanghi led Microchip Technology from 1990 till March 2021 and was one of the longest serving CEOs of a semiconductor company. Mr. Sanghi led the IPO of Microchip (NASDAQ: MCHP) in March 1993 with annual sales of $89M. Under Mr. Sanghi's leadership, Microchip's revenue grew to a $5.4B run rate and a market value of approximately $44B. Microchip returned a cumulative stock-price gain of over 285X, excluding dividends, since the IPO in March 1993. Under Mr. Sanghi's leadership, Microchip completed its 121st consecutive profitable quarter on December 31, 2020, and an achievement unmatched in the semiconductor industry.

Mr. Sanghi relinquished his CEO role in 2021 to his long-time groomed successor within Microchip and became Executive Chairman starting March 1, 2021. In August 2024, he became the non-executive chair of the board of Microchip. He is also Chairman of the Board of Impinj, a leading RFID provider, and Internet of Things pioneer. He is also Chairman of the Board of a private company Advantek. Mr. Sanghi also joined the board of Northern Arizona University Foundation.

Microchip has also been an industry consolidator, having purchased more than 20 companies in the last 13 years. All of them were successfully integrated into Microchip's business—creating enormous value for the shareholders of Microchip through business process improvements that brought them to Microchip's level of financial performance. He is author of the best-selling book "Up and to the right: My personal and business journey building the Microchip Technology juggernaut" published in 2023. He is also co-author of the book "Driving Excellence: How The Aggregate System Turned Microchip Technology from a Failing Company to a Market Leader" (Wiley; April 2006)

Mr. Sanghi is a tireless advocate for science and technology. He is responsible for bringing robotics competitions to high schools in

Arizona that inspire young students in the vital areas of Science, Technology, Engineering, and Math (STEM). He is co-chair of the Arizona First Robotics Planning Committee. In the past, he also co-chaired the state of Arizona Governor's Council of Innovation and Technology. Mr. Sanghi was also a member of the board of *FIRST*® (*F*or *I*nspiration and *R*ecognition of *S*cience and *T*echnology) Robotics, a non-profit company formed to inspire young students in STEM from April 2007 to April 2016, when he termed out after nine years.

Before joining the company, Mr. Sanghi was Vice President of Operations at Wafer Scale Integration, Inc., a semiconductor company, from 1988 to 1990. Mr. Sanghi was employed by Intel Corporation from 1978 to 1988, where he held various positions in management and engineering, the most recent serving as General Manager of Programmable Memory Operations.

In June 1995, Mr. Sanghi received an Arizona Entrepreneur of the Year award. Mr. Sanghi is the only CEO to win the Executive of the Year award twice by Electronic Engineering Times. And Microchip is the only company to win the Company of the Year award twice from the Arizona Association for Corporate Growth (ACG/Arizona). Additionally, Mr. Sanghi has been named to the Phoenix Business Journal's annual list of the Most Admired CEOs, and the Arizona Technology Council selected Mr. Sanghi as the winner of their 2010 Lifetime Achievement Award. The Wall Street Journal ranked Mr. Sanghi second among the top 28 long-serving CEOs of the S&P 500. In April 2022, Arizona State University's W.P. Carey School of business named Mr. Sanghi 2022 Executive of the Year. Finally, in December 2022, Global Semiconductor Industry Alliance honored Mr. Sanghi with Dr. Morris Chang Exemplary Leadership Award, the global semiconductor industry's highest honor.

Mr. Sanghi has served on numerous public and private boards. He was a member of the board of directors of Mellanox Inc (Nasdaq: MLNX), a high-performance Ethernet Interconnect company headquartered in Israel. Mellanox was acquired by Nvidia. Mr.

Sanghi's past board of directors service includes Hittite Microwave (Nasdaq: HITT), sold to ADI in 2014, Xyratex, Ltd. (Nasdaq: XRTX) from 2004 to 2014 (sold to Seagate in March 2014), Chairman of the Board of FlipChip International (sold to TSHT of China in 2015), Chairman of the board of Adflex Solutions (Nasdaq: AFLX) from 1994 to 1999 (sold to Innovex Inc), Artisoft Inc (Nasdaq: ASFT) for two years in the 90s, Vivid Semiconductor (private company funded by Kleiner Perkins, sold to National Semiconductor) and a member of the board of trustees of Kettering University in Flint, Michigan from 2004 to 2012.

Mr. Sanghi holds a Master of Science degree in Electrical and Computer Engineering from the University of Massachusetts, and a Bachelor of Science degree in Electronics and Communication from Punjab University, India.

Northern Arizona University (NAU) awarded Mr. Sanghi an honorary doctorate in Humane letters in 2019.

Printed in Great Britain
by Amazon

27cd5364-4a75-429c-ad9d-9e8e25e75c1dR01